parents aren't supposed to like it

ISSN: 1535-377X

parents aren't supposed to like it

Rock & Other Pop Musicians of Today

Judson Knight
Allison McNeill, Editor

Detroit • New York • San Diego • San Francisco
Boston • New Haven, Conn. • Waterville, Maine
London • Munich

parents aren't supposed to like it
Rock and Other Pop Musicians of Today

Judson Knight

Staff

Allison McNeill, *U•X•L Senior Editor*
Carol DeKane Nagel, *U•X•L Managing Editor*
Julia Furtaw, *Senior Product Specialist, Product Management*
Thomas L. Romig, *U•X•L Publisher*

Michelle DiMercurio, *Senior Art Director*

Dean Dauphinais, *Senior Editor, Image Acquisitions*
Pamela A. Reed, *Imaging Coordinator*
Dan Newell, *Imaging Specialist*
Shalice Shah-Caldwell, *Permissions Associate*

Rita Wimberley, *Senior Buyer*
Evi Seoud, *Assistant Manager, Composition Purchasing and Electronic Prepress*

Marco Di Vita, Graphix Group, *Typesetting*

Cover photos: Macy Gray, Mark Hoppus, Kid Rock, Britney Spears. (Photos by David Atlas. Reproduced by permission); Destiny's Child, Jennifer Lopez. (AP/Wide World Photos. Reproduced by permission); Snoop Dogg. (© Ken Settle. Reproduced by permission).

This publication is a creative work fully protected by all applicable copyright laws, as well as by misappropriation, trade secret, unfair competition, and other applicable laws. The editors of this work have added value to the underlying factual material herein through one or more of the following: unique and original selection, coordination, expression, arrangement, and classification of the information. All rights to this publication will be vigorously defended.

Copyright © 2002
U•X•L, an imprint of the Gale Group
All rights reserved, including the right of reproduction in whole or in part in any form.

ISBN 0-7876-5387-X (3-volume set)
ISBN 0-7876-5388-8 (volume 4)
ISBN 0-7876-5389-6 (volume 5)
ISBN 0-7876-5390-X (volume 6)

ISSN 1535-377X

Printed in United States of America

10 9 8 7 6 5 4 3 2 1

To my daughter Tyler and her cousins
Alex, Caroline, Dana, Drake, Dylan, Henry, Jack, and Narra:
May you always listen to the music in your own hearts.

contents

(update) indicates an update to the original entry

VOLUME 4

Musicians by Genre	xi
Reader's Guide	xvii
Musical Genre Overview	xxi
Words to Know	xxxv
Christina Aguilera	1
Marc Anthony	5
Fiona Apple	10
Backstreet Boys	14
Barenaked Ladies (update)	19
Beastie Boys	23
Beck (update)	28
Mary J. Blige	33
Blink-182	38
Bone Thugs-N-Harmony	43
Garth Brooks	48

Limp Bizkit. (Corbis Corporation. Reproduced by permission.)

Busta Rhymes 54	Enrique Iglesias 196
Mariah Carey 59	Indigo Girls **(update)** 200
Collective Soul **(update)** 64	Ja Rule 203
The Corrs 69	Janet Jackson 206
Counting Crows **(update)** 75	Jamiroquai 210
Creed 79	Jars of Clay 215
Da Brat 84	Jewel 219
D'Angelo 88	R. Kelly 224
Dave Matthews Band **(update)** 93	Kid Rock 229
dc Talk 98	KISS 235
Destiny's Child 102	KoRN 240
Celine Dion 107	Lenny Kravitz **(update)** 245
Dixie Chicks 112	Jonny Lang 249
DMX 117	Lil' Kim 253
Dr. Dre **(update)** 122	Limp Bizkit 257
Missy "Misdemeanor" Elliott 126	LL Cool J **(update)** 261
Eminem 130	Jennifer Lopez 264
Gloria Estefan 136	Marilyn Manson **(update)** 269
Everclear 141	Ricky Martin 273
Everlast 146	Matchbox Twenty 278
Foo Fighters **(update)** 150	Sarah McLachlan **(update)** 282
Kirk Franklin 153	Metallica **(update)** 287
	Mighty Mighty Bosstones 291
Web Sites xliii	Mystikal 295
Index xlv	
	Web Sites xliii
	Index xlv

VOLUME 5

Musicians by Genre xi
Reader's Guide xvii
Musical Genre Overview . . . xxi
Words to Know xxxv

VOLUME 6

Musicians by Genre xi
Reader's Guide xvii
Musical Genre Overview . . . xxi
Words to Know xxxv

Goo Goo Dolls **(update)** 159	Nelly 301
Macy Gray 163	98 Degrees 305
Hanson 168	No Doubt **(update)** 309
Faith Hill 174	'NSync 313
Lauryn Hill **(update)** 179	The Offspring **(update)** 318
Hole **(update)** 183	Ozzy Osbourne 321
Hootie and the Blowfish **(update)** . . 187	
Whitney Houston 191	

Parents Aren't Supposed to Like It

Papa Roach	327
Pearl Jam **(update)**	331
Pink	336
Puff Daddy	340
Queen Latifah **(update)**	344
Radiohead	347
Rage Against the Machine **(update)**	351
The Red Hot Chili Peppers **(update)**	355
R.E.M. **(update)**	360
LeAnn Rimes	364
Santana	369
Brian Setzer	374
Sisqo	380
Sister Hazel	384
Smash Mouth	389
Smashing Pumpkins **(update)**	393
Will Smith **(update)**	399
Snoop Dogg **(update)**	402
Britney Spears	406
Sting	411
Sugar Ray	416
Third Eye Blind	420
311	424
TLC **(update)**	428
A Tribe Called Quest	432
Shania Twain	437
U2 **(update)**	442
The Wallflowers **(update)**	446
Wu-Tang Clan	451
Web Sites	xliii
Index	xlv

musicians by genre

Italic type indicates volume numbers. **Boldface** type indicates main entries in *Parents Aren't Supposed to Like It*. Volumes 4, 5, and 6. Volume numbers 1, 2, and 3 refer to the three-volume *Parents Aren't Supposed to Like It* base set.

(update) indicates an update to the original entry.

Ozzy Osbourne. (© Ken Settle. Reproduced by permission.)

alternative metal

KoRN	*5:* 240
Limp Bizkit	*5:* 257
Marilyn Manson	*1:* 78; **(update)** *5:* 269
Papa Roach	*6:* 327
Rage Against the Machine	*1:* 134; **(update)** *6:* 351

alternative pop/rock

Blink 182	*4:* 38
Collective Soul	*3:* 552; **(update)** *4:* 64
Creed	*4:* 79
dc Talk	*4:* 98
Goo Goo Dolls	*1:* 57; **(update)** *5:* 159
Hootie and the Blowfish	*3:* 572; **(update)** *5:* 187
Jars of Clay	*5:* 215
Matchbox Twenty	*5:* 278

Smash Mouth	6: 389
Sting	6: 411
Sugar Ray	6: 416
Third Eye Blind	6: 420

alternative rock

Afghan Whigs	1: 7
Alice in Chains	1: 11
Fiona Apple	**4: 10**
Babes in Toyland	1: 16
Barenaked Ladies	**1: 20; (update) 4: 19**
Beck	**1: 24; (update) 4: 28**
Bettie Serveert	1: 30
Butthole Surfers	1: 33
Counting Crows	**3: 556; (update) 4: 75**
The Cranberries	1: 37
Crash Test Dummies	1: 42
Dinosaur Jr.	1: 45
Everclear	**4: 141**
Foo Fighters	**1: 49; (update) 4: 150**
Garbage	1: 53; (update) 6: 309
Green Day	**1: 60; (update) 4: 38**
Hole	**1: 65; (update) 5: 183**
Iggy Pop	1: 69
Jane's Addiction	1: 75
Mighty Mighty Bosstones	**5: 291**
Morphine	1: 81
Mudhoney	1: 84
Nine Inch Nails	1: 87
Nirvana	1: 93
No Doubt	**1: 101; (update) 6: 309**
The Offspring	**1: 105; (update) 6: 318**
Pavement	1: 110
Pearl Jam	**1: 115; (update) 6: 331**
Porno for Pyros	1: 123
The Presidents of the United States of America	1: 127
Primus	1: 130
Radiohead	**6: 347**
The Ramones	1: 138
Rancid	1: 145
The Red Hot Chili Peppers	**1: 148; (update) 6: 355**
R.E.M.	**1: 153; (update) 6: 360**
Silverchair	1: 160
Smashing Pumpkins	**1: 163; (update) 6: 393**
Soul Asylum	1: 169
Soundgarden	1: 172
Stone Temple Pilots	1: 178
Sublime	1: 182
311	**6: 424**
Urge Overkill	1: 187
U2	**1: 190; (update) 6: 442**
Veruca Salt	1: 196
The Wallflowers	**1: 199; (update) 6: 446**
Neil Young	1: 203

Brit Pop

The Beautiful South	2: 223
Blur	2: 227
David Bowie	2: 230
Bush	2: 237
Elvis Costello	2: 241
The Cure	2: 248
Elastica	2: 253
PJ Harvey	2: 257
Morrissey	2: 260
Oasis	2: 265
Suede	2: 270

Contemporary Christian and Gospel

dc Talk	4: 98
Kirk Franklin	**4: 153**
Jars of Clay	**5: 215**

Country

Garth Brooks	4: 48
Dixie Chicks	4: 112
Faith Hill	5: 174
LeAnn Rimes	6: 364
Shania Twain	6: 437

Dance Music

Chemical Brothers	2: 280
Deee-lite	2: 283
Jamiroquai	5: 210
Kraftwerk	2: 287
Moby	2: 291
The Orb	2: 295
Tricky	2: 299

Folk and Folk Rock

Jeff Buckley	3: 443
Tracy Chapman	3: 446
Indigo Girls	3: 451; (update) 5: 200
Jewel	5: 219
Sarah McLachlan	3: 454; (update) 5: 282
Michael Penn	3: 458
Michelle Shocked	3: 461

Heavy Metal

Danzig	3: 470
Guns N' Roses	3: 473
KISS	5: 235
Living Colour	3: 470
Megadeth	3: 482
Metallica	3: 485; (update) 5: 287
Ozzy Osbourne	5: 321
Pantera	3: 490
Slayer	3: 493
White Zombie	3: 497

Hip-Hop

Arrested Development	2: 312
Boogie Down Productions	2: 317
Bone Thugs-N-Harmony	4: 43
dc Talk	4: 98
Missy "Misdemeanor" Elliott	4: 126
Kirk Franklin	4: 153
Fugees	2: 343
Hammer	2: 350
Lauryn Hill	2: 343; (update) 5: 179
Puff Daddy	6: 340
Sisqo	6: 380
Will Smith	2: 326; (update) 6: 399
TLC	3: 535; (update) 6: 428
A Tribe Called Quest	6: 432

Jazz-Influenced Pop, Rock, and R&B

Marc Anthony	4: 5
Fiona Apple	4: 10
Dave Matthews Band	3: 584; (update) 5: 93
Jamiroquai	5: 210
Mighty Mighty Bosstones	5: 291
Phish	3: 588
Santana	6: 369
Brian Setzer	6: 374
Sting	6: 411
A Tribe Called Quest	6: 432

Latin

Christina Aguilera	4: 1
Marc Anthony	4: 5
Gloria Estefan	4: 136
Enrique Iglesias	5: 196
Jennifer Lopez	5: 264
Ricky Martin	5: 273
Santana	6: 369

Pop

Christina Aguilera	4: 1
Backstreet Boys	4: 14
Mariah Carey	4: 59
Destiny's Child	4: 102
Celine Dion	4: 107
Gloria Estefan	4: 136
Faith Hill	5: 174
Whitney Houston	5: 191
Janet Jackson	5: 206
Jennifer Lopez	5: 264
Ricky Martin	5: 273
98 Degrees	6: 305
'NSync	6: 313
Pink	6: 336
Will Smith	6: 399
Britney Spears	6: 406
Sting	6: 411
Shania Twain	6: 437

Pop/Rock

The Corrs	4: 69
Hanson	5: 168

Rap

Beastie Boys	4: 23
Bone Thugs-N-Harmony	4: 43
Busta Rhymes	4: 54
Coolio	2: 321
Da Brat	4: 84
DMX	4: 117
Dr. Dre	2: 330; (update) 4: 122
Eazy-E	2: 338
Eminem	4: 130
Gravediggaz	2: 347
Heavy D & The Boyz	2: 355
Ice Cube	2: 360
Ice-T	2: 366
Ja Rule	5: 203
Kool Moe Dee	2: 372
Lil' Kim	5: 253
LL Cool J	2: 376; (update) 5: 261
Mystikal	5: 295
Naughty By Nature	2: 382
Nelly	6: 301
The Notorious B.I.G.	2: 387
Public Enemy	2: 392
Queen Latifah	2: 399; (update) 6: 344
Run-DMC	2: 403
Salt-N-Pepa	2: 410
Tupac Shakur	2: 424
Sir Mix-A-Lot	2: 415
Snoop Dogg	2: 418; (update) 6: 402
Wu-Tang Clan	6: 451

Rap Rock

Everlast	4: 146
Kid Rock	5: 229
KoRN	5: 240
Limp Bizkit	5: 257
Rage Against the Machine	1: 134; (update) 6: 351
311	6: 424

Rhythm and Blues (R&B) and Urban Soul

Babyface	3: 506
Mary J. Blige	4: 33
Boyz II Men	3: 511
Bobby Brown	3: 516
Tevin Campbell	3: 520
D'Angelo	4: 88
Destiny's Child	4: 102
En Vogue	3: 524
Macy Gray	5: 163
Lauryn Hill	2: 343; (update) 5: 179

Whitney Houston	5: 191
Janet Jackson	5: 206
R. Kelly	5: 224
Pink	6: 336
Prince	3: 528
Sisqo	6: 380
TLC	3: 535; **(update)** 6: 428

rock and roll

The Black Crowes	3: 545
Blues Traveler	3: 546
Dave Matthews Band	3: 584; **(update)** 5: 93
Melissa Etheridge	3: 559
Gin Blossoms	3: 562
Grant Lee Buffalo	3: 565
Guided By Voices	3: 568
Lenny Kravitz	3: 630; **(update)** 5: 245
Jonny Lang	5: 249
Live	3: 576
Los Lobos	3: 579
Phish	3: 588
Santana	6: 369
Sister Hazel	6: 384
Son Volt	3: 591
Spin Doctors	3: 594
Bruce Springsteen	3: 597
the subdudes	3: 603
Wilco	3: 606

singers/songwriters

Tori Amos	3: 617
Fiona Apple	4: 10
Beck	1: 24; **(update)** 4: 28
Bjork	3: 621
Mary J. Blige	4: 33
Garth Brooks	4: 48
Sheryl Crow	3: 626; **(update)** 5: 282
D'Angelo	4: 88
Macy Gray	5: 163
Lauryn Hill	5: 179
Jewel	5: 219
k. d. lang	3: 634
Sarah McLachlan	3: 454; **(update)** 5: 282
Alanis Morissette	3: 639; **(update)** 5: 159
Joan Osborne	3: 647
Liz Phair	3: 650
Lou Reed	3: 653
Sting	6: 411

ska revival

Mighty Mighty Bosstones	5: 291
No Doubt	1: 101; **(update)** 6: 309
Smash Mouth	6: 389
Sugar Ray	6: 416

swing revival

Brian Setzer	6: 374

world music

Dave Matthews Band	3: 584; **(update)** 4: 93
Santana	6: 369
Sting	6: 411

Reader's Guide

There's something for just about every young music fan in Volumes 4, 5, and 6 of *Parents Aren't Supposed to Like It: Rock and Other Pop Musicians of Today*. This comprehensive resource, a continuation of U•X•L's 3-volume *Parents* base set, contains 100 biographical entries—70 new entries and 30 update entries—on the hottest bands and musicians of the 1990s and early 2000s, ranging from alternative rock to rhythm and blues, and from hip-hop to folk.

Format

Entries in Volumes 4, 5, and 6 are arranged alphabetically to allow readers quick and easy access to information. This represents a change in format from the 3-volume *Parents* base set, which was arranged by musical genre. Entries are still categorized by musical genre, however, and are accessible via the Musicians By Genre table of contents listed at the front of each volume.

Jennifer Lopez. (Photo by David Atlas. Reproduced by permission.)

Scope

All of the bands and artists selected for inclusion are relevant to current popular music of the 1990s and into the early 2000s. Most have sold a lot of records or are highly influential to today's music. The bands featured in *Parents* provide a representative cross-section of different styles of pop music, reflecting the wide variety of tastes exhibited by the record-buying public. The musicians included differ greatly in musical style, as well as in attitude, image, political messages, belief systems, and lifestyles.

The Musical Genre Overview, found at the front of each volume, describes the progression of musical styles from the latter half of the twentieth century through today. The overview allows readers to quickly obtain a fuller picture of the particular musical scene in which their favorite bands participate. Many modern musicians, of course, play in several genres, or have made hybrid genres. The editors of *Parents* have made an effort to place musicians in the category they are generally associated with, knowing that in many cases the musicians could easily fit well into another category.

Features

- "Update" entries keep readers current on select musicians profiled in the 3-volume *Parents* base set who have remained active on the music scene. Updates are clearly indicated on the first page of an entry as well as in the tables of contents. In addition, readers are directed back to the original essay on the musician appearing in *Parents,* Volumes 1, 2, or 3. For example, the cross-reference "See original entry on the Foo Fighters in *Parents Aren't Supposed to Like It,* Volume 1" appears toward the beginning of the Foo Fighters's update entry.

- A cumulative Musicians By Genre table of contents lists performers by music category. This table of contents is cumulative to include musicians from the 3-volume *Parents* base set as well as those from Volumes 4, 5, and 6.

- Musical genre categories have been clarified and consolidated from the *Parents* base set so as to be more meaningful to readers. Volumes 4, 5, and 6 also include four new categories: contemporary Christian, country, Latin, and pop.

- A comprehensive Words to Know section defines nearly 100 terms relating to the music industry.

- The Musical Genre Overview essay gives readers background into the origins of today's popular music styles.

- 173 portraits and other black-and-white photos of the musicians accompany the entries.

- Over 60 sidebars appear throughout the volumes. Most provide mini-biographies of related performers or brief updates to performers found in previous volumes of *Parents*. Still others supply additional information about or related to the musicians.

- Entries conclude with sections listing selected awards, selected discographies, further reading sources, contact information, and pertinent Web sites.

- A cumulative subject index covers musicians and their works found in the 3-volume *Parents* base set as well as Volumes 4, 5, and 6.

Comments and Suggestions

We welcome your comments on this work as well as your suggestions for entries to be featured in future volumes of *Parents Aren't Supposed to Like It*. Please write: Editors, *Parents Aren't Supposed to Like It,* U•X•L, 27500 Drake Rd, Farmington Hills, Michigan 48331; call toll-free 1-800-347-4253; fax 248-414-5043; or send e-mail via www.galegroup.com.

Musical Genres: An Overview

At the beginning of the twenty-first century, the audience for popular music was more fragmented than it had ever been. No longer did mere rock, pop, and R&B dominate the music world: each of these had splintered into a dozen or more variations, complete with subgroups that crossed genre lines. One of these subgroups, rap rock, proved among the most fascinating developments of the late 1990s.

In this crowded, confusing environment of genres and subgenres, it was sometimes hard, if not impossible, to easily categorize an artist; indeed, much of the music at the end of the twentieth century defied categorization. Despite all the differences, however, most forms of popular music had roots that went back to Africa.

The origins of modern music

During the two centuries of America's slave trade, which began in about 1620, thousands of captured Africans brought to the New World the traditional music of their homelands. As

Nelly. (Liaison Agency. Reproduced by permission.)

slaves toiling on the plantations of the South, they began crafting songs about good times and bad times; but since most times in a slave's life were bad, songs about pain prevailed—and this was the origin of what one day became the blues. On Sundays in church they sang spirituals, and these became the foundation of black gospel.

But African Americans were not the only people fighting to survive in nineteenth-century America; nor were they the only ones giving birth to a musical legacy. From the sweatshops of New York City to the sharecroppers' shacks of Georgia, there were poor whites from Ireland, Scotland, England, and points beyond—people whose musical heritage became the basis for much of folk and country music.

Blues and jazz

Slavery ended in 1865, but within half a century segregation and poor work conditions influenced a mass migration by African Americans out of the Southern states. As a result the blues, which had taken root in the Mississippi Delta, began moving northward toward Chicago.

Closely tied to blues was jazz, which originated around 1890 and likewise soon found a home in the north. During the 1920s, America's white population became aware of the art form, and jazz emerged as the first African-influenced musical strain to gain widespread acceptance. By that point, electronic media—phonograph records and radio—had made possible the development of a national popular culture, one quite different from the various types of folk culture that had prevailed up until that time.

The new recording technology led to a greatly expanded audience for blues and jazz, and influenced the development of country and western music from folk. As for folk, it acquired a dimension of social protest that came to the forefront during the Great Depression of the 1930s. That was the decade when jazz gave birth to swing, the music of World War II (1939–45).

R&B emerges in the 1940s

The end of the war saw the emergence of a new and exciting musical style among transplanted African Americans in the north: jump blues. As its name implied, the new form had a blues influence, but in contrast to the slower pace of the earlier genre, jump blues—closely tied to boogie-woogie—vibrated with a new energy.

During the 1940s, jump blues went by a variety of names, including some—most notably "race music"—that today seem offensive. Then a writer for *Billboard,* the leading trade magazine for the music industry, came up with an all-purpose name to describe recordings by black artists: rhythm and blues, or R&B for short. Over the decades, R&B would spawn a host of styles: soul, funk, disco, and rap. But predating those was its firstborn child—or at least, one of its most famous offspring: rock and roll.

The 1950s: race and rock

Most critics cite the 1954 single "Sh-Boom" by the Chords as the first rock song, but it was not the Chords who made it famous. Fearful that white America would not respond to a black singing group, the record company arranged for a white ensemble (whose name, the Crew Cuts, suggested old-fashioned respectability) to sing it.

The issue of race pervaded the early years of rock and roll. Hence black artists such as Ray Charles, Fats Domino, Chuck Berry, Little Richard, and the Isley Brothers either failed to receive the recognition they deserved, or only received it in later years.

A white man who sings and dances like a black man

In the meantime, an unlikely marriage of blues and country had resulted in the birth of a style known as rockabilly, the first major trend among white rock singers. "Rock Around the Clock" by Bill Haley became the first rockabilly hit in 1955, but Haley lacked the star quality necessary to sustain this new genre. In the 1940s, Frank Sinatra had enraptured female audiences, melting thousands of young girls' hearts. Rock and roll lacked such a star, and audiences—not to mention record-company executives—looked for someone to fill that role.

Specifically, they wanted a white man who could sing and dance like a black man. And in 1955 they found him: a twenty-year-old Mississippi boy named Elvis Presley (1935–1977). For the next half-decade, Elvis thrilled audiences around the nation as he racked up one hit after another: "Heartbreak Hotel," "Hound Dog," "Don't Be Cruel," "Jailhouse Rock," and on and on.

Rock dies its first death

During the second half of the 1950s, rock and roll erupted from the sidelines to center stage. Aside from Elvis and the many black artists who contributed to the formation of rock music, there were a number of country stars who made the transition into rock: Johnny Cash, Jerry Lee Lewis, and Carl Perkins. And there was Buddy Holly, who, unlike Elvis, was a songwriter, and who ultimately may have exerted a greater influence on music than his more famous contemporary.

But as the decade drew to a close, one event after another seemed to point to the end of rock. Elvis was drafted into the army in 1958, and though he lived nearly twenty more years, his greatest work lay far behind him. Holly died in a 1959 plane crash. Chuck Berry went to jail for marijuana possession, and the entire music industry was shaken by the "payola" scandal, involving charges that record companies had paid radio stations to play certain songs.

The 1960s: An explosion of styles

In the next few years, a variety of styles prevailed. R&B flourished, thanks in large part to the influence of Detroit's Motown label, which produced a seemingly endless array of "girl groups" such as the Ronettes.

Among white artists, a vocal style known as "doo-wop" came to the forefront, and "teen-idol" stars such as Fabian and Ricky Nelson dominated. Surf music, led by the Beach Boys, thrived.

So too did another genre that could not have been more different from surf music: folk, led by a nasal-voiced Minnesotan, Robert Zimmermann—better known by his adopted name of Bob Dylan. But old-fashioned rock and roll seemed to have died.

In fact rock was far from over; indeed, it had hardly even begun. This was a theme that would repeat many a time over the years: the apparent death of rock, followed by a sudden burst of new life from an unexpected corner of the music world.

The Beatles and Bob Dylan

In 1964, that unexpected place was England, which had been virtually ignored by American audiences up to that time. But with the February 9, 1964, appearance of the Beatles on the *Ed Sullivan Show*, a popular TV variety program during that era, everything changed.

In addition to generating hit after hit with songs such as "I Want to Hold Your Hand" and "She Loves You," the Beatles brought a vast array of other British groups to the forefront as well. Some of the bands who crossed the Atlantic during the British Invasion of the 1960s would be forgotten; but many others—the Rolling Stones, the Kinks, the Who, the Animals, and the Yardbirds (featuring a young Eric Clapton)—would continue to exert an impact to the present day.

At the same time Dylan, though he did not sell as many albums as the Beatles, held enormous sway in the music world. His use of an electric guitar at the 1965 Newport Folk Festival alienated folk-music devotees, but won him an audience among rock fans. The event heralded the beginnings of folk-rock, and in the aftermath artists such as Simon and Garfunkel and the Byrds emerged. Dylan went on to release a series of critically acclaimed albums, and these in turn influenced the Beatles' turn to folk-rock and later psychedelia.

The ironies surrounding R&B

The Beatles had exposed U.S. fans to the music of African American artists they had long idolized, while the Rolling Stones and other blues-based groups helped popularize the work of bluesmen such as Howlin' Wolf, Muddy Waters, and B. B. King. It was ironic, of course, that white Americans had to learn from foreigners about the rich musical heritage under their noses; equally ironic was the fact that those white foreigners enjoyed much greater popularity playing "black music" than black artists had.

But African American performers, and particularly those with Motown, were far from silent during the mid-1960s. Those years produced some of the greatest artists in R&B and soul (a slower, sexier variation of R&B), including Aretha Franklin, Sam Cooke, Diana Ross and the Supremes, Wilson Pickett, Gladys Knight, Smoky Robinson, Curtis Mayfield, and Marvin Gaye.

Another irony was the fact that, whereas rock and roll had its roots with black artists, virtually all rock musicians were white. But by the mid-1960s, Ike and Tina Turner had become major rock stars, and they were followed in 1967 by

Sly and the Family Stone. That year also saw the debut of a guitarist who became not merely one of rock's great *black* artists, but one of the greatest artists—regardless of race—in music history: Jimi Hendrix.

The hippie movement turns back to the earth

The Jimi Hendrix Experience was one of several major acts, including the Doors and Janis Joplin, to emerge in 1967. The year also saw the famous "Summer of Love" in San Francisco, as well as the release of what many critics regard as the greatest album of all time, *Sgt. Pepper's Lonely Hearts Club Band* by the Beatles. Clearly a full-scale movement was afoot, symbolized by the wild hair, clothes, and lifestyles of the hippies, and this movement reached its height with the Woodstock festival—featuring Hendrix, Joplin, Santana, Jefferson Airplane, and many others—in 1969.

But Woodstock also marked the beginning of the end of the 1960s as a musical era. The murder of a fan by members of the Hells' Angels motorcycle gang at a Rolling Stones concert in 1969; the breakup of the Beatles in 1970; the deaths of Hendrix, Joplin, and the Doors' Jim Morrison in 1970 and 1971—these and many other events indicated that the optimism symbolized by Woodstock had passed.

Meanwhile, Dylan had retreated from the limelight after a motorcycle accident in 1966, and when he reemerged in 1968 the stripped-down sound of his *John Wesley Harding* personified a shift back to basics. In the years that followed, young people increasingly rejected the psychedelic sound that had characterized the Summer of Love, and embraced what became known as the "back to the earth movement"—a return to simpler ways. In music, the popularity of roots-rock groups such as Creedence Clearwater Revival and the Allman Brothers signaled this shift.

The 1970s: From southern rock to disco

The Allman Brothers, along with Lynyrd Skynyrd, spawned an entire movement, southern rock, that shared some similarities with the southwestern style of the Eagles. These were just two of the many musical trends that characterized the 1970s. Yet another was the phenomenon of singer/songwriters such as James Taylor and Carly Simon. Still another was the jazz-influenced rock of groups ranging from Chicago to Steely Dan.

Then there was heavy metal, ear-splitting music laden with magical and sometimes satanic imagery. Its leading proponents were Led Zeppelin and Black Sabbath, the latter particularly notable for lead singer Ozzy Osbourne's terrifying wail. Closely tied in spirit, if not in style, was the art-rock of Pink Floyd and others. Still another form was glam rock, whose greatest stars ranged from the artful David Bowie to the clownish KISS.

There was funk, created by James Brown and expanded by George Clinton and Parliament/Funkadelic, and there was reggae, a Jamaican style whose greatest star was Bob Marley. Reggae had a strong political dimension; by contrast, disco—which melded R&B, pop, and most of all dance music—was all about having a good time.

These were some of the best years in the history of music—and, in some cases, they were also some of the worst. But to a rising generation of disaffected youth in New York City and London during the mid-1970s, the Eagles and Led Zeppelin and disco stars were all the same: money-makers whose music had no connection to harsh realities such as unemployment and racism.

The punk reaction

Thus was born punk rock, whose earliest proponents included the Sex Pistols, the Ramones, and the Clash. The roots of punk could be seen in the work of a late 1960s band called the Velvet Underground, whose most prominent figure was Lou Reed. The Velvets' music was dark and doom laden, but alongside the darkness and anger in much punk, other emerging stars of the era showed a range of emotions.

Elvis Costello may have been an angry young man, but he could also write astonishingly sensitive songs. In any case, at its heart punk called for a return to basics—and it was for this reason that the early Bruce Springsteen was lumped in with punk artists. As it had done before, rock was reviving itself.

The 1980s: Rock takes a back seat

Despite its critical importance—and the later impact it would exert through alternative rock—punk was not a powerful commercial force. As the initial fury of the punk onslaught died in 1979, punk groups either broke up or broadened their style, and what emerged was a movement called new wave, which offered some of the best and worst moments in music history.

The greatest rock music of the late 1970s and early 1980s came from groups such as the Clash, the Police (whose lead singer was Sting), and the Talking Heads, who had started out as punkers and expanded their range. Such groups *truly* went back to roots: the Talking Heads adopted African rhythms, while the other two groups embraced reggae and ska, a more upbeat style from Jamaica. Also important were bands outside punk, such as Dire Straits and the Stray Cats, who likewise favored a return to basics.

Similarly, U2 and R.E.M came out of the musical environment that produced punk, without themselves being punk bands. Both first appeared early in the 1980s and would later become identified with alternative rock, even though they—like an even older star, Neil Young—long predated it.

The video craze

As the 1980s went into full swing and MTV (established in 1981) spurred the craze for music videos, one might have thought that music would become more interesting, but in fact it became less so. New wave merged with watered-down versions of R&B to produce lightweight groups such as Duran Duran and the Culture Club, who were more notable for their appearance than their sound. Video created a whole new array of stars, such as Madonna, who vied with Michael Jackson—an R&B singer who had crossed over into pop to become one of most successful performers of all time—for attention on the TV screens of America.

During the early 1980s, R&B audiences turned, on the one hand, to soul crooners such as Luther Vandross, and on the other hand to party music along the lines of that offered by the Gap Band. Some stars—most notably Jackson and Whitney Houston—crossed over to pop. Though they sold millions of albums, those singers' influence on music as a whole was negligible compared to that of another artist, Prince, who managed to cross over while remaining true to R&B.

A few groups take on the "hair bands"

In the world of rock, The Cure, the Smiths, and a handful of other bands continued to expand musical horizons in the mid-1980s, but R.E.M. and U2 proved the only groups of the era to enjoy large creative *and* commercial success. Meanwhile, center stage belonged to "hair bands," acts that copied the heavy-metal sound of Van Halen while emphasizing hairstyles, clothing, and even—in a glam-rock touch—makeup.

Yet again, however, the elements of music's rebirth lay in unexpected places. Though some of the most excessive 1980s music came from heavy metal, punk-influenced metal bands such as Guns N' Roses and Metallica offered a return to roots. (See overview on Heavy Metal in *Parents Aren't Supposed to Like It*, Vol. 3, p. 465.) At the same time, well outside the rock world, a vibrant new musical form had emerged.

Rap comes of age

The center of energy in the African American musical community during the 1980s lay far from mainstream pop, rock, or even R&B. That center existed in the dance clubs of New York, where rap had been born in the late 1970s. By the early 1980s, it had gained a new political dimension with the work of Grandmaster Flash and the Furious Five, Afrika Bambaataa, and others.

At mid-decade, the world of rap was bursting with a host of new talents: Run-DMC, Public Enemy, Boogie Down Productions, LL Cool J, and even a white group, the Beastie Boys. Soon to follow were Queen Latifah and the rap supergroup N.W.A., whose members included Dr. Dre, Ice Cube, and Eazy-E.

Not all rap was serious: Salt-N-Pepa, for instance, showed that it could be fun. The all-girl rap group was also exceptional in that it enjoyed mainstream success, something beyond the reach of most hardcore rap, with its harsh sounds and lyrics. In any case, rap remained the creative center of music in the late 1980s, while rock—with a few notable exceptions—produced little of lasting interest.

The early 1990s: Grunge and gangstas

Unlike varieties of rock, pop music never goes out of style; it only changes

Musical Genres: An Overview

form, and at times when rock is on the downswing, pop reemerges with a vengeance. Thus it was that the late 1980s and early 1990s witnessed an explosion of new pop superstars: Janet Jackson, Mariah Carey, Celine Dion, and Gloria Estefan. So prevalent were these female artists—along with Madonna and Houston—that the word *diva,* once the exclusive property of opera, entered common usage as a term to describe them.

At the beginning of the 1990s, rap increasingly entered the mainstream, though many of its most popular stars (Vanilla Ice, Young MC) would prove to be one-hit wonders. But the new breed of R&B superstars—Babyface, Boyz II Men, R. Kelly, Mary J. Blige, TLC, and D'Angelo—had much more staying power. (See overview on Rhythm and Blues and Urban Soul in *Parents Aren't Supposed to Like It,* Vol. 3, p. 501.)

Styles proliferated as never before. Folk enjoyed a resurgence, thanks to Tracy Chapman and the Indigo Girls. (See overview on Folk Music and Folk Rock in *Parents Aren't Supposed to Like It,* Vol. 3, p. 439.) And for the first time in history, unabashedly Christian artists such as Amy Grant and Michael W. Smith hit the Top 40, paving the way for the entrance of contemporary Christian music to the mainstream.

May 25, 1991, marked an important event in music history: on that day *Billboard* changed its method of calculating weekly sales to determine the most popular singles and albums in the nation. Up to that time, the magazine had relied upon the reports of record-store owners and employees, data that was highly subject to human error and corruption. Henceforth, *Billboard* would use Soundscan, a computerized system for totalling sales. Not only was Soundscan more accurate, it made clear a fact that keen observers had long noted: there was no longer any one center of the music world—no true Top 40—but rather a dozen competing genres and audiences.

The birth of alternative rock

A second pivotal day in music history came later in 1991, on September 24, when Nirvana released *Nevermind.* Exhibiting influences that ranged from Led Zeppelin to the Sex Pistols, Kurt Cobain and his band almost single-handedly revived rock, and like the Beatles before them, they brought with them a wave of new artists. These new groups, however, came not from Britain but from Seattle, Washington, home to Pearl Jam, Soundgarden, and many others.

Nirvana's gritty, no-frills version of rock quickly earned the name "grunge," but critics also realized that they stood at the head of a movement that was much larger than grunge—or Seattle. Lacking a name for this new, back-to-basics form of hard rock, observers dubbed it "alternative."

The period from 1992 to 1994 saw an explosion of artists known by that term, among them the Red Hot Chili Peppers (actually a band that had been around for several years), Counting Crows, Beck, Hole (fronted by Cobain's wife Courtney Love), The Offspring,

Smashing Pumpkins, Green Day, and Nine Inch Nails.

"Alternative" becomes mainstream

With so many "alternative" bands, the term seemed to have little meaning; and in fact the alternative movement soon splintered in many directions. On the one hand it merged with metal to form the alternative metal (or "alt-metal") of Marilyn Manson, and with metal and rap to create a promising new style in the "rap-metal" of Rage Against the Machine. At the other end of the spectrum, alternative mingled with pop in the songs of hugely successful bands such as Hootie and the Blowfish and Collective Soul.

Seattle-style grunge along the lines of Nirvana and Pearl Jam had been a peculiarly American phenomenon, but across the sea alternative rock linked with an edgy English style called Brit Pop, exemplified by bands such as Blur and Oasis. Then there were numerous American bands, most notably No Doubt and Sublime, whose style suggested ska.

Crossing genre lines

Artists from other genres soon became linked with the "alternative" label, simply because they were young and their music did not fit any well-defined category. Some, such as Alanis Morissette or the Wallflowers, warranted that label; others, among them rockers Lenny Kravitz and the Dave Matthews Band, just happened to be in the neighborhood.

Typical of the cross-pollination between genres that took place during the 1990s was dance music, which enjoyed a brief run of popularity during the early half of the decade. This drew from "house music," a British style that brought together elements of everything from punk to pop. Later it became linked with alternative and electronica, whose roots lay with some of the most creative bands of the 1970s and 1980s: Germany's Kraftwerk and America's very strange punk/new wave band Devo. (See overview on Dance Music in *Parents Aren't Supposed to Like It,* Vol. 2, p. 275.)

Festival tours bring together various artists

During the 1990s, huge festival tours brought together alternative, rock and roll, dance/electronica, and rap artists, as well as latter-day singer/songwriters, on a single stage. The first major festival tour was Lollapalooza, originated in 1991 by Jane's Addiction/Porno for Pyros frontman Perry Farrell.

Next came H.O.R.D.E. (Horizons of Rock Development Everywhere), organized by Blues Traveler in 1992, which concentrated on artists with a blues or roots-rock style. (See overviews on Alternative and Pop Rock in *Parents Aren't Supposed to Like It,* Vol. 1, p. 1; on Rock and Roll in Vol. 3., p. 539; and on Singers/Songwriters in Vol. 3, p. 611.)

Gangsta rap

In the early 1990s, the heavily political rap of groups such as Public Enemy gave way to a style that was in many ways its opposite: gangsta rap. The only politics that interested gangstas were those of inter-gang rivalries, and instead

Musical Genres: An Overview

The Ten Best-Selling Artists of the 1990s

(Numbers represent millions of CDs and cassettes sold.)

- Garth Brooks   60.0
- Mariah Carey   38.3
- Celine Dion   34.6
- Metallica   33.6
- The Beatles   30.2
- Kenny G.   26.7
- George Strait   24.5
- Pearl Jam   22.3
- Reba McEntire   22.0
- Pink Floyd   21.8

Source: Soundscan, as reported in the *New York Times,* April 30, 2000.

---

of confronting large social issues as Public Enemy's Chuck D. had done, gangstas rapped about sex, drugs, and violence.

Though many critics found redeeming social value in the work of Tupac Shakur, and though Dr. Dre's 1993 album *The Chronic* became an instant classic, gangstas were doomed by their own self-proclaimed love for living fast and dying young. Gangstas further courted violence with a war of words that pitted East Coast rappers such as the Notorious B.I.G. against their West Coast counterparts, including Tupac, Dre, and Snoop Dogg.

The war seemed to go beyond words when first Tupac and, six months later, Biggie met their deaths in a hail of bullets. Yet more than a few observers blamed Tupac's September 1996 shooting on Death Row Records chief Marion "Suge" Knight, who was with him at the time and walked away unhurt. Within a short time, federal authorities began investigating Death Row, the nerve center of gangsta rap, and Knight eventually went to prison for his criminal dealings.

In the meantime, Eazy-E had died of complications from AIDS. As for Dre and Snoop, both had sobering brushes with the law: a short jail sentence in the case of the former, and a trial and acquittal for the latter. As a result of these experiences—not to mention the examples of death and destruction that had befallen their old comrades—both sobered up, became family men, and after a few awkward years proved that they still had what it took as rappers. (See overview on Hip-Hop and Rap in *Parents Aren't Supposed to Like It,* Vol. 2, p. 303.)

The late 1990s and beyond: A "big tent"

In a sense, gangsta rap continued to flourish in the work of Bone Thugs-N-Harmony, as well as the many artists on Master P's No Limit label—including Snoop. Yet the character of gangsta had changed, as witnessed by the lifestyle changes of Snoop and Dre, and gangsta would never again dominate the rap scene as it once had.

Dre had turned his attention increasingly to producing, and in fact rap during the late 1990s was dominated by powerful producer/performers such as Puff Daddy. Puff Daddy, who had worked with a host of artists, soon emerged from behind the scenes with "I'll Be Missing You," a tribute to his fallen comrade Biggie (The Notorious B.I.G.). Another producer/performer who appeared at the same time was Missy "Misdemeanor" Elliott, whose success helped bring other female rappers such as Lil' Kim and Da Brat to the forefront.

The class of '97

Puffy and Missy emerged as mainstream stars in 1997, a year that brought an impressive array of new or previously little-known talents to the forefront. There was the rapper Busta Rhymes; "ska-core" alternative rockers the Mighty Mighty Bosstones; sixteen-year-old blues guitarist Jonny Lang; and a host of alternative pop/rock bands that included Matchbox Twenty, Smash Mouth, Sugar Ray, Sister Hazel, and Third Eye Blind.

In addition, established performers returned or hit their stride in 1997. The Wallflowers, Counting Crows, and Foo Fighters released major new albums; No Doubt emerged as superstars; and Marilyn Manson's national audience grew. Radiohead astonished critics and fans alike with their third album, *O.K. Computer*, and Everclear's sophomore effort proved an even greater success than their debut. And though the dance craze of the early to mid-1990s proved shortlived, that did not stop Jamiroquai and Prodigy from scoring big hits that year.

Yet so many female artists held the limelight in 1997 that it came to be known as the "year of the woman." Again, some stars had established themselves earlier, and now returned with new releases. That was the case with Sarah McLachlan, who also made headlines as organizer of Lilith Fair, a festival tour showcasing female talent. Likewise,

---

The Ten Best-Selling Albums of the 1990s

(Numbers represent millions of CDs and cassettes sold.)

- *Jagged Little Pill*— Alanis Morissette 13.5
- *Come On Over*— Shania Twain 12.1
- *Metallica*— Metallica 11.7
- *The Bodyguard* soundtrack— Whitney Houston and others 11.6
- *Falling Into You*— Celine Dion 10.2
- *Cracked Rear View*— Hootie and the Blowfish 9.8
- *Titanic Soundtrack*— Celine Dion and others 9.8
- *Millennium*— Backstreet Boys 9.4
- *Ropin' The Wind*— Garth Brooks 9.4
- *Backstreet Boys*— Backstreet Boys 9.3

Source: Soundscan, as reported in the *New York Times,* April 30, 2000. These figures are lower than those provided by the Recording Industry Association of America (RIAA), the organization that certifies gold and platinum albums. According to the RIAA, for instance, *Come on Over* and *Cracked Rear View* each sold 17 million copies.

Musical Genres: An Overview

Sheryl Crow once again hit the airwaves with a new album.

But 1997 also introduced the world to female performers across the spectrum: from singer/songwriters Jewel, Fiona Apple, and Erykah Badu—representing folk, alternative, and R&B respectively—to bubblegum pop stars the Spice Girls. The year also solidified the influence of Dion, Toni Braxton, and LeAnn Rimes, a highly talented country singer who had recorded her first album at the age of thirteen in 1996.

Not your father's country music anymore

Rimes was but one of several singers who crossed over from the country to the pop charts, but George Strait and Reba McEntire managed to become the seventh and ninth best-selling artists of the 1990s respectively without even making any major attempt to reach a pop audience. On the other hand, Garth Brooks crossed over to pop and even rock on his way to becoming the biggest-selling solo artist of all time.

Though country legends such as Hank Williams and Patsy Cline had gained wide respect, the genre as a whole had been the butt of jokes in the mainstream—but not anymore. Nothing illustrated country's new respect like the rise of female stars such as Rimes, Shania Twain, Faith Hill, and The Dixie Chicks. The music of Twain and Hill, in fact, became virtually indistinguishable from pop, and though country purists complained, the two singers sold millions of albums. So too did the Chicks—and they did so while remaining true to their country roots.

Christian music and other revivals

Billboard's adoption of Soundscan for tracking sales had helped make it clear that there were no longer just a couple of styles capable of drawing large audiences. Therefore record companies and radio stations redirected their efforts, seeking to cater to ever-widening tastes, and the late 1990s acquired a "big tent" atmosphere of inclusiveness.

As a result, a number of amazing things happened. Prior to Amy Grant, it had been virtually impossible to imagine a contemporary Christian artist—someone who, regardless of genre, promoted Christian beliefs in his or her music—turning out a series of hit songs. Even after her success, it was still hard to imagine a contemporary Christian *alternative* band; but then along came Jars of Clay and dc Talk. The latter brought in rap elements, though not to as great an extent as Kirk Franklin, who collaborated with mainstream stars, sold millions of albums, and won a number of Grammy awards.

Christians often talk about "revival," meaning a resurgence of emphasis on spiritual matters. Certainly the world of music in the 1990s was awash in revivals—in more ways than one. There was a revival of interest in ska and even in swing, and perhaps equally surprising was the revival of an old-time favorite: teen pop.

Teen pop makes a comeback

Teen pop, music with an appeal primarily directed toward teenagers, has been around for decades; only the artists themselves change. Critics typically dislike teen pop, and are happy to see it

Parents Aren't Supposed to Like It

disappear, but every few years it returns to the charts. Its reawakening in the late 1990s came with the success of another group from the "class of '97," Hanson.

The Hanson brothers were certainly young, and they had a youthful audience. But they were more than mere teen-pop stars: they actually played their instruments and wrote their own songs. Nonetheless, along with the Spice Girls they resurrected the national interest in teen pop.

The years that followed saw the rise of "boy bands": first the Backstreet Boys, then 'NSync, and later 98 Degrees. Then there were the girl artists, led by Britney Spears and Christina Aguilera, both of whom cultivated a naughty-but-nice image. Still later came a pop-rock band from Ireland that, like Hanson, consisted of siblings who played their own instruments: The Corrs.

The pop charts of 2000 and beyond were also bursting with R&B artists who had crossed over from their own genre. On the one hand, D'Angelo, Mary J. Blige, R. Kelly, and others had spurred a new interest in back-to-roots soul, exemplified by the huge success of Lauryn Hill of the Fugees and, later, Macy Gray and Sisqo. On the other hand, artists such as Destiny's Child and Pink held at least as much interest to pop audiences as to R&B listeners.

Swing, world music, and the Latin beat

The late 1990s' interest in ska and swing was another surprise. Among the leading artists of the swing revival was Brian Setzer, a familiar name to many older listeners from his days with the Stray Cats. In fact the end of the millennium saw the return of several older stars: Santana had a hugely popular album, as did Sting, and Ozzy Osbourne became host to a highly successful festival tour, Ozzfest.

The work of Sting, Santana, and numerous artists helped draw attention to world music. The latter was a loosely defined genre encompassing folk artists from around the planet—and even some pop stars, though typically these were stars from non-English-speaking countries of whom American fans knew little.

But one kind of "world music" took the forefront in 1999: the Latin sound. Starting with Ricky Martin's smash hit "Livin' La Vida Loca," a host of Latin stars—including Marc Anthony, Jennifer Lopez, and Enrique Iglesias —hit the charts, and by the turn of the millennium Latin music was everywhere.

Hip-hop vs. rap

Despite all the energy in so many fields of music at the end of the twentieth century, no area was more dynamic than rap and hip-hop. The latter term came into mainstream use during the late 1990s, but fans often disagreed regarding its meaning. People within the world of rap had varying interpretations that revolved around fine points, whereas outsiders adopted a much simpler distinction: rap had a harder edge, with little singing and often little melody (as opposed to rhythm), whereas hip-hop was much softer, more oriented towards singing and melody.

Numerous hip-hop stars such as Puff Daddy made an art of sampling, or using parts of another recording. On the other hand, A Tribe Called Quest—a hugely influential group that disbanded in 1998—used live musicians. Either way, melody was foremost. And hip-hop stars, unlike most hardcore rappers, had huge pop appeal, as witnessed by the success of Will Smith, who had first established himself with DJ Jazzy Jeff and the Fresh Prince.

Yet pure rap continued to flourish. The nine members of Wu-Tang Clan produced a dizzying array of solo and group albums, sometimes (in the case of ODB) while on the run from the police. Artists such as Nelly, DMX, Ja Rule, and Mystikal even found themselves with radio hits; but none enjoyed the success of Eminem, a white rapper.

The marriage of rap and rock

One of the biggest stories in music at the turn of the millennium was the merger between "white" rock and "black" rap. Certainly the late 1990s and early 2000s had seen the appearance of numerous exciting new bands in the more "traditional" alternative rock category. These ranged from Barenaked Ladies to Blink-182 to Creed to Papa Roach, but nonetheless things were changing. Even Barenaked Ladies, an established group that had a breakthrough in 1998, did so with a quasi-rap on "One Week."

The Red Hot Chili Peppers and Rage Against the Machine had already pointed the way toward the marriage of rap and rock, and their work in turn influenced KoRN, Limp Bizkit, and 311. Despite the fact that they all bore the "rap-rock" label, those three bands could not have been more different from one another. The same was true of the brooding, earnest Everlast and the hilarious Kid Rock, who even figured out how to blend rap with country and western.

Music in the late 1990s and early 2000s was nothing if not diverse. Influences within and across musical genres helped shape new categories while blurring the boundaries between existing genres, thus giving music fans more of what they love.

Words to Know

A

A&R: Artists and repertoire. The A&R section of a record label is devoted to finding new talent.

A cappella: Without musical accompaniment.

advance: Payment made upon signing a contract, in advance of money the artist will later earn from record sales.

airplay: The playing of a song by a radio station.

album: A collection of songs released as a single unit for extended listening. Today's albums are typically in compact-disc format, whereas in the past they appeared on **record** or cassette—but the term "album" applies equally to all.

arranger: A person responsible for adding the background (for example, rhythms or harmonies) to a recording, fleshing it out and giving it its final form.

B

ballad: A slow, very melodic love song.

Da Brat. (Corbis Corporation. Reproduced by permission.)

Billboard: A music trade magazine that publishes weekly charts of the top 200 best-selling albums in the country, as well as the 100 leading **singles** in pop, R&B, and other markets. (See also **Soundscan**.)

Bluegrass: A variety of country music that originated in the mountains of the southeastern United States. Bluegrass places a heavy concentration on instruments such as the banjo and dulcimer, with less emphasis on rhythm instruments.

booking: A scheduled engagement to play a show or concert.

bootleg: A recording made or distributed without an artist's permission.

break dancing: A physically demanding style of movement that involves spinning on the floor like a top. The heyday of break dancing was in the 1980s.

Broadway: The Broadway theatre district in New York City, home to the nation's most prominent plays and musicals. Often the term "Broadway" refers to the highly theatrical style of singing typical of Broadway musical shows.

B-side: Back in the days when music typically appeared on **vinyl** and records had a Side 1 and Side 2, **singles** consisted of an A-side and a B-side. The A-side *was* the single—that is, it was the song the artists and/or management believed would be a hit—whereas the B-side was a song of secondary importance. Sometimes, however, the B-side turned out to be a bigger hit than the A-side.

C

chart: To reach the **Billboard** albums or singles charts.

choreography: The arrangement of dance moves in a stage show.

comeback: The return to fame of an artist long out of the limelight.

concept album: A musical work in which the songs are arranged to form a larger idea or "story."

cover: A recording of a song already made famous by someone else.

creative control: An artist's freedom and legal authority to control the composition, recording, and marketing of his or her music.

crossover: A hit that "crosses over" from one set of **Billboard** charts to another—for instance, from country to pop.

cut: Another name for a song or **track** on an **album**.

D

debut: First. In the music business, *debut* is used as a noun ("the group's debut"); adjective ("debut album"); or verb ("the album debuted").

demo: A demonstration recording, which an artist or group uses to attract the attention of record-label **A&R** representatives.

disco: A type of dance music that flourished in the late 1970s, which placed a strong emphasis on repetitive beats.

distribution: The process of getting an artist's work into stores and other points of sale.

diva: A female solo artist with an enormous following and legendary talent, who is known primarily as a singer rather than as a songwriter.

DJ or deejay: Disk jockey. In rap, a DJ is the person who "spins" records on a turntable, creating a musical backdrop to the words of the **MC**.

E

EP: An extended-play recording—not as long as an **LP**, but longer than a **single**. Typically an EP consists of four to six songs.

eponymous: Self-titled. For example, *Indigo Girls* and *Ricky Martin* are eponymous albums.

F

fanzine: A music fan magazine that typically focuses on **teen pop** music.

festival tours: A concert tour package that includes a large and sometimes diverse lineup of performers. Examples of festival tours are Lollapalooza (1991–97) and Lillith Fair (1997–99).

follow-up: A song or album with which an artist hopes to "follow up" the success of an earlier release.

frontman: The most prominent member of a group, almost always a lead singer. (And of course there are front*women*, such as Courtney Love of Hole and Gwen Stefani of No Doubt.)

G

gangsta rap: A style of rap that flourished in the early- to mid-1990s, dominated by artists with either real or claimed connections to gangs.

genre: (Pronounced ZHAHN-ruh); a particular strain or variety within a larger art form. In modern music, some of the major genres are rock, rap, R&B, and pop. There are also multiple subgenres—for instance, alternative rock, heavy metal, and many others.

glam rock: Glam or glamour rock, which had its heyday in the mid-1970s, combined outlandish music with bizarre costumes and makeup.

gold certification: Recognition by the Recording Industry Association of America (RIAA) that a particular release (whether a **single, album,** or music video) has sold 500,000 copies. (See also **platinum certification.**)

gospel: A style of music that originated in churches, as opposed to contemporary Christian music, which like rock or pop originated in concert halls and recording studios.

goth: A movement that began in the late 1980s and took **glam rock** several steps further, placing a much greater emphasis on death imagery.

Grammy award: The National Academy of Recording Arts and Sciences highest award, and one of the top honors in the music industry.

grunge: A gritty, no-frills version of alternative rock influenced by heavy metal punk rock.

H

hardcore: A term used to describe an intense form of music, whether it be rap, heavy metal, or some other form.

headliner: The main group appearing at a concert; usually the last act after one or more **openers.**

hook: The key part of a song, usually a short, very catchy section.

I

independent: Independent record labels are ones not connected to a large corporation. (See also **label.**)

industrial: A noisy, discordant style of music that often uses tapes of noise or sounds created by nonmusical instruments.

J

jam: An extended session in which musicians start with a basic theme and improvise on it, playing off of both the theme and each other's instrumental work.

L

label: A record company.

lick: A powerful sound from a guitar, often constituting part of a **hook.**

lip-synch: To go through the motions of singing, without actually making any sound, while a recording of someone singing plays in the background.

live album: A recording of a concert, part of a concert, or selections from several concerts.

LP: A long-playing record. The term is still used today as a synonym for **album,** though "LP" more accurately describes a **vinyl** record, as opposed to a compact disc.

lyrics: The words to a song.

M

MC or emcee: Master of ceremonies or microphone controller; the "singer," as opposed to the **DJ,** in rap music.

merchandising: The sale of items related to a musical performer—not just singles and albums, but books, tee shirts, and other forms of merchandise.

mixing: The combining of various **tracks** to form a finished recording. In mixing a song, the **producer** and sound engineer bring all these tracks together, controlling noise levels and ensuring that certain parts—in particular, the singer's vocal track—are more prominent than others.

moshing: Violent and unruly dancing, usually at very close quarters in an area known as a mosh pit.

MTV: Music Television, a cable music/entertainment network started in 1981.

N

Napster: The name of a controversial Internet file-sharing service allowing fans to download music for free.

Nashville: Not only the capital of Tennessee, but the capital of the country music industry. A reference to "Nashville" can mean the entire world of country music.

new wave: The dominant form of rock during the first half of the 1980s that combined elements of dance music, electronica, and even soul.

O

opening act: A band or singer that "opens" a show for a **headliner.**

P

platinum certification: Recognition by the Recording Industry Association of America (RIAA) that a particular release (whether a single, album, or music video) has sold 1 million copies. Recordings that sell multiple millions are designated as *multi-platinum.* (See also **gold certification.**)

playlist: The list of songs that a radio station will play over a given period.

pop culture: Popular culture, or the social backdrop created in modern life by music, movies, television, magazines, books, fashion, lifestyles, and fads.

producer: The person who holds the principal artistic authority behind the creation of a musical recording. A producer oversees everything from choosing backup performers to **arranging** instruments to **mixing** the record.

psychedelia, psychedelic: Terms describing both a form of music and a lifestyle that flourished in the 1960s. *Psychedelic* comes from two Greek roots that together mean "to show the mind," and indeed psychedelia first emerged with the use of so-called consciousness-altering drugs such as LSD in the period from 1966 to 1968. Elements of psychedelia include jangly guitars and hazy lyrics.

punk: A musical movement that originated simultaneously but separately in Britain and America between 1975 and 1977 featuring a raw, stripped-down style and angry commentaries on social issues.

R

record: Like **LP,** "record" technically refers to a **vinyl** recording, but in practice it can often mean a CD.

recording contract: A legal agreement between a record **label** and an artist. Generally, a contract states that an artist agrees to record a certain number of **albums** in exchange for some sort of financial compensation.

reggae: Combining elements of African music, traditional Caribbean styles, and American R&B, reggae originated in Jamaica during the 1960s.

rhythm guitar: A "second" guitar, typically played by the singer in a band that also has a (typically non-singing) lead guitarist. The lead guitarist fingers specific notes and may play solos, whereas a rhythm guitarist strums the strings and provides a backdrop for the lead.

rotation: The frequency of **airplay** for a given **single.**

S

Salsa: A musical style that blends elements of Latin, rock, jazz, and R&B.

sampling: To use parts of another recording, typically one that another artist has made famous, in a new recording.

scratching: Moving a record back and forth, thus making a scratching sound as the needle skates across the grooves. Rhythmic scratching as practiced by **DJ**s has long been a part of rap, especially in the 1980s.

self-distributed: A type of recording that an artist arranges to record and sell (typically at concerts) without the help of *any* record company—even an **independent.**

show tune: A song popularized in a **Broadway** musical.

single: A song which, in the view of the artist and/or management, has hit potential, and which therefore is released in a relatively inexpensive short format.

Soundscan: A computerized system for tracking record sales, which in 1991 became the basis for calculating the ***Billboard*** charts.

speed metal: A fast, aggressive form of heavy metal, reflecting a **punk** influence, that arose in the late 1980s.

spot: An engagement to play in a club or on a concert lineup, or a place on the ***Billboard*** charts or some other charting system (as in "the album reached the number-one spot.")

studio album: A non-**live** recording, usually rehearsed and recorded in a music studio.

T

teen pop: Usually a light form of music, marketed primarily toward teenagers, that emphasizes the performers' looks and a catchy sound.

teenybopper: A negative term referring to teenagers who obsessively follow musical fads.

Top 40: The 40 most popular **singles**, according to the ***Billboard*** pop charts, in a given period. Though the number 40 might seem arbitrary (why not 25, for instance, or 50?), at some point in time station programmers determined that 40 was an ideal number of singles to keep in **rotation.**

tour: A series of concerts. Often artists go on tour to support a new album or a hit single.

track: A song or **cut** from an **album,** or a recording of one or more voices or instruments that will be **mixed** with other tracks for a finished recording.

V

VH1: Video Hits One, a cable music channel owned by **MTV** Networks and established in 1985.

vinyl: A term for old-fashioned **records**—the kind people played on a turntable. With the rise of compact discs in the late 1980s, vinyl became virtually obsolete, but record companies still produce vinyl versions of some **singles** and **albums.**

W

Woodstock: A three-day music festival that took place in upstate New York in August 1969. Revivals of Woodstock were held in 1994 and 1999.

parents aren't supposed to like it

NELLY

American rap artist
Born Cornell Haynes, Jr., on November 2, 1979, in Texas

When Nelly's *Country Grammar* sold 5 million copies within six months of its release in June 2000, it seemed the rapper had come out of nowhere. Indeed, in the New-York- and Los-Angeles-dominated world of rap, Nelly's hometown of St. Louis, Missouri, might as well be nowhere. But thanks to the infectious title track, reminiscent of a jump-rope rhyme, Nelly has helped put the Midwest on the hip-hop map.

Moving from town to town

"Nelly" is a nickname that developed in childhood from his given name of Cornell. Because his father was in the Air Force, Nelly spent his early years moving from town to town, but around the time he reached seventh grade, he wound up in the St. Louis suburb of University City.

Unfortunately, his parents' divorce canceled out any stability the family might have gained by settling down. "There was a point in time when my mother couldn't afford to keep me," he later told

> "I don't sound like anyone. I've got a style that's all my own. I'm rappin' the blues. I like to think of my music as a jazz form of hip-hop."
>
> –Nelly, *Jet*, October 30, 2000

Nelly. (Archive Photos. Reproduced by permission.)

The *Other* Nelly

Unlike Cornell Haynes, Jr.—a.k.a. Nelly—Canada's Nelly Furtado (b. 1979) was actually born with that name. Of Portuguese descent, she comes from Victoria, British Columbia, where she played trombone in the high school band.

Released in the fall of 2000, her debut, *Whoa Nelly!*, reflects the broad range of her musical influences, from hip-hop to jazz to a variety of Latin strains, including Brazilian bossa nova. Indeed, it could be said that Nelly Furtado does not just perform world music; this promising newcomer *is* world music.

Rolling Stone, "and my father couldn't afford to keep me, so I lived with friends, grandparents. When you [are] a kid, that kind of [stuff] affects you."

Either a rapper or a drug dealer

A talented shortstop, in his teens Nelly landed a position in the St. Louis amateur baseball league. He might have gone pro, but at age sixteen he became a father. (In addition to his daughter, born in 1996, Nelly has a son three years younger.) Determined to support his girlfriend and child, he turned to selling drugs.

> "Nelly was going to either be a number-one rapper or a number-one drug dealer."

"Nelly was going to either be a number-one rapper or a number-one drug dealer," fellow rapper Murphy Lee explained to *Rolling Stone*. Fortunately rap won out: while playing baseball, Nelly had met Murphy's older brother Kyjuan, and in 1992 the two thirteen-year-olds recorded a single, "Addiction."

A year later, in 1993, Nelly formed the St. Lunatics with Kyjuan and Murphy, as well as rappers Ali and Jason—and his own younger brother, known as City Spud. By 1996 they had a local hit with "Gimme What Ya Got," but DJ 618, a leading figure in the St. Louis club scene, told them they had an even bigger potential smash on their hands with their song "Country Grammar."

A number-one jump-rope rhyme

Nelly later told *Rolling Stone* that the support of DJ 618 "was actually what got our faith behind the song. We just felt like we were holding the winning lottery ticket." But in order to cash it in, the St. Lunatics decided they would have more success if they billed Nelly—who is as handsome as he is smooth and articulate—as a solo artist.

Eventually they got a tape of "Country Grammar" to the rapper Mase, who helped them make a quality demo recording. After considerably more effort to market the demo, Nelly and his crew finally got a deal with Universal Records, which in June 2000 released both the single and the album of the same title.

"Country Grammar" combined elements of "Shimmy, Shimmy, Ko-Ko-Bop," a 1959 hit for Little Anthony and the Imperials, with what Rob Sheffield in *Rolling Stone* described as a "singsong

Nelly, along with Britney Spears, 'NSync, and Aerosmith, lights up the stage during a halftime performance at the 2001 Super Bowl in Tampa, Florida. (AP/Wide World Photos. Reproduced by permission.)

hook from the classic clapping song 'Down Down Baby,' currently in heavy rotation on a jungle gym near you. Talk about old school: you probably learned the original in kindergarten, watching the first-grade girls at recess clap their hands in those mystical patterns...."

The song may have been based on a schoolgirls' jump-rope rhyme, and the singer may have a girl's name, but Nelly is as macho as they come. His stage shows proved a huge hit with female fans, while "Country Grammar"—a top-ten single and a popular MTV video during the late summer of 2000—spurred the album's phenomenal sales.

A memorable MTV Video Awards performance

After **DMX** (see entry) failed to show up to rehearse a performance at the MTV Video Music Awards in September 2000, the ceremony's organizers recruited Nelly instead. The result was a memorable one: his belt buckle broke just before he was scheduled to go on, and his pants fell down on stage. "It was nothing I did on purpose," he told *Rolling Stone*. "But I did get a lot of good reviews from it. The ladies like[d] it."

Late in 2000, as he once again hit the Top 10 with "E.I.," Nelly prepared to make his motion-picture debut in a film

Nelly 303

titled *Snipes*. The year that followed would see the first St. Lunatics album, but for the time being, Nelly planned to get some rest. He intended, he told *Rolling Stone* in late December 2000, to "relax with my son and daughter. I'm missing my son. He's walking, he's starting to talk, and I'm missing all of that."

Selected Awards

Multi-platinum certification (5 million sales), *Country Grammar*, 2000.

Grammy Award nomination, Best Rap Solo Performance, for "Country Grammar," 2001.

Grammy Award nomination, Best Rap Album, for *Country Grammar*, 2001.

Selected Discography

Country Grammar (Universal), 2000.

Further Reading

Binelli, Mark. "People of the Year: Nelly." *Rolling Stone,* December 14–21, 2000, p. 98.

Bozza, Anthony. "Nelly: Hip-hop's Heartland Hero." *Rolling Stone,* November 9, 2000, p. 55.

"Debut Solo CD 'Country Grammar' Making Nelly and City of St. Louis Big Names in Hip-hop." *Jet,* October 30, 2000, p. 40.

Moon, Tom. "Nelly/Cash Money Millionaires." *Rolling Stone,* December 7, 2000, p. 40.

Sheffield, Rob. "Shimmy-Shimmying to Nelly's Playground Chic." *Rolling Stone,* October 26, 2000, p. 32.

Contact Information

Universal/Motown Records Group
1755 Broadway
New York, NY 10019

Web Sites

Nelly (official site). http://www.nelly.net (accessed on January 23, 2001).

Nelly Lyrics and Pictures. http://www.nellyhq.com (accessed on January 23, 2001).

98 Degrees

American pop group

Formed 1996 in Los Angeles, California

The members of 98 Degrees are quick to distinguish the group from "boy bands" such as the **Backstreet Boys** and **'NSync** (see entries). They formed their ensemble without the help of a pop starmaker, and they write many of their own songs. Performers who see themselves as working in the tradition of Boyz II Men, the members of 98 Degrees are among the few white artists on the highly respected Motown label.

The Ohio contingent in Los Angeles

After studying psychology at Ohio's Kent State University, Jeff Timmons (born April 30, 1973) moved to Los Angeles with plans of becoming a singer. He met fellow Ohioan Nick Lachey (born November 9, 1973), who introduced him to his friend Justin Jeffre (born February 25, 1973).

Lachey, Jeffre, and Lachey's brother Drew (born August 8, 1976) had all attended the Cincinnati School for Creative and Performing Arts. Drew had since entered the Army Reserves, and

> "People automatically assume we're from Florida, that we were put together (by someone else), and that there are five of us—all wrong."
>
> —Nick Lachey, *Interview*, May 2000

(L–R) Justin Jeffre, Nick Lachey, Drew Lachey and Jeff Timmons. (AP/Wide World Photos. Reproduced by permission.)

after completing his training as a medic, he went to work as an emergency medical technician (EMT) in New York City. But when his older brother asked him to join the new group, who called themselves 98 Degrees, he decided to move westward and seek his fortune.

The four worked a variety of odd jobs while searching for their big break. One night they tried to get backstage at a Boyz II Men concert without passes, and in the process they attracted enough attention that they got an opportunity to sing on a local radio station. As a result of the radio spot, they met manager Paris D'Jon, who arranged for them to record a demo and got them a contract with Motown in 1996.

Riding the pop wave to chart success

Their self-titled debut appeared in July 1997, just as pop resurfaced with groups ranging from **Hanson** to the Spice Girls (see entry and sidebar). The single "Invisible Man" hit No. 12 on the singles charts, and 98 Degrees followed it up in 1998 with two more hits.

> "When we put the group together . . . we thought of ourselves as similar to Boyz II Men. Then along the way we got pigeonholed into the boy-band phenomenon."

First came the top-forty "True to Your Heart," recorded with Stevie Wonder (see sidebar to **Jamiroquai** entry) for the soundtrack of Disney's *Mulan;* and then the top-ten "Because of You." The latter came from the group's sophomore release, *98 Degrees and Rising,* which put them on the Top 10 twice in 1999 with "The Hardest Part" and "I Do (Cherish You)."

Late 1999 and early 2000 found 98 Degrees back on the Top 20 with "This Gift" from their holiday release, *This Christmas,* and on the Top 10 singing backup for **Mariah Carey** (see entry) on "Thank God I Found You." Meanwhile they prepared to record their next LP, which would include far more songs written by group members.

One fast-food meal short of a million dollars

As they made their way into the limelight, 98 Degrees had to fight critics' and fans' attempts to lump them in with their competitors. "When we put the group together in 1995," Nick told Michael Musto in *Interview,* "we thought of ourselves as similar to Boyz II Men. Then along the way we got pigeonholed into the boy-band phenomenon."

But Nick, who described 'NSync and Backstreet as "very talented bands," was not always so serious. When David A. Keeps of *Rolling Stone* asked him "Did you become a millionaire this year?" (2000), he said, "It's borderline. It all hinges on whether I get the Value Meal today."

An interview with *People* revealed a traditional brother-to-brother rivalry between Nick and Drew, who said they had often fought over girlfriends in high school. By 1999, however, the elder Lachey had become involved with another pop sensation, Jessica Simpson, and sang with her on her March 2000 hit "Where You Are."

A lawsuit and a wedding

The bilingual "Give Me Just One Night (Una Noche)" hit the charts in

98 Degrees perform at the 2000 Radio Music Awards show, where their song "Give Me Just One Night" won for Most Requested Song of the Year. (Archive Photos. Reproduced by permission.)

2000, reaching the Top 10 by September. Also that month *Revelation* was released, which debuted at No. 2 on the *Billboard* charts.

Group members hoped the album, which included more of their own songs than any preceding release, would help to distance them from the boy-band label. But in October 2000, they acquired at least one highly unfortunate similarity with Backstreet and 'NSync when, like those groups, they found themselves in a legal disagreement with their manager. The latter had sued 98 Degrees for $25 million, claiming he should receive a better share of their earnings since he had helped them reach a national audience.

Also in October, one of the Lachey brothers got married—but instead of Nick it was Drew, who wed childhood sweetheart Lea Dellecave in Cincinnati. During the following month, the group again entered the Top 40 with "My Everything."

Selected Awards

Platinum certification, "Because of You" (single), 1998.

Platinum certification, *This Christmas*, 1999.

Radio Music Award, Most Requested Song of the Year, for "Give Me Just One Night (Una Noche)," 2000.

Multi-platinum certification (4 million sales), for *98 Degrees & Rising*, 2000.

98 Degrees

Multi-platinum certification (2 million sales), for *Revelation,* 2000.

(With Mariah Carey and Joe) Grammy Award nomination, Best Pop Collaboration with Vocals, for "Thank God I Found You," 2001.

Selected Discography

98 Degrees (Motown), 1997.
98 Degrees & Rising (Motown), 1998.
This Christmas (Motown), 1999.
Revelation (Motown). 2000.

Further Reading

Degnen, Lisa and Deborah Law. *98°: Ninety-Eight Degrees.* New York: MetroBooks, 2000.

Keeps, David A. "People of the Year: 98 Degrees." *Rolling Stone,* December 14–21, 2000, p. 124.

Musto, Michael. "98 Degrees." *Interview,* May 2000, p. 66.

"Oh, Brother!: Nick and Drew Lachey." *People,* November 15, 1999, p. 182.

Squires, K. M. *98 Degrees: The Official Book.* New York: MTV/Pocket Books, 1999.

Thomas, Harry. "Raves: Justin Jeffre of 98 Degrees." *Rolling Stone,* November 9, 2000, p. 50.

Contact Information

Top Forty Entertainment
156 W. 56th St.
4th Floor
New York, NY 10019

Web Sites

Hot 98 Degrees. http://www.angelfire.com/oh3/98degreesandrising/ (accessed on January 23, 2001).

98 Degrees (official site). http://www.98degrees.com (accessed on January 23, 2001).

98 Degrees Dimension. http://www.98-degrees.org (accessed on January 23, 2001).

Pure 98 Degrees. http://pure98.hypermart.net/ (accessed on January 23, 2001).

NO DOUBT

American alternative pop/rock band

Formed 1987 in Orange County, California

If Mick Jagger and Little Orphan Annie had a daughter, she would probably be a little something like No Doubt's vocalist Gwen Stefani. The band's combination of a sweet-looking but sexy girl singing with a bunch of hard-rocking boys has given them an irresistible appeal that rocketed 1995's *Tragic Kingdom* past 10 million in sales. In 2000, No Doubt came out with their first new studio album in half a decade, *The Return of Saturn,* which spawned a number of new hits and showed a maturing style

Punk singer John Spence formed No Doubt, which he named after one of his favorite expressions, with high-school friend Eric Stefani. Eric "forced" his little sister Gwen (born October 3, 1969) to sing backup, and soon afterward bassist Tony Kanal (born August 27, 1970) joined them. Playing ska mixed with rock, the band had a multicultural character from the beginning: Spence was black, and Kanal from India. Gwen fell in love with Kanal, and they began a seven-year relationship.

The other band members were devastated when Spence committed suicide at the age of eighteen in December 1987.

"In the past, we tended to overheat on our songs, load them up, turn the volume to 10. I think we've matured enough to realize it's good enough to leave space for the songs to breathe."

–Gwen Stefani, *New York Times Upfront,* April 24, 2000

(L–R) Tom Dumont, Adrian Young, Gwen Stefani, and Tony Kanal. (AP/Wide World Photos. Reproduced by permission.)

Garbage. (Archive Photos. Reproduced by permission.)

Garbage

Like No Doubt, Garbage is an all-male band fronted by a female lead singer. Bassist Steve Marker, drummer Butch Vig, and guitarist Duke Erickson began playing together in Wisconsin during the late 1980s. Vig had already made a name for himself as producer of a great classic, Nirvana's *Nevermind*, but Garbage did not take shape until Shirley Manson—originally from Scotland—joined them in 1994.

The group's self-titled 1995 debut, with its hit singles "Only When It Rains" and "Stupid Girl," soon got them noticed. *Garbage* went on to sell over 4 million copies worldwide, and earned the group an MTV Video Music Award, as well as a slew of Grammy Award nominations. (See original entry on Garbage in *Parents Aren't Supposed to Like It,* Volume 1, p. 53.)

In 1998 Garbage released *Version 2.0,* which earned them a host of further nominations, both for Grammys and MTV Video Music Awards, as well as the hits "Special" and "When I Grow Up." Garbage, which has been nominated for numerous Grammy Awards without actually receiving one, earned two more nominations—but no Grammy—in 2000. In April of that year, Manson announced that the group was working on a new album.

But they pulled themselves together, recruiting guitarist Tom Dumont (born January 11, 1968) and drummer Adrian Young (born August 26, 1969). Opening for bands such as the **Red Hot Chili Peppers** (see entry), whose bassist Flea became a friend and mentor, they attracted the attention of Inter-

Parents Aren't Supposed to Like It

scope Records, which signed them to a record deal in 1991.

It seemed their challenges were over; but in fact they had just begun. *No Doubt* (1992) sold poorly, and with Interscope unwilling to finance another tour or album, the group released *The Beacon Street Collection* (1995) with their own funds. (Later, when No Doubt became an explosive success, Interscope re-released the album.) In the meantime, they had begun recording what would emerge, during some thirty months of recording sessions, as *Tragic Kingdom*.

The latter included a song, "Don't Speak," which Gwen wrote after Kanal broke up with her. Another parting soon followed, when Eric left No Doubt to become animator for *The Simpsons* cartoon. Now a foursome, the group toured in support of *Tragic Kingdom*—and to their shock, watched both "Don't Speak" and the album shoot to No. 1. **(See original entry on No Doubt in *Parents Aren't Supposed to Like It*, Volume 1, p. 101.)**

Not just Gwen's backup band

Tragic Kingdom sold more than 10 million copies in the United States, yielding two other hits with "Sunday Morning" and "Spiderweb," while "Just a Girl" became a huge concert favorite. No Doubt spent much of 1997 and 1998 touring in support of—and accepting awards and nominations for—music they had begun creating in 1993.

The members of the group spent 1998 writing songs for a new album. All of them worked on the compositions, a fact that may seem surprising to observers who think of No Doubt as nothing but Stefani and her backup band. In fact the band's sound and style draw enormously from the energies and talents of all four.

Toure in *Rolling Stone* described Young as having "an energetic punk soul," and quoted the consensus of the other band members: "Adrian's the adrenalin of the whole project." Regarding Dumont, who Toure referred to as "a shy, intellectual sort," the others said, "Tom is the musician of the band." Kanal, Toure wrote, is "an intensely cool cat. . . . He's the kid in your high school who was somehow down with everyone."

As for Stefani, "She's the one who fills the room with her presence, playing coy, cartoonish sexy as well as badass hot mama—a little bit Betty Boop, a little bit Buffy [the Vampire Slayer]. . . . She's also the creative leader. . . . Gwen, the other members say, was the major force behind the direction of *Return to Saturn*."

The return of No Doubt

Released in April 2000, *The Return of Saturn* was a commercial success, selling 200,000 copies in its first week; but it also showed the maturing of No Doubt's sound. "Ex-Girlfriend," which hit the Top 40 early in the year, was a classic No Doubt tune with a frenetic ska-rock beat, but the poppish "Simple Kind of Life"—a second hit in June—revealed a strong Beatles influence.

For No Doubt's members, *The Return of Saturn* was a satisfying experience on both a personal and professional level.

Right after the album came out, Toure wrote, "The gang laughs at the few bad reviews they've gotten," and Stefani said, "This is a magical night. I can't believe it! Our record is out! When I woke up this morning, it was like Christmas!"

"[T]he story of No Doubt," Toure concluded, "is the story of people who let nothing—school, work, breakups, early departures, psychic pain—get in the way of the band." Kanal said, "We can go on with our lives knowing we spent these years together and made this amazing thing happen. It doesn't even matter at this point. We wanna sell records, of course, but we're already so fulfilled."

Selected Awards

MTV Video Music Award, Best Group Video, for "Don't Speak," 1997.

(Gwen Stefani and Eric Stefani), Grammy Award nomination, Song of the Year, Songwriter, for "Don't Speak," 1998.

Grammy Award nomination, Best Pop Performance by a Duo or Group with Vocal, for "Don't Speak," 1998.

Multi-platinum certification (10 million sales), *Tragic Kingdom*, 1999.

Platinum certification, *Return of Saturn*, 2000.

Grammy Award nomination, Best Rock Album, for *Return of Saturn*, 2001.

Selected Discography

No Doubt (Interscope), 1992.

Beacon Street Collection (independent), 1995; re-released on Interscope, 1997.

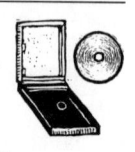

Tragic Kingdom (Interscope), 1995.

The Return of Saturn (Interscope), 2000.

Further Reading

Baker, Ken. "Heart to Heart." *Us*, December 11, 2000, p. 20.

Dunn, Jancee. "People of the Year: Gwen Stefani of No Doubt." *Rolling Stone*, December 14-21, 2000, p. 151.

Eliscu, Jenny. "Raves: Gwen Stefani of No Doubt." *Rolling Stone*, May 25, 2000, p. 28.

Punter, Jennie. "New Doubt." *New York Times Upfront*, April 24, 2000, p. 21.

Toure. "No Doubt: Music from Big Pink." *Rolling Stone*, July 6-20, 2000, p. 68.

Contact Information

No Doubt
P.O. Box 8899
Anaheim, CA 92812

Web Sites

The Don't Doubt No Doubt Homepage. http://www.trappedinabox.com (accessed on January 11, 2001).

No Doubt (official site). http://www.nodoubt.com (accessed on January 11, 2001).

No-Doubt.net. http://no-doubt.net (accessed on January 11, 2001).

'NSync

American pop group

Formed 1995 in Orlando, Florida

To people not familiar with 'NSync's music, it might be a little difficult to tell them apart from the **Backstreet Boys** (see entry). Both consist of five handsome young men, and both rode the teen-pop wave of the late 1990s to stardom with a combination of catchy tunes, smooth dance moves, and appeal with the girls.

Both have had the same management: Johnny and Donna Wright—who helped create 1980s boy band New Kids on the Block—and Orlando, Florida, businessman Lou Pearlman. And both eventually became entangled in court battles with Pearlman. With all these similarities, the members of 'NSync work hard to distinguish themselves—which they have done with a growing string of hits.

The first three members

The founder of 'NSync is Chris Kirkpatrick (born October 17, 1971). From a poor family in Clarion, Pennsylvania, Kirkpatrick had a tough childhood, losing his father at an early age and being forced to move from school to school as his mother—who remar-

> "It's like Mr. Toad's Wild Ride at Disney. It just keeps going. We knew we were going to be successful, but we didn't know it was going to happen as fast as it did, or as big."
>
> –Joey Fatone, *People*, February 8, 1999

(L–R) J.C. Chasez, Chris Kirkpatrick, Joey Fatone, Justin Timberlake, and Lance Bass. (Corbis Corporation. Reproduced by permission.)

313

ried several times—struggled to support him and his four half-sisters. He attended college in Orlando, where he took choir alongside future Backstreet Boy Howie Dorough. Kirkpatrick, who excelled in musical theatre, briefly sang in a five-voice group that ended when one of its members left—ironically, to join an early version of the Backstreet Boys.

Determined to form a group, Kirkpatrick signed on with an agent who helped him contact Justin Timberlake (born January 31, 1981). Timberlake, destined to become the leading heartthrob of 'NSync, had grown up singing in the Baptist church back in Memphis, Tennessee, and had arrived in Orlando at age twelve as a cast member on the TV show *The New Mickey Mouse Club*. The show, a revival of an early 1960s show, produced a virtual who's who of teen stars: **Britney Spears, Christina Aguilera** (see entries), Keri Russell of *Felicity*, Timberlake, and Joshua "J. C." Chasez (born August 8, 1976).

Raised the oldest of three children in Maryland, Chasez had a happy childhood, judging by his account of family vacations: "Every summer we used to caravan wherever for a few weeks," he told *Rolling Stone*. "We'd just pick a direction and go. . . . I've seen every state on the continent from the car. I've seen the World's Largest Ball of Twine, the Largest Rubber Ball Band, the Largest Bean Farm—I've seen 'em all, dude."

'NSync gets its name

"J. C. was the cool older guy," Aguilera later told *Rolling Stone*, "and Justin wanted to be just like him." The two wrote songs together, and after a few false starts—Chasez tried to make it in Los Angeles, and ran into management problems—they hooked up with Fitzpatrick. All three tended to sing on the tenor end of the scale, so they needed lower voices: a baritone and a bass.

The baritone came from Joey Fatone, Jr. (born January 28, 1977), who they met one night at a local club. A New Yorker, Fatone had moved to Florida with his family when he was thirteen, and in high school he had been an enthusiastic participant in extracurricular activities such as singing, acting, and dance. His father, who had once sung in a minor "doo-wop" vocal group during the 1950s, encouraged these interests.

With Fatone, the quartet still needed a bass, and initially they recruited a young man named Jason. He did not work out, but in the meantime Timberlake's mother had given the group a name that described their style while incorporating the last letters of all five members' names: Justi*n*, Chri*s*, Joe*y*, Jaso*n*, and J. C.

It was a great name, but there was just one problem: they found they could not work with Jason, and had to let him go. Therefore when they recruited a singer named Lance, they jokingly "renamed" him Lans*ten* to fit with the name scheme. That was not the only funny thing about the name of this Clinton, Mississippi native, who they found through Timberlake's former vocal coach in Tennessee: not only did he sing bass, but his *name* was Lance Bass (born May

'NSync performs "Bye Bye Bye" live for the morning crowd at NBC's *Today* show. (David Atlas. Reproduced by permission.)

4, 1979)—though it is pronounced with a short "A," like the fish.

First hits

In 1997 the group signed a recording contract with RCA Records and released a single, "I Want You Back," the following year. The song first attracted attention not in the United States but in Germany and the Netherlands. By February, however, it had hit the Top 40 back home. Riding the wave of popularity created by the teen-pop explosion of 1997 and the success of other acts—including the Backstreet Boys—the group's self-titled debut album, released in March, was a smash hit and produced a number-one single, "Tearing Up My Heart."

At the end of 1998 'NSync released a holiday CD, *Home for Christmas,* and appeared as opening act on the latter part of **Janet Jackson**'s (see entry) *Velvet Rope* Tour. They finished out the year with *'NSync* as the fifth best-selling album of 1998, and in January had another top-ten hit with "(God Must Have Spent) A Little More Time on You."

Interesting collaborations— and lawsuits

In the spring of 1999, 'NSync engaged in a couple of interesting collaborations. First they sang backup for country group Alabama on the latter's cover of "(God Must Have Spent) A Little More Time on You," and later they teamed up with **Gloria Estefan** (see entry) on "Music of My Heart." Both collaborative efforts won numerous awards and nominations.

> "We're not going to pierce everything that we have and paint our faces trying to get a different market. We'll grow with our audience. We're just going to keep doing what we do."

'NSync hit the Top 10 again in May 1999 with "I Drive Myself Crazy," and again reached the Top 10 by year's end with their appearance on Blaque's "Bring It All to Me." The latter part of the year also saw a flurry of lawsuits. 'NSync had recently left RCA, and in October RCA sued them for breach of contract (that is, not sticking to a legal agreement). At the same time, 'NSync sued Pearlman. Both lawsuits ended in a settlement: in other words, the parties concluded the situation by reaching an agreement outside of court.

Changing with their audience

The group had recorded most of *No Strings Attached,* whose release was delayed until March 2000 due to the legal problems, without a record-label contract. But with their growing string of hits, it was a safe bet that a record company would sign them, and in fact Jive Records—the same label that handles Backstreet—did.

During 2000, 'NSync cranked out the hits: "Bye Bye Bye" (No. 1, April); "It's Gonna Be Me" (No. 1, July); and "This I Promise You" (Top 10, October). Meanwhile *No Strings Attached* broke first-day sales records by selling 1.1 million copies in one day and 2.4 million during the first week. In addition, the group's 2000 tour broke single-day sales records for Ticketmaster.

Barely stopping to catch their breath, 'NSync embarked on another summer tour in support of the 2001 release *Celebrity.* Asked about their success, the band took a philosophical view toward their fame and the ever-changing tastes of teen-pop record buyers. "We're not going to pierce everything that we have and paint our faces trying to get a different market," Kirkpatrick told *People* in early 1999. "We'll grow with our audience. We're just going to keep doing what we do."

Selected Awards

American Music Award, Best New Pop Artist, 1999.

Multi-platinum certification (2 million sales), *Home for Christmas*, 1999.

(With Gloria Estefan) Grammy Award nomination, Best Pop Collaboration with Vocals, for "Music of My Heart," 2000.

(With Alabama) Grammy Award nomination, Best Country Collaboration with Vocals, for "(God Must Have Spent) A Little More Time on You," 2000.

MTV Video Music Awards, Viewer's Choice and Best Pop Video, for "Bye Bye Bye," 2000.

Multi-platinum certification (10 million sales), *'NSync*, 2000.

Multi-platinum certification (9 million sales), *No Strings Attached*, 2000.

Grammy Award nominations, Record of the Year and Best Pop Performance by a Duo or Group with Vocal, both for "Bye Bye Bye," 2001.

Grammy Award nomination, Best Pop Vocal Album, for *No Strings Attached*, 2001.

Selected Discography

'NSync (RCA), 1998.
Home for Christmas (RCA), 1998.
No Strings Attached (RCA), 2000.
Celebrity (RCA), 2001.

Further Reading

Adams, Ashley. *Omnibus Presents the Story of 'NSync*. New York: Music Sales Corporation, 1999.

Bozza, Anthony. "'NSync." *Rolling Stone*, March 30, 2000, p. 52.

Galt, Jasmine. *'NSync: The Unofficial Book*. New York: Billboard, 1999.

Helligar, Jeremy, et al. "Boy Power." *People*, February 8, 1999, p. 93.

Pearl, A. *'NSYNC Now and Forever: Backstage Pass*. New York: Scholastic, 2000.

Stein, Joel. "'NSync's Latest Dish." *Time*, March 27, 2000, p. 93.

Contact Information

Stellar Worldwide, LLC.
P.O. Box 608640
Orlando, FL 32860-8640

Web Sites

'NSync (official site). http://www.nysnc.com (accessed on December 18, 2000).

'NSync 411. http://www.angelfire.com/fl/nsyncinfo/home.html (accessed on December 18, 2000).

'NSync Studio. http://www.nsyncstudio.com (accessed on December 18, 2000).

THE OFFSPRING

American alternative rock band

Formed 1984 in Orange County, California

> "I don't feel all grown up. I feel I can relate to teens and even feel a little stuck in that, but in a good way."
> —Dexter Holland, *Rolling Stone*, February 4, 1999

After a decade of laboring in obscurity, the Offspring scored in a big way with the aptly titled *Smash* in 1994. Their last release with punk label Epitaph, *Smash* sold 6 million copies. By contrast, sales of *Ixnay on the Hombre* (1997)—issued on Columbia after the group signed a lucrative contract—were relatively disappointing. But with *Americana* (1998), the Offspring, with their punkish but funky (and fun) sound, had their biggest hit yet with "Pretty Fly (For a White Guy)."

The evolution of the Offspring began in 1984. During high school in southern California, Brian "Dexter" Holland (born 1966?), the Offspring's vocalist and guitarist, and bassist Greg Kriesel, both of whom ran for the cross-country team, formed a band called Manic Subsidal. Later both went off to college, where they met guitarist Kevin "Noodles" Wasserman. Soon they took on drummer Ron Welty, and by 1987 the group (now called the Offspring) had recorded a single that they released independently. (Valedictorian of his high-school class, Holland entered a pre-med program in college and even after his group hit

The Offspring. (Photo by Sam Levi. WireImage.com. Reproduced by permission.)

the big time, continued work on his Ph.D. in microbiology.)

Their self-titled debut album (1989) attracted the attention of Epitaph Records owner, and Bad Religion guitarist, Brett Gurewitz. He signed them and released *Ignition* (1992), which sold over 30,000 copies. The real success, however, came with *Smash* two years later, which got the Offspring major airplay with the single "Come Out and Play (You Gotta Keep 'Em Separated)."

Disagreements with Epitaph led to a 1996 deal with Columbia, which released *Ixnay on the Hombre* a year later. The latter sold over a million copies, which prior to *Smash* would have seemed like a huge success. **(See original entry on the Offspring in *Parents Aren't Supposed to Like It*, Volume 1, p. 105.)**

Biggest hit yet with "Pretty Fly"

In November 1998, the Offspring came back strong with *Americana*. The album yielded "Pretty Fly (For a White Guy)," a satire on white kids from sheltered suburban homes who listen to rap and try to pretend they come from the 'hood. "Pretty Fly" hit the Top 10 in February 1999, by which time *Americana*—only out for three months—had sold 3 million copies.

In May 1999, the Offspring again hit the charts with the top-forty hit "Why Don't You Get a Job?" They performed at Woodstock '99 in July, and in November received an MTV Europe Music Award. During 2000, the Offspring toured and worked on their next album, *Conspiracy of One*.

Involved in free music downloading controversy

Like many other artists, the Offspring became involved in the controversy over the Internet music-sharing service Napster (see **Metallica** entry), but unlike **Dr. Dre** (see entry) and Metallica's Lars Ulrich, Holland maintained that free downloading did not hurt CD sales. Therefore the group announced in September 2000 that it planned to make the album available for free online.

This led to threats of a lawsuit by the record company, and as a result the group reduced the scope of its offer to free downloads of the single "Original Prankster." The song topped MTV's Top 20 list in October 2000, and a month later, the group released the new album to stores. By January 2001, "Original Prankster" had hit the Top 40.

Families and priorities

All the members of Offspring have families. In March 1999, Kriesel's wife had a baby, making him, as Wasserman observed in *Melody Maker,* "the last one to enter into parenthood. [Holland, Welty,] and I all have kids as old as eleven."

This is hardly the reality one would expect of a loud punk band, but with their emphasis on family and making music on their own terms, the members of Offspring are far from ordinary punkers.

Selected Awards

Platinum certification, *Ixnay on the Hombre*, 1997.

MTV Video Music Award nomination, Best Rock Video, for "Pretty Fly (For a White Guy)," 1999.

Multi-platinum certification (4 million sales), *Americana*, 1999.

Multi-platinum certification (6 million sales), *Smash*, 2000.

Platinum certification, *Conspiracy of One*, 2000.

Selected Discography

The Offspring (Nemesis), 1989.
Ignition (Epitaph), 1992.
Smash (Epitaph), 1994.
Ixnay on the Hombre (Sony/Columbia), 1997.
Americana (Sony/Columbia), 1998.
Conspiracy of One (Sony/Columbia), 2000.

Further Reading

Ali, Lorraine. "Q&A: Dexter Holland of the Offspring." *Rolling Stone*, February 4, 1999, p. 31.

Clerk, Carol. "The Offspring: Just the Job." *Melody Maker*, March 27, 1999, p. 7.

Eliscu, Jenny. "The Offspring Go Offline." *Rolling Stone*, November 9, 2000, p. 33.

Eliscu, Jenny. "Raves: Noodles of the Offspring." *Rolling Stone*, December 14-21, 2000, p. 51.

Watson, Ian. "Psycho Babble: Dexter Holland of the Offspring." *Melody Maker*. January 16, 1999, p. 15.

Contact Information

Sony Music
550 Madison Ave.
New York, NY 10022

Web Sites

Chasms Funky Offspring Page. http://www.geocities.com/SunsetStrip/Venue/5783/ (accessed on December 18, 2000).

The Offspring (official site). http://www.offspring.com (accessed on December 18, 2000).

The Offspring Net. http://theoffspring.net/main.html (accessed on December 18, 2000).

The Offspring Unofficial Homepage. http://www.geocities.com/SunsetStrip/Alley/1675/index.html (accessed on December 18, 2000).

Ozzy Osbourne

British heavy-metal artist

Born John Michael Osbourne on December 3, 1948, in Birmingham, England

As lead singer for Black Sabbath in the 1970s, Ozzy Osbourne influenced a generation of heavy-metal and grunge rockers. After his abuse of drugs and alcohol got him kicked out of the band—no small feat, considering Sabbath's own bad reputation—he went it alone in the 1980s, forging a highly successful solo career.

Along the way, Ozzy created a legend around himself, as a madman who bit the heads off of bats. It was all an act; but his addiction to drugs and alcohol was frighteningly real. With the help of his wife and manager, Sharon, however, he has kicked most of his worst habits, created a happy family, and even—thanks to Ozzfest in the late 1990s—enjoyed a third run in the musical limelight.

Aston's own Black Sabbath

Like many another musical great, John "Ozzy" Osbourne had a miserable childhood. Raised in Aston, a grim industrial section of Birmingham in northern England, Osbourne was the son of work-

> "Ozzy's special, I think. He remains somewhat of a mystery. He's always been the underdog, never been tragically hip, and I think that's one reason why he's survived."
>
> –Sharon Osbourne, *Rolling Stone*, July 2000

Ozzy Osbourne. (Ken Settle. Reproduced by permission.)

ing-class parents. A hyperactive child, he suffered from dyslexia, a learning disorder that impairs one's ability to read and write. Teachers told him he was stupid, and he set out to prove them right.

Suicidal from the age of fourteen, Osbourne got himself thrown in jail for burglary. Then he learned that some boys from his school were forming a band, and needed a lead singer. The boys were guitarist Tommy Iommi, who had bullied Osbourne when they were younger, bassist Terry "Geezer" Butler, and drummer Bill Ward. After going through a number of names, in 1969 they settled on Black Sabbath.

Influences music history

Sabbath followed on a heavy-metal trail blazed by another English band, Led Zeppelin, but their sound was much grittier, and their lyrics more laden with frightening imagery. With crunchy guitars and a fuzzy bass, an insistent backbeat and Osbourne's weird, frightening wail, they turned songs such as "Paranoid," "War Pigs," and "Iron Man" into downer rock anthems. These in turn influenced the work of Nirvana, Soundgarden, Megadeth, **Metallica, Smashing Pumpkins, Rage Against the Machine**, (see entries), and many others.

Yet during his years with Black Sabbath, Osbourne cared little about his impact on music history: he just wanted to lose himself in a haze of drugs and alcohol. "People would run up to me [and say], 'Do you realize the profound effect you've had on rock and roll?'," he told Erik Hedegaard of *Rolling Stone*. " . . . The

Where Are They From? Outside the Continental United States

Though both Jewel and Ricky Martin are Americans, they come from far outside the continental United States. (Jewel was actually born in Utah, but raised in Alaska.) Included here are two artists, Gloria Estefan and Enrique Iglesias, who have spent most of their lives in Florida but have significant roots overseas.

Alaska
- Jewel (Homer)

Canada
- Barenaked Ladies (Scarborough, Ontario)
- Celine Dion (Charlemagne, Quebec)
- Shania Twain (Windsor and Timmins, Ontario)

Cuba
- Gloria Estefan (lived in Florida since childhood)

England
- Jamiroquai (London)
- Ozzy Osbourne (Birmingham)
- Radiohead (Oxford)
- Sting (Wallsend)

Ireland
- The Corrs (Dundalk)
- U2 (Dublin)

Puerto Rico
- Ricky Martin

Spain
- Enrique Iglesias (lived in Florida since childhood)

only thing that concerned me was how fast we could get to the pub [bar]."

Meets his future wife

By 1978, the other members of Sabbath were fed up with Osbourne's shenanigans, and booted him out of the band. He spent the next six months drunk and stoned, hiding out in a hotel room, and it was there that his future wife found him. Osbourne was already married at the time, with two children, but he had made a mess of his first marriage and was well on his way to divorce. Then along came Sharon Arden, who knocked on his door and demanded payment of a debt to her father, his manager.

Intrigued by Ozzy, Sharon tricked him into checking himself into the Betty Ford Clinic, an alcohol treatment facility that she billed as "this place where they teach you to drink properly." As Osbourne recalled, "So I walk in there and go, 'Where's the bar?' And they go, 'Oh, you're definitely in the right place!'"

The infamous head-biting incident

That was far from the end of Osbourne's struggles with addiction: he relapsed shortly after leaving the clinic, and continued to pass in and out of sobriety after he and Sharon married in 1982. Meanwhile with her help, he created a new band. Thanks in part to the dazzling guitar work of youthful virtuoso Randy Rhoads, *Blizzard of Oz* (1980) yielded the hit "Crazy Train." *Diary of a Madman,* which earned radio play with "You Can't Kill Rock and Roll," followed in 1981. But Osbourne's behavior on stage drew even more attention.

> "People would run up to me (and say), 'Do you realize the profound effect you've had on rock and roll?'" ... The only thing that concerned me was how fast we could get to the pub (bar)."

Around this time, at a meeting with record-company executives, Sharon had instructed him to release two doves into the air "as a peace offering." Out of his mind on drugs, he bit the head off one bird. This became a part of his show—and of his growing legendary status. Then at a concert in Des Moines, Iowa, Ozzy bit the head off of what he was thought was a rubber bat—but which turned out to be a real one. As a result, he had to undergo an excruciating series of rabies shot, and his head-biting days were over.

The death of Randy Rhoads

Tragedy struck Osbourne's band in Florida on March 19, 1982. Ozzy and Sharon were asleep in the tour bus while Rhoads went up in a small plane flown by their bus driver. The pilot saw his wife, who had recently filed for divorce, leaving the bus, and decided to fly threateningly close to the vehicle. He misjudged the distance, however: the plane hit the bus and went careening into a house, killing both Rhoads and the pilot.

Osbourne was devastated. "He thinks about Randy every day," wrote Hedegaard, "and knows that had he been awake, he would have been on the plane and been killed." Yet once again Sharon

Ozzy Osbourne with old Black Sabbath bandmates, (left to right, standing) Bill Ward, Tony Iommi, and Geezer Butler. (AP/Wide World Photos. Reproduced by permission.)

forced him to get back on his feet, and the result was a new band, which recorded the double-live LP *Speak of the Devil* (1982) and, after more personnel changes, *Bark at the Moon* in 1983. Two years later at Live Aid—a set of concerts to benefit victims of famine in Africa—Ozzy played with his old Sabbath bandmates for the first time since 1978.

More success followed with *Ultimate Sin* (1986); *Tribute* (1987), an album to honor Rhoads's memory; *No Rest for the Wicked* (1989); and *No More Tears* (1991). On the last two shows of his "No More Tours" tour, Sabbath opened for him. The tour also included a show in San Antonio, Texas, a town from which Osbourne had once been banned because he had urinated on the Alamo in a drunken stupor.

Confronting his substance abuse

Despite his successes, Osbourne had not successfully dealt with his addictions. He and Sharon had three children, Aimee, Kelly, and Jack, and as they began coming up through school, he began wanting to change his life. Osbourne, who with characteristic wit gave a vivid account of his struggles on a VH1 *Behind the Music* special, finally kicked his drinking and drug habits. He even gave up caffeine and began a lifestyle of healthy eating and exercise. Hedegaard, who found Osbourne in the throes of giving up cigarettes as well, observes that at fifty-one, he looked far better than he had a decade or even two decades earlier.

Ozzy returned to touring with *Ozzmosis* (1995), at a time when most observers assumed his career was over. But the tour proved such a success that Sharon—with the help of Jack—created the highly successful Ozzfest tour. The tour has featured heavy-metal artists, including **Marilyn Manson** (see entry), who were young children (or not even born) when Sabbath recorded its first album.

A model citizen

Rather than financially gouge concertgoers, as many tours do, Sharon explained to *Billboard* that Ozzfest "give[s] back" to the kids by providing "free water, CDs, and posters, so they leave with something." When Ozzy protested her suggestion that he put on a concert to benefit Jack's school, a place for children with dyslexia, she said, "We have to give back, Ozzy. That's what life is about."

Osbourne has come under fire for his lyrics and stage antics, particularly when a teen killed himself in the 1980s, allegedly under the influence of his song "Suicide Solution." Actually the song was both anti-alcohol and anti-suicide. Likewise he explained to *Billboard* that imagery surrounding shows at Ozzfest is not supposed to be Satanic; rather, "it's like a Halloween party."

He may have done and said some highly outrageous and controversial things, but today Ozzy Osbourne is something of a model citizen: a committed family man and a survivor of all the excesses he brought on himself. "Sometimes I forget how lucky I am," he told *Billboard*. "I've tried all the way to be as true as possible."

Selected Awards

Grammy Award nomination, Best Metal Performance, for "I Don't Wanna Change the World," 1992.

Multi-platinum certification (3 million sales), *Diary of Madman*, 1994.

Multi-platinum certification (4 million sales), *Blizzard of Oz*, 1997.

Multi-platinum certification (4 million sales), *No More Tears*, 2000.

Multi-platinum certification (3 million sales), *Bark at the Moon*, 2000.

Selected Discography

(With Black Sabbath) *Black Sabbath* (Warner Brothers), 1970.

(With Black Sabbath) *Paranoid* (Warner Brothers), 1971.

(With Black Sabbath) *Master of Reality* (Warner Brothers), 1971.

(With Black Sabbath) *Black Sabbath, Vol. 4* (Warner Brothers), 1972.

(With Black Sabbath) *Sabbath, Bloody Sabbath* (Warner Brothers), 1973.

(With Black Sabbath) *Sabotage* (Warner Brothers), 1975.

Blizzard of Oz (Epic), 1980.

Diary of a Madman (Epic), 1981.

Speak of the Devil (Epic), 1982.

Bark at the Moon (Epic), 1983.

Tribute (Epic), 1987.

No More Tears (Epic), 1991.

The Ozzman Cometh: Greatest Hits (Sony), 2000.

Further Reading

Conte, Robert V. and C. J. Henderson. *Black Sabbath: The Ozzy Osbourne Years.* New York: Studio Chikara, 2000.

Hedegaard, Erik. "Ozzy: The Prince of Darkness Would Like a Little Peace." *Rolling Stone,* July 6-20, 2000, p. 112.

Vaziri, Aidin. "The Wizard of Ozzfest: The Woman Behind the Man Is the One Who Calls the Shots." *San Francisco Chronicle,* August 20, 2000, p. D-34.

Waddell, Ray. "Hard Music: Bigger Is Better–Festival Tours Continue to Grow." *Billboard,* June 24, 2000, p. 36.

Wall, Mick. *Ozzy Osbourne: Diary of a Madman.* London: Zomba Books, 1985.

Wiederhorn, Jon. "Ozzy Osbourne." *Rolling Stone,* June 26, 1997, p. 28.

Contact Information

c/o Monowise, Ltd.
9048 Santa Monica Blvd.
Los Angeles, CA 90069

Web Sites

Ozzy Net. http://www.ozzynet.com (accessed on January 22, 2001).

Ozzy Osbourne. http://www.geocities.com/SunsetStrip/Club/9783/ozzy.htm (accessed on January 22, 2001).

Ozzy Osbourne—The Official Site. http://www.ozzy.com (accessed on January 22, 2001).

Papa Roach

American alternative metal band
Formed 1993 in Vacaville, California

> "We looked at ourselves like cockroaches—we're survivors."
> —Coby Dick, *Rolling Stone*, August 31, 2000

The name "Papa Roach" might sound like it belongs to one individual (see sidebar), but in fact it is a hard-rocking quartet out of Vacaville in northern California. The band plays what is known as alternative metal or "alt metal," a genre that has its roots in the work of Nirvana and other groups. But like **Everclear** (see entry), Papa Roach combines a head-banging sound with lyrics about the pains of childhood and adolescence that are as sensitive as they are brutally honest.

"A town with no scene"

Prior to Papa Roach, Vacaville's principal claim to fame was as "Onion Capital of the World." It was, as vocalist Coby Dick (born Jacoby Shaddix in 1976) told *Rolling Stone*, "a town with no [music] scene." In school, Dick played football with drummer Dave Buckner (born 1976), but "We weren't that good. . . . Neither of us wanted to be jocks; we wanted to be rockers."

The result was Papa Roach, named after Dick's grandfather, "Papa Roatch," who was alive and in his mid-nineties as of 2000.

Papa Roach. (Mitch Schneider Organization. Reproduced by permission.)

Dick and Buckner met Jerry Horton (born 1975), a guitarist who, though he had a fondness for industrial music and death-metal, was a straight-arrow when it came to drugs and alcohol. "I don't even hear him cuss," bassist Tobin Esperance (born 1980) told *Rolling Stone*. "We used to try to get him to drink and smoke, but after a while we realized how cool it was. We gotta let Jerry be Jerry."

Turning point in 1996

Thirteen years old when the band was formed in 1993, Esperance started out as the band's roadie—that is, someone responsible for setting up equipment before a live show. By 1996, the band members—who included bassist Will James—were out of high school and pursuing a relentless schedule of touring. It was then that the others agreed to part ways with James, whose involvement in a church summer camp would have made it impossible for him to keep up with practicing and playing concerts.

Therefore Esperance took James's place, and the band hired Bret Bair as their manager. Up to this point, they had released an EP (extended-play) in 1994 and a single a year later, but in 1996 they finally decided it was time for a full-length CD. The result was *Old Friends From Young Years* (1997), which they recorded for $700 at a studio in Pittsburg, California.

A false start, and then a record deal

Despite the fact that it was independently released and had no major mar-

Papa Roach lead singer Coby Dick. (Corbis Corporation. Reproduced by permission.)

"He's the coolest guy," Dick explained. "But the name took on its full meaning after we were together a few years." Not only are cockroaches survivors, "the thing about roaches is that if you see one, there's a million, and your whole house is infested."

keting support, the album began to attract attention with independent and college radio stations. This, combined with seemingly endless work on the road, helped build a following throughout central and northern California. After the EP *5 Tracks Deep* (1998) sold a thousand copies, and *Let 'Em Know* (1999) did even better, record companies began to take notice.

Yet a deal with Warner Brothers failed to materialize: the label financed the recording of a demo, but never signed Papa Roach. But as Dick recalled in *Rolling Stone,* "literally the next day, we got the call from DreamWorks," which signed the group. Finally in April 2000, the band's seven years of hard work paid off with their first major release, *Infest.*

Dick and Davis

The album is hardly what one would call lighthearted; indeed, it calls to mind the work of another non-L.A.-or-San-Francisco, California hard-rock band: **KoRN** (see entry). Though Dick is not nearly as angry or tortured as KoRN lead singer Jonathan Davis, and it appears that his family was more supportive than Davis's, there are similarities: both had troubled childhoods; both were attracted to gruesome jobs; both found release in music, and, later, in family life. (Dick has been married since 1997.)

His brother was diagnosed with attention deficit disorder (ADD), and Dick told *Rolling Stone* that he believes he has it. "I'm pretty hyperactive and mood-swingy," he revealed. "I had a bed-wet-

That's Not "His" Name

Papa Roach is just one example of a group whose name has led unsuspecting fans to conclude, incorrectly, that "they" are a "he" (or in some cases a "she"). A great example of this is the 1970s art-rock band Jethro Tull: led by flautist (flute-player) Ian Anderson, it is indeed named after a real person—but Jethro Tull, inventor of the seed-driller, died in 1741.

Other examples of bands often mistaken for individuals (and the real sources of their names) include:

Led Zeppelin (Who guitarist Pete Townsend's incorrect prediction that the group would "go over like a lead zeppelin" or airship)

Lynyrd Skynyrd (a strict high-school teacher, Leonard Skinner, who was always after the boys to cut their hair)

Pink Floyd (named after two blues musicians)

Sister Hazel [see entry]

Steely Dan (a term used in the 1950s underground novel *Naked Lunch* by William S. Burroughs)

Uriah Heep (after a character in *David Copperfield* by Charles Dickens)

ting problem until I was sixteen. It was not cool; I had some issues." Whereas Davis went to work as a mortician, Dick got a job at an intensive-care unit (ICU) where, in an incident he would never forget, he once opened a freezer to find a human head, stripped of skin so that medical students could study it.

Finding comfort and meaning

Though he tried drugs, Dick ultimately found release in a different way: "I decided to write my life down on paper. And on this record I'm venting my emotions. It's blunt." The title of "Broken Home" tells its own story; but "Last Resort" is not about a vacation—it is about a friend's suicide attempt.

> "We've gotten so many e-mails from people who tell us 'Last Resort' saved their lives."

To most people over twenty-five, it might be hard to imagine how the fierce sound and harrowing lyrics of a group such as Papa Roach can bring comfort to a teenager, but it does. "We've gotten so many e-mails from people who tell us 'Last Resort' saved their lives," Dick told *Rolling Stone*. "A lot of people tell us they're thinking about suicide and don't know what to do. All we can say is, 'Keep your head up; find a friend, family member, or counselor you can talk to. And if that doesn't work, write a song. . . .'"

Selected Awards

MTV Video Music Award nomination, Best New Artist, for "Last Resort," 2000.

Multi-platinum certification (2 million sales), *Infest,* 2000.

Grammy Award nomination, Best New Artist, 2001.

Selected Discography

Infest (DreamWorks), 2000.

Further Reading

Binelli, Mark. "All Punked Up and Ready to Go." *Rolling Stone,* August 17, 2000, p. 100.

Bozza, Anthony. "Papa Roach: New Metal Heroes." *Rolling Stone,* August 31, 2000, p. 42.

Bozza, Anthony. "People of the Year: Papa Roach." *Rolling Stone,* December 14–21, 2000, p. 90.

Guzman, Rafer. "Papa Roach." *Rolling Stone,* October 26, 2000, p. 34.

Jenkins, Sacha. "Papa Roach: No Way Home." *Spin,* December 2000.

Contact Information

Papa Roach
666 N. Robertson Blvd.
Suite A-2
Los Angeles, CA 90069

Web Sites

Broken Home. http://brokenh.net/ (accessed on January 24, 2001).

Papa Roach (official site). http://www.paparoach.com (accessed on January 24, 2001).

Papa Roach 2000. http://www.paparoach2000.com (accessed on January 24, 2001).

Pearl Jam

American alternative rock band
Formed 1990 in Seattle, Washington

Loud and proud, honest or arrogant (depending on whether one is a fan or not), Pearl Jam was one of the biggest bands of the 1990s. Through all the changes in the musical landscape, including a dip in sales at mid-decade, they remained the flagship of grunge in particular, and alternative rock in general. With the decade over, they entered the new millennium with a bang, releasing an unprecedented twenty-five live CDs of their European shows. It was an event marred by tragedy, however, as a twenty-sixth show—at Roskilde, Denmark—ended in the deaths of nine fans.

The band had its roots with guitarist Stone Gossard (born July 20, 1966) and bassist Jeff Ament (born March 10, 1963), who played in a Seattle hard-rock outfit called Green River. Joining with vocalist Andrew Wood and drummer Jeff Turner, they formed Mother Love Bone in 1988. Two years and two albums later, Wood died of a heroin overdose and the group fell apart, whereupon Gossard and Ament formed a new band with guitarist Mike McCready (born April 5, 1965) and drummer Dave Krusen.

> "By recording and releasing their 2000 European tour as twenty-five double CDs . . . [Pearl Jam] is drawing up a new blueprint for marketing live music, *and* beating bootleggers at their own game."
>
> –Bill Crandall and others, *Rolling Stone*, September 26, 2000

Eddie Vedder. (AP/Wide World Photos. Reproduced by permission.)

Soon they were joined by vocalist Eddie Vedder (born December 23, 1966), who gave the new band its name, a reference to his aunt Pearl's homemade preserves.

Ten (1991) initially failed to attract attention, but in 1992, fellow Seattle grunge-rockers Nirvana exploded into the limelight. At the same time, tracks such as "Jeremy," "Evenflow," and "Alive" gained Pearl Jam extensive exposure on the radio and MTV.

By late 1993 Pearl Jam had a new drummer, Dave Abbruzzese, and a new album, *Vs.* "Daughter," "Dissident," "Animal," and "Go" got airplay even though the group refused to release singles, and in 1994 their opposition to the commercialization of rock led to a showdown with Ticketmaster over the high cost of concert tickets (see sidebar). *Vitalogy,* released late in the year, yielded a number of radio hits, most notably the Grammy-winning "Spin the Black Circle."

In early 1995, Jack Irons (born July 18, 1962), formerly of the **Red Hot Chili Peppers** (see entry), replaced Abbruzzese. The band toured and recorded with Neil Young, and in August 1996 released *No Code,* their least commercially successful album. **(See original entry on Pearl Jam in** *Parents Aren't Supposed to Like It,* **Volume 1, p. 115.)**

Disenchantment with Pearl Jam?

Some observers attributed diminished sales to fans' growing disenchantment with the group's hard, angry sound and image. Pearl Jam, however, refused to change, and though the period since *Vitalogy* (which sold more than 4 million copies) has seen no smash albums, the band maintains a solid following. In 1999, in fact, they enjoyed their biggest hit single yet with "Last Kiss," a remake of a song from the early 1960s.

Yet the late 1990s saw a number of challenges for Pearl Jam. The first of these came in June 1997, when McCready broke his collarbone while playing baseball and was forced to take six weeks off. Later that year, attorneys for a teenage boy who killed three people at his high school cited the "Jeremy" video as having influenced his violent act.

Dealing with bootleggers

A challenge of a different kind came in 1998, when songs from *Yield* appeared on the Internet before the album itself made it to the stores. Tracks such as "Given to Fly," available on the then-new mp3 format, sounded almost as good as they did on the CD. Like **Metallica** (see entry) and many another band, Pearl Jam had come face-to-face with Internet piracy, which potentially posed a greater threat to artists' profits than Ticketmaster ever could. The group and its management chose a clever response: they got in the game themselves, offering free downloads of the single "Nothing As It Seems" a day before it went out to radio stations in April 2000.

A number of artists have likewise chosen an "if you can't beat 'em, join em" policy for dealing with another form of piracy: bootlegging, or the making of ille-

Ticketmaster

Undisputed leader in the area of ticket sales for musical and sporting events, Ticketmaster began life in 1978 as the creation of two college students who were unhappy with the way tickets were sold. Initially Ticketmaster failed to make much headway against industry leader Ticketron; but when a wealthy Chicago investor bought the company in 1982, it began a decade of rapid expansion.

Before Ticketmaster, ticket vendors only had a set amount of tickets to a given concert or sports event. This meant that some vendors did not have enough tickets for their customers, while others had too many. Concert promoters—the people who undertook the financial responsibility of putting on musical shows—typically lost money because not all the seats were filled.

Ticketmaster overcame this inefficient situation with computerized ticket sales, which made it possible for any vendor in a city to sell as many tickets as possible to a given event. Naturally, concert promoters loved Ticketmaster, and its strategy—including convenient ticket sales over the phone—helped ticket-buyers as well. By 1991, Ticketmaster had bought out Ticketron, and virtually owned the market.

To some critics, however, it began to seem that Ticketmaster really did "own" the market. They called Ticketmaster a monopoly, a company so big it does not allow fair competition. Among the leading critics were the members of Pearl Jam. Concerned about Ticketmaster's profits from sales of tickets to their shows, the group in 1994 filed a request with the U.S. Justice Department to investigate Ticketmaster's sales tactics.

Guitarist Stone Gossard and bassist Jeff Ament testified in June before a subcommittee of the House of Representatives looking into the subject of ticket sales agencies. Meanwhile, the Justice Department proceeded with its investigation—which in January 1995 ended with a ruling favorable to Ticketmaster.

In June 1998, Pearl Jam went on its first tour in two years. Instead of using Ticketmaster, the group sold tickets to its shows almost entirely through local, typically independent, ticket agencies.

---

gal recordings, often at concerts. Thus the **Dave Matthews Band** (see entry) and others flooded the market with live albums, undercutting the bootleggers. In September 2000, Pearl Jam adopted this strategy as well—and in a big, big way—simultaneously releasing twenty-five double CDs of concert recordings made throughout Europe during the spring and early summer.

Tragedy in Denmark

It was also during Pearl Jam's European tour that eight fans were crushed or suffocated by surging crowds during a show at Roskilde, Denmark, on June 30. A ninth died a few days later of injuries sustained during the concert. It was the second-worst concert-related tragedy in history, after the December 3, 1979, concert by the Who in Cincinnati,

Ohio—an event in which eleven people were trampled

To say that Pearl Jam's members were badly shaken is an understatement, as revealed in a press release reportedly written by Vedder during the early morning hours after the event. "This is so painful," it began. " . . . I think we are all waiting for someone to wake us and say it was just a horrible nightmare. And there are absolutely no words to express our anguish in regard to the parents and loved ones of those precious lives that were lost. . . . Our lives will never be the same, but we know that is nothing compared to the grief of the families and friends of those involved. It is so tragic . . . there are no words. Devastated, Pearl Jam."

Later, McCready revealed that the band considered breaking up after the tragedy in Denmark; but as he said, "it wouldn't have been a good way to end it all." In October 2000, Pearl Jam made *Billboard* history when five of the live CDs debuted on the Top 200 LPs chart.

Selected Awards

MTV Video Music Awards, Video of the Year, Best Group Video, Best Metal/Hard Rock Video, and Best Direction (Mark Pellington), all for "Jeremy," 1993.

Multi-platinum certification (4 million sales), *Vitalogy*, 1995.

Grammy Award, Best Hard Rock Performance, for "Spin the Black Circle," 1996.

American Music Award nomination, Favorite Alternative Artist, 1999.

Multi-platinum certification (11 million sales), *Ten*, 1999.

Multi-platinum certification (7 million sales), *Vs.*, 2000.

Grammy Award nomination, Best Hard Rock Performance, for "Grievance," 2001.

Selected Discography

Ten (Epic), 1991.
Vs. (Epic), 1993.
Vitalogy (Epic), 1994.
No Code (Epic), 1996.
Yield (Epic), 1998.
Live on Two Legs (Epic), 1998.
Binaural (Epic), 2000.
Twenty-five live "bootlegs" (various cities) (Epic), 2000.

Further Reading

Clarke, Martin. *None Too Fragile: Pearl Jam and Eddie Vedder.* London: Plexus, 1998.

Cohen, Jonathan. "Pearl Jam Goes to the Web to Market." *Billboard,* May 27, 2000, p. 126.

Crandall, Bill et al. "The Complete Pearl Jam Live Album Guide." *Rolling Stone,* September 26, 2000.

Fricke, David. "Nine Dead at Pearl Jam Concert." *Rolling Stone,* August 17, 2000, p. 27.

Neely, Kim. *Five Against One: The Pearl Jam Story.* New York: Penguin, 1998.

Power, Martin. *Pearl Jam: Dark Corners: An Illustrated Biography.* London: Omnibus, 1997.

Contact Information

Epic Records
2100 Colorado Ave.
Santa Monica, CA 90404

Web Sites

Five Horizons: A Pearl Jam Fanzine. http://www.fivehorizons.com (accessed on January 8, 2001).

Pearl Jam (official site). http://www.pearljam.com (accessed on January 8, 2001).

Pearl Jam Synergy. http://www.sonymusic.com/artists/PearlJam/ (accessed on January 8, 2001).

The Pearl Jam Vault. http://www.pauserecord.com/john/pjvault/ (accessed on January 8, 2001).

Pink

American pop and R&B singer

Born Alecia Moore on September 8, 1979, in Philadelphia, Pennsylvania

> "... Pink sings about being less interested in a man who's successful than one who understands her and offers real love."
>
> –Chuck Taylor, *Billboard*, June 17, 2000

Pink. (AP/Wide World Photos. Reproduced by permission.)

Even as the media ignored her and critics panned her work, Pink's songs permeated the airwaves during 2000 and 2001. Her sometimes-racy videos likewise became popular fare on MTV. Though her hair color makes her a standout, the most surprising thing for anyone who has never seen her is that the singer with the soulful voice, who records on the R&B and hip-hop label LaFace, is white.

How Alecia Moore turned Pink

Growing up in Philadelphia, Alecia Moore's biggest hero was her father, but though she seems to have had a happy childhood, her nickname emerged during what must have been a painful incident at YMCA summer camp. "This kid pulled my pants down in front of everybody," she later told *Rolling Stone*. "When I get embarrassed, I turn bright pink. So then he called me Pink, and I never lived it down."

Later, when she became famous, the name "Pink" acquired new meaning due to the color of her hair, which she began dying in 1998. When she met her idol, Stevie Wonder (see sidebar with **Jamiroquai** entry), who is blind, he had to rely on his bodyguard to explain what she looked like. "Your hair is pink?" he said. "I wish I could see that."

Singing on a dare

Blessed with a powerful voice, Moore began singing backup for a friend's rap group, Schools of Thought, when she was thirteen years old. A year later, she was at a Philadelphia club near the end of an all-night "rave" or dance party, and the DJs were packing up their equipment when a friend dared her to step up to the microphone. She took the dare, belting out a song by **Mary J. Blige** (see entry). This woke a sleeping DJ, who was so impressed that he offered her a guest spot on his Friday-night shows.

Supported by her family, the high schooler began pursuing a musical career. In time she would sing backup for Diana Ross, **98 Degrees** (see entry), and Tevin Campbell, and eventually MCA Records invited her to record with an all-girl trio called Basic Instinct. The group did not last long enough to make a single, but Moore soon joined another such trio, Choice.

From Choice to solo

Choice made a demo and mailed it to LaFace, whose executives liked what they heard and flew the girls down to Atlanta for a formal audition. They signed them immediately, but Choice, too, soon fell apart. By then, however, Pink—as Moore now called herself—had a recording contract. Working with a number of producers, including Babyface, she made recordings that would appear in April 2000 as *Can't Take Me Home*.

Pink performs at the 2001 American Music Awards. (Photo by Steve Granitz. WireImage.com. Reproduced by permission.)

The album's first single, released early in the year, was "There U Go," which had hit the Top 10 by June. With its lyrics about a cheating man, the song set the tone for much of Pink's music. She followed it with "Most Girls," which made the Top 40 in August, and by the following month *Can't Take Me Home* was certified platinum (1 million copies sold).

Critics vs. fans and MTV

Critics typically were unkind to Pink: Chuck Taylor of *Billboard* dismissed "Most Girls" as "assembly-line, paint-by-numbers fare," and Douglas Wolk of *Rolling Stone* wrote that "She's got a dazzling, gymnastic R&B voice, without a hint of style that's all her own." But the fans, who catapulted her album to double-platinum status by years' end, had a different view; so too did MTV and *Teen People,* which put her face on its cover.

December 2000 saw a third single, "You Make Me Sick," whose lyrics played on the idea of being simultaneously attracted to, and repelled by, a cheating lover. While maintaining that "This song is a far cry from art," Taylor in *Billboard* conceded that "it punches hard in the dead center of today's R&B-flavored landscape."

Taylor also noted that Pink is strong on image and attitude, and that these features help her stand apart from the many performers vying for airtime. Pink herself describes her style as a combination of Annie Lennox, who established herself with the Eurythmics and later as a solo performer, and Method Man (see **Wu-Tang Clan** entry). Early in 2001, she returned to the recording studio for a followup album, to be released that summer.

Selected Awards

Multi-platinum certification (2 million sales), *Can't Take Me Home,* 2000.

MTV Video Music Award nomination, Best New Artist, for "There U Go," 2000.

Billboard Music Video Award nomination, Best Pop New Artist Clip of the Year, for "There U Go," 2000.

American Music Award nomination, Favorite Soul/R&B New Artist, 2000.

Selected Discography

Can't Take Me Home (LaFace), 2000.

Further Reading

"Pink Chat Transcript." *Teen People Online.* http://www.teenpeople.com/teenpeople/chat/transcriptsarchive (accessed on January 24, 2001).

Roth, Kristin. "Pink." *Rolling Stone,* March 30, 2000, p. 22.

Taylor, Chuck. "Pink: Most Girls." *Billboard,* June 17, 2000, p. 31.

Taylor, Chuck. "Spotlight: Pink: 'You Make Me Sick.'" *Billboard,* December 9, 2000, p. 36.

Wolk, Douglas. "Can't Take Me Home." *Rolling Stone,* April 27, 2000, p. 75.

Contact Information

LaFace Records
3350 Peachtree Street
Suite 1500
Atlanta, GA 30326-1040

Web Sites

Always Pink. http://ba.smxiexplore.com/pink/ (accessed on January 24, 2001).

The Official Pink Fan Site. http://pinkfanz.homestead.com/splash~ns4.html (accessed on January 24, 2001).

Pink's Nest on the Web. http://www.pinksnest.com (accessed on January 24, 2001).

Pinkspage (official site). http://www.pinkspage.com (accessed on January 24, 2001).

Puff Daddy

American hip-hop artist, producer, and record company executive
Born Sean Combs on November 4, 1970, in New York, New York

> "I'm in love with what I do. It's like if you're in love, you can't sleep at night. You wake up excited . . . and you're skipping around."
> –Puff Daddy, *Jet*, September 13, 1999

Widely credited as the father of hip-hop soul, which merges those two styles, Sean "Puffy" Combs is a busy man. As a producer, he has worked with a variety of performers; as a record company executive, Combs presides over Bad Boy Entertainment; and as a recording artist performing under the name Puff Daddy, he has enjoyed enormous success.

Puffy gets his name

Sean Combs was born in Harlem, but his mother, Janice—his father was shot when he was a small boy—worked three jobs and managed to buy a house in Mount Vernon, a suburb of New York. As a child, he had a habit of "huffing and puffing," and soon acquired the nickname "Puffy."

In 1988, Combs enrolled at Washington, D.C.'s Howard University, and soon afterward obtained an internship, an unpaid work-study program, at Uptown Records. Recalled Andre Harrell, a former rap star and later director of Uptown, "The first thing I

Sean "Puffy" Combs. (AP/Wide World Photos. Reproduced by permission.)

Grandmaster Flash and the Furious Five

As a youngster, Sean "Puffy" Combs often went to see shows by Grandmaster Flash and the Furious Five, widely credited as the first rap group to make a mainstream impact. (Rap itself dates back at least to the time of the Last Poets in the 1960s—see *Parents Aren't Supposed to Like It*, Vol. 2, p. 305). Unlike the Sugarhill Gang, whose 1979 release "Rapper's Delight" was the first rap record to reach the *Billboard* charts, the Furious Five did not simply come together in a studio to record a hit. They had performed for years in the New York club scene before they scored with "The Message," a gritty, powerful 1982 single.

The group soon split in two, with both Grandmaster Flash and Melle Mel at the helm of bands who called themselves "the Furious Five." They reunited briefly in 1987, but by then the revolution they helped create had been all too successful, and they seemed like old-timers. However, a listen to any of their classic works—available on compilations such as *The Best of Grandmaster Flash, Melle Mel & the Furious Five* (Rhino Records, 1994)—makes it clear how a few young men from the streets changed the future of music.

---

asked him to do was get me a tape from the studio. He came back with it in five minutes. The studio was ten blocks away."

Impressed by Puffy's energy and penchant for hard work, Harrell soon gave him a full-time job with the label's A&R (artists and repertoire) wing. This meant that Puffy, just out of his teens, had the power to decide artists' futures. By 1991, he was vice-president of Uptown, and had established himself as a producer working with such up-and-coming stars as Jodeci and **Mary J. Blige** (see entry).

From Uptown to Bad Boy

Despite his successes, Combs found himself at odds with Harrell, who in 1993 fired him. Just two weeks later, however, he signed a deal with Arista Records to take over distribution for his newly formed company, Bad Boy Entertainment. The new label would bring in somewhere between $100 and $200 million during the period from 1993 to 1997.

At Bad Boy, Combs made friends with gangsta rapper Biggie Smalls (a.k.a. The Notorious B.I.G), and as a result became involved in the world of gangsta rap. Gangstas emphasized violence in their lyrics, and for many artists the violence spilled over to their lives. Thus Smalls's rival Tupac Shakur was shot and killed in Las Vegas in September 1996, and on March 9, 1997, Smalls himself was shot in Los Angeles. Neither crime has been solved, but as the smoke cleared, one thing was certain: gangsta rap had seen its day.

No Way Out

As gangsta gave way to more moderate versions of hip-hop, one of the figures leading the charge was Combs.

Ironically, his hit song "I'll Be Missing You" was a tribute to Smalls. By then Combs was performing as "Puff Daddy and the Family," the latter a loose collection of talents that on the 1997 album *No Way Out* included Faith Evans, **Lil Kim,** and **Busta Rhymes** (see entries).

Sampling—using parts of another recording, typically one that another artist has made famous, in a new recording—is a major element in Puffy's work. "I'll Be Missing You" used a hook, or key part, from the 1983 Police hit "Every Breath You Take"; less obvious was its use of "I'll Fly Away," an old Christian hymn, as well as "Adagio for Strings" by American composer Samuel Barber (1910–1981). Other songs lifted pieces from hits by Diana Ross, Grandmaster Flash (see sidebar), David Bowie, Lisa Stansfield, and others.

This earned Puffy a great deal of criticism, to which he responded by saying that what he does—bringing together diverse styles in a coherent whole—is more difficult than it appears. In addition, it is important to remember that Combs is first and foremost a behind-the-scenes figure, a producer who also performs rather than the other way around. In any case, he received a resounding endorsement from a music legend when former Led Zeppelin guitarist Jimmy Page joined him in recording "Come with Me," which sampled Zeppelin's 1975 classic "Kashmir."

"The Great Puffy"

Though *Forever* (1999) did not equal the multi-platinum success of *No Way Out,* Puffy's name stayed in the headlines. He opened a restaurant, started a magazine, established a film company, and spent time with his two sons Justin and Christian, born 1994 and 1998 respectively. (The boys have different mothers.) "He wants to be everywhere," wrote the *Village Voice*'s Eric Weisbard, who compared Puff Daddy to Jay Gatsby, hero of the classic novel *The Great Gatsby* by F. Scott Fitzgerald (1896—1940).

Like Gatsby, Puffy came from obscurity to wealth: he owns a mansion in the Hamptons, an exclusive area of New York's Long Island, and reportedly earns more than $50 million a year. Gatsby, who also lived in a fictionalized version of the Hamptons, was known for his materialism (love of possessions) and financial excess. Similarly, Puffy has come under fire for his glorification of commercialism, and his use of brand names in songs.

Puffy on trial

Early in 2001, the legend of Puff Daddy grew even larger as he went on trial for his role in an incident that took place more than a year before. He and then-girlfriend **Jennifer Lopez** (see entry) were at a New York club on December 27, 1999, when Puffy allegedly fired shots at the ceiling. He was arrested and charged with possession of an illegal firearm; even more serious was the charge that he offered his driver, Wardel Fenderson, $50,000 to claim that the gun belonged to *him.*

"It's like a show," an Italian reporter covering the case told *USA Today.* Indeed, the Puff Daddy trial had all the makings of the circus-like cases of the

1990s, especially the O. J. Simpson trial in 1995—and it so happened that Puffy had secured the services of Simpson's celebrated lawyer, Johnny Cochran. In March 2001, Puffy was acquitted of both gun possession and bribery charges. Later that month, he announced on MTV that he would no longer call himself Puff Daddy: adopting a name he said Smalls had given him, he said he wanted to be known as "P. Diddy."

Selected Awards

Songwriter of the Year Award, ASCAP, 1997.

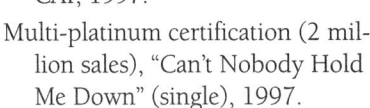

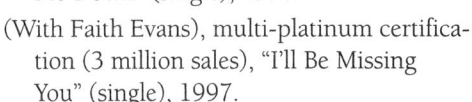

Multi-platinum certification (2 million sales), "Can't Nobody Hold Me Down" (single), 1997.

(With Faith Evans), multi-platinum certification (3 million sales), "I'll Be Missing You" (single), 1997.

(With The Family), Platinum certification, "Been Around the World" (single), 1997.

(With The Family), multi-platinum certification (6 million sales), *No Way Out,* 1998.

(With Jimmy Page), platinum certification, "Come with Me" (single), 1998.

Howard University Alumni Award for Distinguished Postgraduate Achievement in the Field of Entertainment, 1999.

Platinum certification, *Forever,* 1999.

Selected Discography

No Way Out (Bad Boy), 1997.
Forever (Bad Boy), 1999.

Further Reading

Cable, Andrew. *A Family Affair: The Unauthorized Sean "Puffy" Combs Story.* New York: Ballantine Books, 1998.

Chappell, Kevin, "The Puff Daddy Nobody Knows," *Ebony,* January 2000, p. 74.

Christian, Argena A., "Sean 'Puffy' Combs Discusses: The Love He's Never Been Able to Shake, His Impact as a Black Performer, and Why He's a Role Model," *Jet,* September 13, 1999, p. 54.

Oldenburg, Ann. "The People vs. Puff Daddy: The Hot Ticket in Town?" *USA Today,* February 5, 2001, p. 1-D.

Toure, "What Makes Puffy Run?," *Rolling Stone,* October 14, 1999, p. 48.

Weisbard, Eric, "The Gatsby of Gats," *Village Voice,* September 7, 1999, p. 69.

Contact Information

Bad Boy Entertainment
1540 Broadway
30th Floor
New York, NY 10036

Web Sites

Bad Boy Records. http://www.badboyonline.com (accessed on September 6, 2000).

Puff Daddy (official site). http://www.puffdaddy.com/start.html (accessed on September 6, 2000).

Queen Latifah

American rap artist

Born Dana Elaine Owens on March 18, 1970, in Newark, New Jersey

> "... I think it's important to be real and to relate to people now. I'm not coming from a holier-than-thou, self-righteous point of view."
>
> –Queen Latifah in her autobiography *Ladies First, Ebony,* November 1999

Queen Latifah's first three albums made music history by popularizing the idea that a woman could rap, and that she could do so without losing her feminine qualities. During the early 1990s, the singer remained highly visible, but by the midpoint of the decade her acting career increasingly took her away from music. Finally in 1998, five years after *Black Reign,* Latifah released *Order in the Court.* The album showed her experimenting with new styles, and in 1999 she suggested that she was working on a follow-up. By then, however, she had a new daytime TV talk show, a book, and more movie roles, and the prospect of a new Latifah album was uncertain.

A native of New Jersey, Dana Elaine Owens chose the performing name Latifah, Arabic for "delicate and sensitive." Her background was middle class, but when she got behind the mike she could sound as though she had come from the same rough streets that produced many well-known male rappers. Her message was different, however: instead of promoting violence, Latifah's lyrics called for men in the rap community to give women greater respect.

Queen Latifah. (AP/Wide World Photos. Reproduced by permission.)

That was the theme of "Ladies First," her popular anthem from *All Hail the Queen* (1989), and in 1991 she delivered much the same message with "Fly Girl" from *Nature of a Sista*. The album marked a departure from the type of material normally used in rap backing tracks: instead of repetitive recorded sounds, Latifah used live instruments, along with singing. But it was *Black Reign* that would prove her greatest commercial and critical success. "U.N.I.T.Y." became a hit both with black and white audiences, and earned her a Grammy Award.

Latifah had meanwhile launched a successful acting career, starting with *Jungle Fever* in 1991, and in 1993 she joined the cast of the Fox TV situation comedy *Living Single*. Her performance in *Set It Off* (1996) won her acclaim, and more roles followed. She also launched her own music management company, Flavor Unit, with ShaKim Compere, and her client list included talents such as **LL Cool J** (see entry).

Not everything was positive for Latifah in the mid-1990s, however. She lost her brother in a motorcycle accident, an event that affected her deeply, and in July 1995 she was the victim of a carjacking. That created more problems: fearful for her safety, she began carrying an unregistered handgun, and was arrested on weapons charges when police stopped her for speeding in February 1996. They also found a small quantity of marijuana in her car. **(See original entry on Queen Latifah in *Parents Aren't Supposed to Like It*, Volume 2, p. 399.)**

Order in the Court

Latifah later gave up drugs, and in her 1999 autobiography, *Ladies First,* she frankly discussed her problems not only with marijuana, but with cocaine and mescaline as well. She also opened up about past difficulty in accepting her own appearance: "People look at me now," she wrote, "and think, 'WOW, there's a full-sized woman who has it together. Puh-lease! It took me years to get to the point where I love my body."

> "People look at me now and think, 'WOW, there's a full-sized woman who has it together. Puh-lease! It took me years to get to the point where I love my body."

Living Single was cancelled in 1997, but in 1998 Latifah appeared alongside Dustin Hoffman, Samuel L. Jackson, and Sharon Stone in the film *Sphere*. She also began making a return to music, playing shows on the Lilith Fair (see **Sarah McLachlan** entry), and in June 1998 released *Order in the Court*. The album marked a return to the rougher sounds of her first record, but despite its tone, Latifah was in the process of perfecting a kinder, gentler image.

She played a jazz singer and sang in the film *Living Out Loud* (1998), and at the end of the year was named one of the "Most Fascinating Women of 1998" by the traditional women's magazine *Ladies Home Journal*. She also debuted *The Queen Latifah Show,* which she described thus in *Ebony:* " . . . it's going to be positive, because I'm not tacky and sleazy, so my show won't be tacky and sleazy." Referring to a notorious shock-talk show, she added, "It won't be a *Jerry Springer*."

Another Latifah album?

Latifah told *Ebony* that she was working on a new album: "Beats and rhymes, that's the way I would describe it," she said. "No real complicated subject matter, just bringing that Latifah you loved on the first album into the year 2000." The album did not materialize, however, probably because Latifah was busy with her TV show, which had poor ratings in its initial run. Through hard work, however, she built a following, and the program was moved into a more favorable time slot in 2000.

Latifah performed in a February 2000 benefit show for the gay and lesbian Human Rights Campaign, along with **Garth Brooks** (see entry), Melissa Etheridge, k. d. lang, and others. She also sang at the Academy Awards in March, and in June announced that she would appear as Glenda the Good Witch in a remake of the 1939 classic *The Wizard of Oz*. "People have been continuously surprised by my next moves," she told the New Orleans, Louisiana, *Times–Picayune*. "Don't count Queen Latifah out when it comes to, 'Hey, she can do this, she can do that.' Don't even waste your time."

Selected Awards

Grammy Award nomination, Best Rap Solo Performance, for "Latifah's Had It Up to Here," 1991.

Grammy Award, Best Rap Solo Performance, for "U.N.I.T.Y.," 1993.

Gold record certification, for *Black Reign*, 1994.

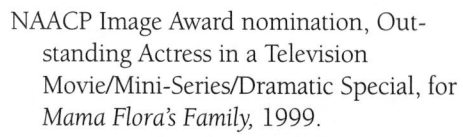

NAACP Image Award nomination, Outstanding Actress in a Television Movie/Mini-Series/Dramatic Special, for *Mama Flora's Family*, 1999.

NAACP Image Award nomination, Outstanding Supporting Actress in a Motion Picture, for *Living Out Loud*, 1999.

Selected Discography

All Hail the Queen (Tommy Boy), 1989.

Nature of a Sista (Tommy Boy), 1991.

Black Reign (Motown), 1993.

Order in the Court (Motown), 1998.

Further Reading

Lorando, Mark. "So You Want to Be in Show Business: Three Stars, Three Very Different Roads to NATPE." *Times–Picayune* (New Orleans), January 26, 2000, p. E-1.

Norment, Lynn. "Queen Latifah Has a New TV Show, A New Movie, and New Sass." *Ebony*, November 1999, p. 116.

Queen Latifah. *Ladies First: Revelations of a Strong Woman*. New York: Pocket Books, 1999.

Ruth, Amy. *Queen Latifah*. Minneapolis, Minnesota: Lerner Publications, 2001.

Washington, Bobby. *Queen Latifah*. New York: Dell Publishing, 1992.

Contact Information

Queen Latifah Fan Club
151 El Camino Dr.
Beverly Hills, CA 90212

Web Sites

Queen Latifah Home Page (official site of TV show). http://latifahshow.warnerbros.com (accessed on September 18, 2000).

RADIOHEAD

British alternative rock band
Formed 1987 in Oxford, England

"I can still remember buying *O.K. Computer* the night it came out in America," wrote British journalist Barney Hoskyns in the Manchester, England, *Guardian*. He went on to recount "driving up the New York Thruway in a state of feverish bliss as 'Airbag' and 'Lucky' and 'Let Down' enveloped me in their webs of sound."

Hoskyns was hardly alone in judging Radiohead's 1997 release one of the great musical events of rock history: in a 2000 poll, British music fans voted it the fourth-greatest album of all time, just behind *Sgt. Pepper's Lonely Hearts Club Band* (1967) by the Beatles. With *O.K. Computer*, Radiohead created a glittering jewel of an album, and as the music world awaited the release of the follow-up, everyone—even the band members themselves—wondered if they could top their earlier success.

On A Friday becomes Radiohead

A five-man ensemble from the English university town of Oxford, Radiohead consists of Thom Yorke (vocals and guitar; born October 7, 1968); Jonny Greenwood (guitar, keyboards, xy-

"We just got bored with being a rock band, and we started considering what else was going on around us."
-Ed O'Brien, *Guitar Player*, October 1997

Radiohead. (Photo by Tom Sheehan. EMI Ltd. Reproduced by permission.)

Radiohead lead singer Thom Yorke. (Ken Settle. Reproduced by permission.)

lophone; born November 7, 1971); Ed O'Brien (guitar; born April 15, 1968); Colin Greenwood (bass; born June 26, 1968); and Phil Selway (drums; born May 23, 1967).

During the mid-1980s, Yorke and Colin Greenwood played briefly in a band called TNT before leaving in 1987 to form a new group with Colin's brother Jonny. Joined by O'Brien and Selway under the name "On A Friday," they played their first show at Jericho's Tavern in Oxford. Soon they realized that their name was not getting attention, so in 1989 they chose a new one, taking as their inspiration the title of the Talking Heads song "Radio Head."

Surprise hit with "Creep"

A 1992 EP, or extended-play recording, called *Drill* attracted the attention of Capitol Records, who signed the band and in 1993 released *Pablo Honey*. The latter yielded a surprise hit in "Creep," a song recorded at the last minute and tacked on near the beginning of the album. As a result of attention from U.S. college radio stations, the band went on an American tour opening for Belly and Tears For Fears.

The Bends (1995) did not prove a great commercial success, but it won the adoration of critics, and in time fans would celebrate it as one of music history's greatest albums. Radiohead went on another U.S. tour, again as an opener—but this time with a much more significant band, **R.E.M.** (see entry). In 1996, they toured with Alanis Morissette (see sidebar with **Goo Goo Dolls** entry) before going into the studio to record *O.K. Computer*.

A "shimmering, densely textured masterpiece"

Yorke later explained the title of their blockbuster release, saying that while they were recording it, group members had made a joke of walking around the studio like robots and saying "O.K., computer!" to each other. Neither he nor the others seemed to have any idea that they were creating a masterwork, and as the album began attracting attention and respect, they shrugged off suggestions that they were making music history.

But other musicians, ranging from Don Henley to members of **Counting Crows, Jars of Clay,** and **KoRN** (see entries), were not shy about singing the praises of *O.K. Computer*. Nor were critics and journalists such as Hoskyns, who called it a "shimmering, densely textured masterpiece . . . an album that took the moribund [dying] 'rock' genre and resurrected it in [twelve] astonishing tracks of ecstatic, multi-layered genius."

Comparisons to the Beatles

This was an opinion echoed by the thousands of British music fans who voted in the Virgin Music All Time Top 1,000 Albums poll in 2000. Such polls are typically dominated by artists from the 1960s and 1970s, and thus it was a surprise when *O.K. Computer* placed in the top five. But even more surprising was the showing for *The Bends*.

Over the years, *Sgt. Pepper* (see sidebar with **A Tribe Called Quest** entry) has remained the standard for rock albums, and people speak about a group's best release as their *Sgt. Pepper*. But judging from the Virgin Music poll, *O.K. Computer* is not Radiohead's *Sgt. Pepper* since *The Bends,* in the number-two slot, actually placed higher than *Sgt. Pepper* itself. In fact, the top five consisted purely of the Beatles and Radiohead, with *The Beatles* (a.k.a. "The White Album," 1968) in fifth place and *Revolver* (1966) in the number-one position.

A number of critics noted with interest the fact that, whereas Oasis had positioned themselves as "the next Beatles"— a claim made by numerous bands ever since the Beatles themselves became international superstars in 1964—it was Radiohead that most clearly deserved comparison with the Fab Four. Like the Beatles, who spent a then-unheard-of four months recording *Sgt. Pepper,* Radiohead in the late 1990s found themselves in a position to take their time crafting an album. This could be both good and bad.

Great expectations

"One possible pitfall," wrote Hoskyns, "is the open-ended time frame Radiohead have been permitted on this album. Unlike its three predecessors, this one has been recorded at their own pace, with no gun to their heads. 'The problem we have found is that we are essentially in limbo—for the first time in our lives we have nothing to get ready for,' confessed O'Brien [in August 1999]. 'It's taken us seven years to get this sort of freedom, but it could be so easy to [mess] it all up."

'The problem we have found is that we are essentially in limbo—for the first time in our lives we have nothing to get ready for. It's taken us seven years to get this sort of freedom, but it could be so easy to [mess] it all up."

As the music world awaited the release of *Kid A* in October 2000, the legendary status of Radiohead only grew, and many observers wondered if expectations for the *O.K. Computer* follow-up might be too high. The answer was both yes and no. Fans who hoped for "O.K. Computer II" were bound to be disappointed; but anyone who wanted to hear the sound of Radiohead stretching their musical boundaries would find *Kid A* an enthralling experience. In summer 2001 Radiohead released their fifth album,

Amnesiac, composed of further material recorded during the *Kid A* sessions.

Selected Awards

Platinum certification, *Pablo Honey,* 1995.

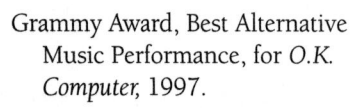

Grammy Award, Best Alternative Music Performance, for *O.K. Computer,* 1997.

Grammy Award nomination, Album of the Year, for *O.K. Computer,* 1998.

MTV Video Music Award nominations, Best Group Video, Best Direction (Jonathan Glazer), Best Cinematography (Stephen Keith-Roache), and Best Alternative Video, all for "Karma Police," 1998.

Platinum certification, *O.K. Computer,* 1998.

Grammy Award nomination, Best Alternative Music Performance, for *Airbag/How Am I Driving?,* 1999.

Platinum certification, *The Bends,* 1999.

Gold certification, *Kid A,* 2000.

Grammy Award nomination, Album of the Year, for *Kid A,* 2001.

Grammy Award, Best Alternative Music Album, for *Kid A,* 2001.

Selected Discography

Pablo Honey (Capitol), 1993.
The Bends (Capitol), 1995.
O.K. Computer (Capitol), 1997.
Airbag/How Am I Driving? (EP; Capitol), 1998.
Kid A (Capitol), 2000.
Amnesiac (Capitol), 2001.

Further Reading

Clarke, Martin. *Radiohead: Hysterical & Useless.* London, England: Plexus, 2000.

Hoskyns, Barney. "No Surprises: After the Success of *O.K. Computer,* Radiohead's Next Album Is One of the Most Eagerly Awaited Records Ever." *Guardian* (Manchester, England), April 14, 2000, p. 14.

Kelso, Paul. "Radiohead Challenge Fab Four as *Bends* Leaves *Sgt. Pepper* Cold." *Guardian* (Manchester, England), September 4, 2000, p. 5.

Randall, Marc. *Exit Music: The Radiohead Story.* New York: Delta Trade Paperbacks, 2000.

Vaziri, Aidin. "Radiohead: British Pop Aesthetes." *Guitar Player,* October 1997, p. 27.

Contact Information

Capitol Records
1750 North Vine Street
Hollywood, CA 90028

Web Sites

Green Plastic Radiohead. http://www.greenplastic.com (accessed on October 26, 2000).

kinetic: radiohead unofficial. http://wezl.org/rhead/ (accessed on February 9, 2001).

Radiohead (official site). http://www.radiohead.com (accessed on September 19, 2000).

Radiohead Planet. http://members.tripod.com/~Planettelex/ (accessed on September 19, 2000).

Rage Against the Machine

American alternative metal and rap-rock band

Formed 1991 in Los Angeles, California

Opinions on Rage Against the Machine have long been sharply divided, though more because of their far-left radical politics than because of their sound. The politics, in the view of many critics, are merely simple-minded (see sidebar), but the music—hard-driving metal riffs and machine-gun raps—is anything but dull, as the band proved again on *The Battle of Los Angeles* (1999). But with the departure of vocalist Zach de la Rocha in October 2000, *Renegades* may very well turn out to be Rage's final statement.

Rage is known for its support of socialist revolutionary movements around the world, and its outspoken opposition to wealth and the capitalist free-market economic system. Therefore it may seem a little ironic that the group members came from privileged backgrounds. De la Rocha (born January 1970) and bassist Tim Commerford both came from upscale Irvine, California; guitarist Thomas Morello (born May 1964) attended the nation's most prestigious school, Harvard University; while drummer Brad Wilk was from a well-to-do Portland, Oregon, family.

> "I feel that it is necessary to leave Rage because our decision-making process has completely failed."
> —Zach de la Rocha, press release, October 18, 2000

Zach de la Rocha and Tim Commerford. (AP/Wide World Photos. Reproduced by permission.)

Rage guitarist Tom Morello. (David Atlas. Reproduced by permission.)

In Los Angeles during the early 1990s, the members of Rage got together and self-produced a cassette that sold more than 5,000 copies, leading to a deal with Epic Records in 1992. Their hugely successful self-titled debut album spawned such memorable songs as "Bullet in the Head" (which had also appeared on the earlier independent release) and "Freedom," which became an MTV favorite in 1994. Epic had not known quite what to make of Rage's style, which they initially promoted as rap. But by the mid-1990s it became clear that a new musical genre, rap metal or "rap-core," had come into existence—and Rage, along with the **Red Hot Chili Peppers** (see entry), was at the forefront.

In 1996 the group solidified its position with *Evil Empire,* which included the hit single "Bulls on Parade."

Also in 1996, Rage made headlines when they appeared on *Saturday Night Live* with upside-down American flags hanging from their amplifiers. This was just another example of the group's political stance, which has included support for a guerrilla uprising in Chiapas, Mexico, as well as advocacy for the release of jailed African American journalist Mumia Abu-Jamal and Native American activist Leonard Peltier. At Lollapalooza III in 1993, group members stood nude, with duct tape across their mouths, to protest censorship. **(See original entry on Rage Against the Ma-**

Rage, Revolution, and Responsibility

Fans of Rage Against the Machine's politics (as opposed to their music) believe that the group's political positions are daring and dangerous. But to many critics it seems more like a case of "radical chic," a term coined by author Tom Wolfe in the 1960s to describe a type of radicalism that was fashionable but intellectually and spiritually empty.

Serious political action involves a great deal of study and thought. Rare examples of rock musicians making that effort are Bono of **U2** (see entry) in his work for Third World debt relief, and **Sting** (see entry) in his efforts on behalf of rain forests and other political causes. Yet despite the fact that Rage's Tom Morello is well-educated, political statements by him and other members of the band suggest a preference for image over substance.

To many observers, some of the group's stances have been downright irresponsible, as when Morello advocated violence in his famous statement, "A good song should make you wanna tap your feet and get with your girl. A great song should destroy cops and set fire to the suburbs. I'm only interested in writing great songs." Rage has also attached its name to terrorist organizations such as the Shining Path, a group responsible for the murder of thousands of people, which was a major force behind the cocaine trade, in its homeland of Peru during the 1980s.

---

chine in *Parents Aren't Supposed to Like It,* Volume 1, p. 134.)

Tim C. rushes the stage

On the heels of *Evil Empire,* the band released an EP—extended-play, a collection of songs shorter than a regular album—called *People of the Sun* in 1997. They continued to tour, and in 1999 released *The Battle of Los Angeles,* their first album in three years. Like its predecessors, *Battle* sold several million copies and showed that the group's sound was as powerful as ever, though many critics maintained that their debut album remained their best.

Not surprisingly, in the controversy over Napster (see **Metallica** entry), Rage came down solidly on the side of the Internet file-sharing service and against record companies. But perhaps the group's most noticeable "statement" in 2000 came when Commerford—who at times has gone by the stage name of "Tim C."—rushed the stage at the MTV Video Music Awards. **Limp Bizkit** (see entry) had just won the Best Rock Video award, a category in which Rage's "Sleep Now in the Fire" had also been nominated. Commerford was arrested, and many music fans condemned his behavior as evidence of a sore-loser mentality.

De la Rocha departs

In retrospect, some observers may have seen in Commerford's outburst a sign that Rage was coming apart at the seams. Just a few weeks after the awards show, de la Rocha announced that he was leaving Rage, which he maintained was "no longer meeting the aspirations [goals] of all four of us collectively. . . ." Furthermore, he said, the group (or perhaps it successes) had "undermined [gone against] our artistic and political ideals."

The other three members maintained that Rage would go on, though obviously in a much-changed form. Late in 2000, the group released *Renegades,* a collection of cover tunes. In May 2001 it was announced that Morello, Commerford and Wilk had created a new band with former Soundgarden lead singer Chris Cornell. At the time of the announcement, the band did not have a name, but it was not to be called Rage Against the Machine. Said an Epic Records publicist, "Rage Against the Machine doesn't exist anymore."

Selected Awards

Grammy Award nomination, Best Metal Performance, for "No Shelter," 1999.
Multi-platinum certification (2 million sales), *The Battle of Los Angeles,* 1999.
MTV Video Music Award nomination, Best Rock Video, for "Sleep Now in the Fire," 2000.
Multi-platinum certification (3 million sales), *Rage Against the Machine,* 2000.
Multi-platinum certification (3 million sales), *Evil Empire,* 2000.
Grammy Award nomination, Best Rock Album (for *The Battle of Los Angeles*), 2001.
Grammy Award, Best Hard Rock Performance, for "Guerrilla Radio," 2001.

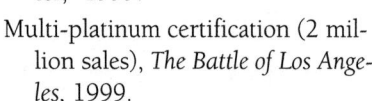

Selected Discography

Rage Against the Machine (Epic), 1992.
Evil Empire (Epic), 1996.
People of the Sun (EP; Revelation), 1997.
The Battle of Los Angeles (Epic), 1999.
Renegades (Epic), 2000.

Further Reading

Blackett, Matt. "Funk-Rock Freedom Fighter." *Guitar Player,* July 2000, p. 76.
Christensen, Thor. "In a Blaze of Glory, Rage Bows Out with Power Riffs, Fresh Guitar Licks." *Dallas Morning News,* December 10, 2000, p. 8-C.
Doherty, Brian. "Rage On." *Reason,* October 2000, p. 48.
Tyrangiel, Josh. "One Less Cog in the Machine." *Time,* October 30, 2000, p. 107.

Contact Information

Rage Against the Machine
P.O. Box 2052
Los Angeles, CA 90069

Web Sites

Fitz's Rage Against the Machine Site. http://www.geocities.com/TimesSquare/5618/rage.html (accessed on December 18, 2000).
House of Rage. http://www.bullsonparade.com/index.html (accessed on December 18, 2000).
Rage Against the Machine (official site). http://www.ratm.com (accessed on December 18, 2000).
Township Rebellion. http://www.geocities.com/CapitolHill/2822/ (accessed on December 18, 2000).

THE RED HOT CHILI PEPPERS

American alternative rock and rap-rock band

Formed 1983 in
Los Angeles, California

Most bands experience personnel changes over the years, but usually the drummers are the ones that get rotated. Not so with the Red Hot Chili Peppers, which have had no less than six guitarists. In 1998 Dave Navarro quit amid rumors of drug abuse, and on *Californication* (1999)—the group's biggest success since *Blood Sugar Sex Magik* put them on the map eight years before—the Peppers introduced a "new" guitarist: former member John Frusciante.

Back in 1977, two boys at Fairfax High School in Los Angeles, California, became inseparable friends. One, Anthony Kiedis (born November 1, 1962) was charming and magnetic; the other, Michael Balzary (born October 16, 1962)—better known as Flea—was intense and withdrawn. Flea played trumpet, but at seventeen he started playing bass, and by 1983 he and vocalist Kiedis had formed the Red Hot Chili Peppers with guitarist Hillel Slovak and drummer Jack Irons.

Slovak left a year later, was replaced by Jack Sherman, then returned in 1985. By 1988, the Peppers had released three al-

"If I've learned anything through the freaky tribulations of this business, it's that all of the setbacks, all of the losses and all of the gains—it's all for a reason."

-Anthony Kiedis, *Rolling Stone*, April 29, 1999

(L–R) Chad Smith, Anthony Kiedis, John Frusciante, and Flea. (AP/Wide World Photos. Reproduced by permission.)

bums and an EP called *Abby Road*—the title and cover a parody of the Beatles' *Abbey Road* (1969). They had also gone through a number of personnel changes. On June 25, 1988, Slovak died of a heroin overdose, and after a brief stint with Duane McKnight on guitar, the Peppers invited eighteen-year-old John Frusciante (born March 5, 1970) to join the band. Meanwhile, Irons left (he later wound up in **Pearl Jam**; see entry), to be replaced by Chad Smith (born October 25, 1962).

Their cover of "Higher Ground" by Stevie Wonder (see sidebar with **Jamiroquai** entry) on *Mother's Milk* (1989) got the Peppers considerable airplay. But their real breakthrough came in 1991 with *Blood Sugar Sex Magik*, which yielded massive radio and video hits with "Give It Away" and "Under the Bridge." Just as the group catapulted to stardom, however, Frusciante quit, and the Peppers replaced him with a succession of guitarists: Arik Marshall, Jesse Tobias, and finally former Jane's Addiction member Dave Navarro. **(See original entry on the Red Hot Chili Peppers in *Parents Aren't Supposed to Like It*, Volume 1, p. 148.)**

Navarro, Frusciante, Kiedis—and heroin

One Hot Minute (1995), as it turned out, would be the only Red Hot Chili Peppers studio album with Navarro. As for Navarro, during the late 1990s rumors increasingly associated him with a problem that has dogged several band members: heroin. While touring with the reunited Jane's Addiction in 1997, Navarro began behaving strangely, and *USA Today* quoted the Peppers' publicist Ken Phillips as saying that Navarro was using "hard drugs." Navarro denied rumors of drug use, but in 1998 announced that he was leaving the Peppers.

Navarro's departure led to the return of Frusciante, who had gone down his own dangerous road of addiction. He had quit the group in reaction to the rock-star lifestyle, but unfortunately retained a part of that lifestyle: specifically, an addiction to heroin. The drug nearly killed him, but he finally checked himself into a treatment facility.

Kiedis had also struggled with heroin, as documented in "Under the Bridge," and had relapsed in 1997. ". . . [W]hen I'm using" the drug, he told MTV, "my life sucks, and when I'm clean my life gets really beautiful. . . . I'm just happy to be back here and not using." Having once more kicked the habit, Kiedis visited Frusciante at the rehab center in 1997. He had not taken Frusciante's departure well, and the two had not spoken for years, but after Navarro left, he and the others invited the newly clean Frusciante to return.

Flea's challenges

"Kiedis credits Flea and Smith with keeping the Chili Peppers alive, if barely at times, over the past seven years," David Fricke wrote in *Rolling Stone*. "Flea was beyond patient and beyond compassionate," Kiedis told Fricke. "There was me going back and forth, John quitting, things not panning out with Dave. I can't

Peppers on the Silver Screen

The Red Hot Chili Peppers are known for their onstage theatrics, but they have also performed in plenty of movies as well. Vocalist Anthony Kiedis played bit parts in *F.I.S.T.* (1978), *Less Than Zero* (1987), *The Chase* (1994), and several other films—most notably *Point Break* (1991), where he appeared as a thuggish surfer punk. Drummer Chad Smith has also had a few roles, including *Ski Hard* in 1995. But Flea is by far the most experienced actor in the Red Hot Chili Peppers lineup.

The bassist, who also appeared in *Less Than Zero* and *The Chase,* had his first film role in *Suburbia* in 1984, and has been in more than two dozen movies (as well as a handful of TV spots) since then. Movies with Flea include *Back to the Future,* parts II (1989) and III (1990); *My Own Private Idaho* (1991); *Son in Law* (1993); *Liar's Poker* (1997); *The Big Lebowski, Fear and Loathing in Las Vegas,* and *Psycho* (all 1998).

Then of course there is *Woodstock '94* (1995), which features all of the group members—as themselves, performing on stage. For more information, see the *Internet Movie Database* (http://www.imdb.com).

---

believe he was willing to hang in there as long as he did. Chad, too."

Flea himself had his own personal challenges: a very painful breakup with his girlfriend of five years, an event that clouded his life during the recording of *Californication*. Flea, who like Smith is a parent, told Gavin Edwards of *Rolling Stone* that while they were on tour in Australia, "I was crying one day, and [my daughter Clara, born in 1989] said, 'Look, Papa, I don't know why you're sad, but no matter what, it's going to be OK. You're such a good person.' It was an amazingly touching thing."

As Edwards observed, Flea is an upstanding parent who makes sure his daughter does her homework and eats healthy food. He even prays before meals. Regarding the group's influence on the current rap-metal trend, he expressed distaste for much of the "angry, screaming metal now." As for the Peppers' ability to weather all the challenges they have faced, he told Edwards, "we still get in each others' hair. But now we say, 'Sorry for being in your hair.'"

Scarred but stronger than ever

In addition to everything else, the Peppers have sustained a number of physical injuries over the years. Kiedis suffered a dislocated wrist from a July 1997 motorcycle accident—an event that also led to a prescription for painkillers, which helped him down to the road his drug relapse. A month later, Smith also had a motorcycle accident, and dislocated his shoulder. The Chili Peppers were also the band who happened to be playing at Woodstock '99 when the crowd got out of control and began setting fires—an event that led to the closing of the festival.

No wonder, then, that the first of several hits from *Californication* was called "Scar Tissue." The song became a top-ten hit and won a Grammy in 2000, only one of many awards showered on the newly reinvigorated Peppers. At the same time, *Californication* rapidly proved to be their most popular release in years. The group again hit the Top 10 in May 2000 with "Otherside," and later that year had another hit with "Californication."

The Peppers performed the latter at the MTV Video Music Awards, where in September 2000 they received a Video Vanguard Award. But they performed fully clothed, not in the signature "costume"—nothing but a white athletic sock covering their privates—that for years defined the Peppers on stage. Edwards brought up the group's lack of clothing with the drummer: "'We've done it so many times,' groans Smith. 'It's like putting the **KISS** [see entry] makeup back on. Give us $100 million for the reunion tour of 2022, we'll do it in every town. You won't be able to see the sock under our fat bellies, but it'll be on."

Selected Awards

Grammy Award, Best Hard Rock Song, for "Give It Away," 1993.
Grammy Award, Best Rock Song, and Grammy Award nomination, Best Rock Performance by a Duo or Group, both for "Scar Tissue," 2000.
Grammy Award nomination, Best Rock Album, for *Californication,* 2000.
American Music Award, Favorite Alternative Artist, 2000.
MTV Video Music Video Vanguard Award, 2000.
Multi-platinum certification (6 million sales), *Blood Sugar Sex Magik,* 2000.
Multi-platinum certification (4 million sales), *Californication,* 2000.
Grammy Award nominations, Best Rock Performance by a Duo or Group with Vocal and Best Rock Song (Songwriter), both for "Californication," 2001.

Selected Discography

Red Hot Chili Peppers (Warner Brothers), 1984.
Freaky Styley (Warner Brothers), 1985.
The Uplift Mofo Party Plan (Warner Brothers), 1987.
Mother's Milk (Warner Brothers), 1989.
Blood Sugar Sex Magik (Warner Brothers), 1991.
What Hits!? (greatest hits; Warner Brothers), 1992.
Out In L.A. (rarities; Warner Brothers), 1994.
One Hot Minute (Warner Brothers), 1995.
Best of Red Hot Chili Peppers (greatest hits; Warner Brothers), 1997.
Californication (Warner Brothers), 1999.

Further Reading

Blackett, Matt. "Return of the Prodigal Son." *Guitar Player,* September 1999, p. 72.
Bozza, Anthony. "People of the Year: Anthony Kiedis of the Red Hot Chili Peppers." *Rolling Stone,* December 14-21, 2000, p. 116.
Edwards, Gavin. "Red Hot Chili Peppers." *Rolling Stone,* April 27, 2000, p. 56.
Fricke, David. "Red-Hot Reunion." *Rolling Stone,* April 29, 1999, p. 38.

Contact Information

Red Hot Chili Peppers
75 Rockefeller Plaza

20th Floor
New York, NY 10019

Web Sites

Red Hot Chili Peppers. http://home1.swipnet.se/~w-10622/ (accessed on January 8, 2001).

Red Hot Chili Peppers Online (official site). http://www.redhotchilipeppers.net (accessed on January 8, 2001).

The Red Hot Page. http://redhotpage.hem.netlink.se (accessed on January 8, 2001).

The Red Hot Place. http://hem.passagen.se/stuven/rhcp (accessed on January 8, 2001).

R.E.M.

American alternative rock band
Formed 1980 in Athens, Georgia

update

(L–R) Bill Berry, Mike Mills, Peter Buck, and Michael Stipe. (AP/Wide World Photos. Reproduced by permission.)

> "We depended on Bill, because he's a real pop person. He was the one to say, 'Get to the chorus. The verse gets too long, it's draggy.' Without Bill, the verses go on forever."
>
> –Peter Buck, on drummer Bill Berry. *Newsweek*, October 26, 1998

Pioneers of the 1990s alternative rock sound, R.E.M. emerged from Athens, Georgia, in the early 1980s to become one of the world's most influential bands. They were unlikely candidates for the role: singer Michael Stipe mumbled lyrics that seemed to make no sense, and Peter Buck's jangly guitar, combined with the rhythm section provided by bassist Mike Mills and drummer Bill Berry, added to the hazy, dream-like feel of their music. Nearly twenty years later, however, they stood at the summit of the rock world, but with Berry's departure, the remaining three had to reassess their identity as a group.

Stipe (born January 4, 1960) grew up in a military family that moved around the country; he and met Buck (born December 6, 1956) at the University of Georgia. Eventually they teamed up with Mills (born December 17, 1958) and Berry (born July 31, 1958) to form the Twisted Kites. By 1980, however, they were calling themselves R.E.M., a reference to "rapid eye movement," which a person experiences in deep sleep and especially while dreaming.

Signed with IRS Records in 1982, the group released an EP called *Chronic Town,* followed in 1983 by the album *Murmur.* The latter, with its single "Radio Free Europe," began winning them a small but loyal audience. During the mid-1980s, the group released several memorable albums—their best work, in the opinion of many fans—but only experienced pop-chart success with *Document* (1987), which included "The One I Love," "Finest Worksong," and "It's the End of the World As We Know It (And I Feel Fine)."

Green (1988), with hits such as "Stand" and "Orange Crush" that showed a new, more poppish R.E.M., catapulted the group to international superstardom. But their biggest album was yet to come: *Out of Time* (1991), with "Shiny Happy People," "Radio Song," and their biggest hit, "Losing My Religion." R.E.M. collected three Grammys in 1992, and spent the next five years winning numerous other awards while racking up a string of further hits with *Automatic for the People* (1992), *Monster* (1994), and—after signing an $80 million recording contract—*New Adventures in Hi-Fi* (1996). **(See original entry on R.E.M. in** *Parents Aren't Supposed to Like It,* **Volume 1, p. 153.)**

A "three-legged dog"

In October 1997, Berry announced that he was leaving the group. Although he gave a number of reasons, including a desire to work on other projects, health was a factor: during R.E.M.'s 1995 European tour, he suffered a ruptured aneurysm (swollen blood vessel) in his brain, and had to undergo surgery. All four group members assured the press that they were parting on the best of terms, and Mills told reporters, "As sad as this is, the fact that Bill is still around to be my friend puts everything in perspective. I look forward to playing golf with Bill, and music with Michael and Peter."

" ... [A]re we still R.E.M.? I guess a three-legged dog is still a dog. It just has to learn how to run differently."

In his own statement to the press, Stipe said, "I'm happy for Bill; it's what he really wants, and I think it's a courageous decision. . . . [A]re we still R.E.M.? I guess a three-legged dog is still a dog. It just has to learn how to run differently." They would remain a trio: the remaining members had chosen not to replace Berry, but to record and tour with hired drummers.

Filling the void

The group did not tour in support of their album *Up* (1998), primarily due to Berry's departure. His loss was also reflected in the album itself, which saw yet another change in sound for R.E.M., with far more keyboards and electronic instruments—including drums from a synthesizer. "It was unlike any other recording process," Buck told *Newsweek.* " . . . [T]here were no rules. Mike's our bass player, and he mostly played keyboards. I played bass. There's not a lot of guitar."

The writer for *Newsweek* observed that Berry's departure "shouldn't have been a big deal. Come on—he was just the drummer." However, "the loss was symbolic. R.E.M., ascendant [rising] in popularity since its first release in 1982, had reached its first downturn." In confronting this situation, *Newsweek*'s writer commented, R.E.M. had chosen to reinvent its sound.

During 1999, the group's music could be heard in the soundtrack of *Man on the Moon,* and they put in an appearance on the popular TV show *Party of Five.* That summer saw their first tour in four years, as well as a spot in the Tibetan Freedom Concert (see sidebar with **Beastie Boys** entry.) In 2001, they released the album *Reveal.* "I think we're going to be less predictable about where we play and what we play," Stipe told *Melody Maker* in 1998. "Hopefully we'll confuse each other as well as our audience!"

Selected Awards

MTV Video Music Awards, Best Video, Best Group Video, Best Direction, Best Art Direction, Best Editing, and Breakthrough Video, all for "Losing My Religion," 1991.

Grammy Awards, Best Pop Performance by a Duo or Group with Vocal; Best Music Video, Short Form, both for "Losing My Religion," 1992.

Grammy Award, Best Alternative Music Album, for *Out of Time,* 1992.

Multi-platinum certification (4 million sales), *Out of Time,* 1992.

Multi-platinum certification (2 million sales), *Green,* 1994.

MTV Video Music Awards, Video Vanguard Award, 1995.

Multi-platinum certification (4 million sales), *Automatic For the People,* 1995.

Multi-platinum certification (4 million sales), *Monster,* 1995.

Grammy Award nomination, Best Song Written for a Motion Picture, Television, or Other Visual Media (Songwriter), for "The Great Beyond" (from *Man on the Moon*), 2001.

Selected Discography

Out of Time (Warner Brothers), 1991.
Automatic For the People (Warner Brothers), 1992.
Monster (Warner Brothers), 1994.
New Adventures in Hi-Fi (Warner Brothers), 1996.
Up (Warner Brothers), 1998.
Reveal (Warner Brothers), 2001.

Further Reading

Clerk, Carol. "Stipe on Make-Up and Making 'Up'!" *Melody Maker,* November 28, 1998, p. 9.
Hogan, Peter. *R.E.M.* New York: Omnibus Press, 1997.
McCarthy, Rebecca. "R.E.M. Plays to Promote a Greener Hometown." *Atlanta Constitution,* October 23, 2000, p. E-3.
Platt, John A. *Murmur: R.E.M.* New York: Schirmer Books, 1999.
"R.E.M. Reinvents Itself." *Newsweek,* October 26, 1998, p. 83.
Rosen, Craig. *R.E.M. Inside Out: The Stories Behind Every Song.* London, England: Carlton, 1997.

Contact Information
R.E.M.
P.O. Box 8032
Athens, GA 30603

Web Sites
Murmurs. http://www.murmurs.com (accessed on November 9, 2000).
John Michael Stipe: In the Spotlight. http://janavision.com/jms/ (accessed on November 9, 2000).

Talk About the Passion. http://talkaboutpassion.8m.com (accessed on November 9, 2000).

LeAnn Rimes

American country and pop singer
Born August 28, 1982, in Jackson, Mississippi

> "Hopefully, what's made me so big so fast is my music and my voice, and I hope that's what people are enjoying, not my age."
>
> —LeAnn Rimes, *Texas Monthly*, September 1997

LeAnn Rimes. (AP/Wide World Photos. Reproduced by permission.)

When music fans first heard LeAnn Rimes sing, few could believe they were hearing the voice of a thirteen-year-old girl. Yet her voice, with its range—both in terms of vocal quality and emotion—sounded like that of a grown woman, and critics immediately compared her to country legend Patsy Cline (see sidebar).

On the heels of *Blue* (1996), Rimes found herself catapulted into the sort of superstar circus atmosphere that would boggle the mind of someone twice her age. The first country singer ever to win the Best New Artist Grammy Award in 1997, she finished that year with a staggering $96 million in record sales. Yet disappointments followed, both at the 1998 Grammy Awards and in a 2000 lawsuit. The latter pitted her against her former agent—who happened to be her father.

Wins first talent contest at age six

Margaret LeAnn Rimes, only child of Wilbur, a pipe salesman, and Belinda Rimes, won her first talent contest at age six with a rendition of the show tune "Getting to Know You." The

Patsy Cline

People may think that the idea of a country crossover star—a singer who "crosses over" from country to mainstream chart success—is a relatively new one. But long before **Shania Twain, Faith Hill** (see entries), and LeAnn Rimes, country star Patsy Cline crossed over by scoring a hit on the pop charts with "Walkin' After Midnight" in 1957.

Cline was born Virginia Hensley on September 8, 1932, in Winchester, Virginia. She went to Nashville at the age of sixteen in 1948, but it took her nearly a decade to experience a full-scale breakthrough. Along the way, Cline carefully distinguished herself from the "hillbilly" or "cowgirl" image that characterized many country stars at the time; from the beginning, she was determined to be a superstar with an influence far beyond Nashville.

In 1961 she hit the pop charts with "I Fall to Pieces," and scored later that year with "Crazy"—a song written by a young man named Willie Nelson. By then Cline had long achieved the superstardom she sought, with all its trappings—including a private plane to take her from show to show. On March 5, 1963, a single-engine craft piloted by her manager crashed near Kansas City, Missouri. More than 25,000 people attended her funeral.

Interest in Cline remained strong two decades later, when Jessica Lange portrayed her in *Sweet Dreams* (1985). By then her influence had extended throughout the world of music, affecting not only country stars but a number of pop artists as well.

Patsy Cline. (Archive Photos. Reproduced by permission.)

family moved from Mississippi, to Garland, Texas, and when she was eight she won the first of two consecutive competitions on the then-popular television show *Star Search*.

In 1993 the eleven-year-old Rimes attracted the attention of Dallas, Texas, music personality Bill Mack, who arranged for her to record an independent LP. Mack helped her to book concert and television appearances during the next few years, and early in 1996, he presented her with a song called "Blue," which he said he had written for Patsy Cline before she died. Rimes's recording of it became an instant country-radio hit.

Two Grammys and a string of hits

June 1996 saw the release of the album *Blue,* destined to sell more than 6 million copies. Later that year, Rimes became the youngest artist ever nominated for a Country Music Award when she received two nominations, though she did not win in either category. By February 1997, however, she had the ultimate in consolation prize: two Grammys.

> "Anybody can relate to hurt, to being alone, to love, because you've had it in some part of your life, in some way. It doesn't matter how, but you've had it."

In 1997 she released *The Early Years: Unchained Melody,* recorded before *Blue,* as well as *You Light Up My Life—Inspirational Songs,* which would finish the year as the tenth best-selling album in America. In addition to the title track, a cover of a song made famous by Debby Boone two decades earlier, Rimes had a major hit with "How Do I Live," from the soundtrack to the film *Con Air.* The song received a Grammy nomination in 1998, but lost to another version recorded by fellow country star Trisha Yearwood.

The "age thing"

In the opinion of many observers, Rimes's Grammy loss was due to what John Morthland in *Texas Monthly* referred to as "the age thing." Writing well before the Grammy nomination, Morthland noted that Disney, which produced *Con Air,* had decided not to include Rimes's version because it "didn't fit the scene"—yet they had arranged for Yearwood to record the same song for the soundtrack. The reason, observers suggested, was that with lines such as "How do I get through one night without you?" the song seemed more appropriate coming from Yearwood, at thirty-three years old, than from Rimes.

From the earliest days of *Blue's* successes, many had wondered how Rimes could sing with such emotion, often about subjects that were presumably beyond her experiences of most girls in their early teens. Quoting a line from the classic title track of *Unchained Melody,* Morthland wrote that "you wonder what she knows about a line like, 'Oh, my love, my darling, I hunger, hunger for your touch'"—yet he conceded that at the same time, "you're stunned and dazzled by [her] vocal acrobatics." For her own part, Rimes told Morthland, "Anybody can relate to hurt, to being alone, to love, because you've had it in some part of your life, in some way. It doesn't matter how, but you've had it."

"Sittin' on top of the world" . . . ?

Rimes herself was about to experience a new kind of hurt when her father suddenly divorced her mother and remarried in late 1997. By then Wilbur and business partner Lyle Walker had taken over management of Rimes's career, and this continued even as LeAnn and her mother moved into a new house in Sherman Oaks, California, while Wilbur settled with his new wife in Nashville.

On the heels of her parents' divorce and her Grammy disappointment, Rimes came down with a viral infection in June

1998, and had to cancel a concert in Colorado. All of this made the title of *Sittin' On Top of the World*, released the previous month, seem a bit ironic. In August, she had to cancel three more concerts because of a respiratory infection.

In some ways, however, Rimes *was* sitting on top of the world. As of September 1998, "How Do I Live" had spent more time on the Hot 100 (seventy weeks) and Top 10 (thirty-two weeks) than any single in the history of *Billboard* magazine. By the end of the year, the song had become the biggest-selling country single of all time.

A bitter legal battle

Rimes sang a duet with Elton John (see sidebar with **Collective Soul** entry) on "Written in the Stars" from *Elton John and Tim Rice's Aida* early in 1999, and in October released *LeAnn Rimes*. Though "Big Deal" hit the Top 40, sales of the album were sluggish compared to its predecessors. Then in May 2000, Rimes shocked the entertainment world by suing her father and his partner Walker for more than $7 million, which she claimed the two had siphoned off of her earnings between 1996 and 1999.

The legal battle promised to last through many more painful rounds. Meanwhile, in June 2000, Rimes had to cancel her summer tour because of a strained vocal cord. Her doctor ordered her to rest for several months, and diagnosed her with Epstein Barr virus, which causes the infectious condition called mononucleosis. Returning to the concert circuit in the fall of 2000, Rimes released *I Need You* in early 2001.

Selected Awards

American Music Award, Best New Country Artist, 1997.

Grammy Awards, Best New Artist and Best Country Performance, Female (for "Blue"), 1997.

Billboard Music Awards, Artist of the Year, Country Artist of the Year, and Country Album of the Year (for *Blue*), 1997.

Multi-platinum certification (2 million sales), *The Early Years: Unchained Melody*, 1997.

Grammy Award nomination, Best Female Country Vocal Performance, for "How Do I Live," 1998.

Multi-platinum certification (4 million sales), *You Light Up My Life—Inspirational Songs*, 1998.

Multi-platinum certification (3 million sales), "How Do I Live" (single), 1998.

Platinum certification, *Sittin' On Top of the World*, 1998.

Multi-platinum certification (6 million sales), *Blue*, 1999.

Platinum certification, *LeAnn Rimes*, 2000.

Selected Discography

Blue (Curb/Atlantic), 1996.
The Early Years: Unchained Melody (Curb/Atlantic), 1997.
You Light Up My Life—Inspirational Songs (Curb/Atlantic), 1997.
Sittin' On Top of the World (Curb/Atlantic), 1998.
LeAnn Rimes (Curb/Atlantic), 1999.
I Need You (Curb/Atlantic), 2001.

Further Reading

Britton, Tamara L. *LeAnn Rimes*. Edina, MN: Abdo, 1999.

Hewitt, Bill, et al. "Pall in the Family: Singer LeAnn Rimes and Her Father Wage a Legal War Over $7 Million She Claims He Bilked from Her." *People,* May 29, 2000, p. 141.

McCracken, Kristin. *LeAnn Rimes.* New York: Children's Press, 2000.

Morthland, John. "LeAnn Rimes." *Texas Monthly,* September 1997, p. 106.

Powell, Joanna. "'I Had to Learn Fast.'" *Good Housekeeping,* November 1997, p. 210.

Zymet, Cathy Alter. *LeAnn Rimes.* Philadelphia: Chelsea House, 1999.

Contact Information
Curb Records
47 Music Square East
Nashville, TN 37203

Web Sites
Rimestimes.com (official site). http://www.rimestimes.com (accessed on November 6, 2000).

"LeAnn Rimes at Atlantic Records." *Atlantic Records.* http://www.atlantic-records.com/frames/Artists_Music/main.html?artistID=508 (accessed on November 6, 2000).

The Beautiful LeAnn Rimes. http://www.leann-rimes.org (accessed on November 6, 2000).

Santana

American rock and roll, Latin, and world music artist/band
Born Carlos Santana on July 20, 1947, in Mexico

When Santana hit the scene in a big way with the 1999 album *Supernatural*—which sold more than 13 million copies and won him eight Grammys—a lot of older fans talked about a "comeback." But in fact Santana had never gone away. The name Santana refers both to a group with an ever-changing lineup, as well as to its one constant, frontman Carlos Santana, a guitar virtuoso whose distinctive international sound has colored the world of music for more than three decades.

First three albums

Born in Mexico, Santana moved to California with his family when he was in his teen years. His father played violin in a mariachi band, a traditional type of Mexican group. In later years, Santana would insist that his music is entirely African and not Latin, as most people claim. Certainly there is a multicultural aspect to his sound—but there is also an unmistakable Spanish flavor.

Santana gravitated to San Francisco at the very time when the music scene there was exploding with innovative groups such as

"... [The success] gives us an enormous capacity to be of service to people, especially young people, to let them know what they need to strengthen their aspirations and visions."

–Carlos Santana, *Hispanic*, May 2000

Carlos Santana. (Ken Settle. Reproduced by permission.)

the Jefferson Airplane and the Grateful Dead (see sidebar with **Dave Matthews Band** entry). By 1966, Santana—then just nineteen years old—had formed the Santana Blues Band, which renamed itself Santana prior to appearing at Woodstock three years later.

Also in 1969, Santana released his self-titled debut album, which contained "Evil Ways" and "Jingo." This he followed in 1970 with *Abraxas*, which yielded the classics "Black Magic Woman" and "Oye Como Va." A year later came *Santana III*, an album that included "Everybody's Everything" and "No One to Depend On." Together these first three albums constituted an early high point of Santana's career, and though he had many hits in the years that followed, nothing would equal their success until *Supernatural*.

Quiet years

"I had only one concern when making my new record," Santana told *Guitar Player* in 1999. "Would Jimi Hendrix like it if he were here?" Santana had known the legendary guitarist (see sidebar in **Lenny Kravitz** entry), shared the Woodstock stage with him, and in 1972—two years after Hendrix's death from a drug overdose—joined forces with a former Hendrix collaborator, drummer Buddy Miles, on a powerful album, *Carlos Santana and Buddy Miles Live!*

During the 1970s, his band's lineup changed a number of times. At one point, for instance, it included Neil Schon, who left in 1972 to form the pop-rock outfit Journey. Santana released a string of albums during those years, but did not produce another hit until 1981, with "Winning" from *Zebop!* A year later, "Hold On" from *Shango* also made the charts.

Of course a performer such as Santana is not really concerned about making hits; he plays guitar for the sheer joy found in the artistry itself. Nonetheless, most musicians want to reach a wider audience and enjoy greater recognition; but though Santana received recognition in the form of a 1988 Grammy, his audience still consisted primarily of fans who had been attracted by the first three albums.

The years continued quietly as Santana toured and released albums, but without gaining much attention beyond his loyal fan base. He received occasional honors, including a star on the Hollywood Walk of Fame in 1996, but these were primarily in recognition of his past work. All of that would change, however, after Clive Davis, the executive with whom he had worked at Columbia Records in the 1960s, brought him to the Arista label in the mid-1990s.

Wildly successful collaborations

Collaboration comes naturally to Santana, who never sang on his albums. But he had never worked with as wide, talented, and prominent a variety of singers as on *Supernatural*. There was first of all Eric Clapton, who like Hendrix and Santana himself had been one of the great guitarists of the 1960s. But there were also plenty of younger artists: **Lauryn Hill,** Wyclef Jean (see entry and

Carlos Santana, with Latin singer Mana, performs at the first annual Latin Grammy Awards in 2000. (AP/Wide World Photos. Reproduced by permission.)

accompanying sidebar), Dave Matthews of the **Dave Matthews Band,** Rob Thomas of **Matchbox Twenty,** and **Everlast** (see entries).

"Smooth," recorded with Thomas, began climbing the charts in summer 1999, and by October had hit No. 1. By then *Supernatural,* released just four months before, had already sold 3 million copies—more than *Santana* and *Santana III,* two of his most successful albums, had sold in nearly thirty years. Six months after that, it had sold 11 million copies, far more than his first three albums combined.

Santana and his collaborators cleaned up at the 2000 Grammys, walking away with eight awards. (In addition, "Love of My Life" with Dave Matthews had been nominated for Best Pop Collaboration with Vocals.) In March 2000, the single "Maria, Maria" (with The Product G&B) hit the Top 10, and top-forty hits followed as "Put Your Lights On" (with Everlast) and "Love of My Life" climbed the charts.

"A great waiter"

During 2000, Santana continued to collect awards and nominations, including three Latin Grammys, a Blockbuster Award, and a California Music Award. But when fans and journalists started asking about a followup, he let it be known that he was in no hurry: having finished touring for the year in October, he intended to devote himself to his wife, Deborah, and their children. Family came first, and career would have to wait.

> "I equate myself with a great waiter. My napkin is tucked, my apron is clean, the water is pure, and the flowers are fresh. And what (I'm) serving is always tasty."

For all his monumental successes, as well as the range of his experience as a performer, the depth of his contribution to music, and his astounding artistry as a master of the guitar, Santana is a very humble person. "I equate myself with a great waiter," he told *Rolling Stone*. "My napkin is tucked, my apron is clean, the water is pure, and the flowers are fresh. And what [I'm] serving is always tasty."

On the other hand, as he went on to point out, he has never been one to scramble for a big hit, or to change his standards to fit the demands of the market. "I hope you're hungry," he said, continuing the waiter analogy. "If you're not, no problem. I'm going to commit suicide because people don't like me? I have seen a lot of musicians go through that, and it's really pathetic."

Selected Awards

Grammy Award, Best Rock Instrumental Performance, for *Blues for Salvador,* 1988.

Grammy Awards, Album of the Year and Best Rock Album, both for *Supernatural,* 2000.

(With Rob Thomas) Grammy Awards, Record of the Year and Best Pop Collaboration with Vocals, both for "Smooth," 2000.

(With The Product G&B) Grammy Award, Best Pop Performance by a Duo or Group with Vocal, for "Maria Maria," 2000.

Grammy Award, Best Pop Instrumental Performance, for "El Farol," 2000.

(With Eric Clapton) Grammy Award, Best Rock Instrumental Performance, for "The Calling," 2000.

(With Everlast) Grammy Award, Best Rock Performance by a Duo or Group with Vocal, for "Put Your Lights On," 2000.

Multi-platinum certification (13 million sales), *Supernatural,* 2000.

Multi-platinum certification (7 million sales), *Santana's Greatest Hits,* 2000.

Multi-platinum certification (5 million sales), *Abraxas,* 2000.

Selected Discography

Santana (Columbia), 1969.
Abraxas (Columbia), 1970.
Santana III (Columbia), 1971.
Santana's Greatest Hits (Columbia), 1974.
Moonflower (Columbia), 1977.
Zebop! (Columbia), 1981.
Shango (Columbia), 1982.
Blues for Salvador (Columbia), 1988.
Sacred Fire: Santana Live in South America (Polydor), 1993.
Supernatural (Arista), 1999.

Further Reading

Ellis, Andy. "Quest for Fire." *Guitar Player,* August 1999, p. 74.
Green, Michelle Y. "Interview: Carlos Santana on Recruiting Minority Teachers." *NEA Today,* May 2000, p. 21.
Leng, Simon. *Soul Sacrifice: The Santana Story.* London: Firefly Publishers, 2000.
Shapiro, Marc. *Carlos Santana: Back on Top.* New York: St. Martin's Press, 2000.
Varela, Chuy. "Santana: In the Open." *Hispanic,* May 2000, p. 82.
Wild, David. "Cosmic Carlos." *Rolling Stone,* August 19, 1999, p. 47.

Contact Information

New Santana Band, Inc.
P.O. Box 10348
San Rafael, CA 94912-0348

Web Sites

Carlos-Santana.com. http://www.carlos-santana.com (accessed on December 18, 2000).
Klaus's Page of Santana Links and MIDI Files. http://home2.inet.tele.dk/krytved/midi.htm (accessed on December 18, 2000).
SANTANA (official site). http://www.santana.com (accessed on December 18, 2000).
"Santana." *Arista Records.* http://www.aristarec.com/aristaweb/CarlosSantana/main.html (accessed on December 18, 2000).

Brian Setzer

American swing revival and rock and roll artist
Born April 10, 1959, in Long Island, New York

> "I can't say that I started a craze myself. There are a lot of bands out there who have been doing a lot of swing music different from the way I was doing this."
>
> –Brian Setzer on the late 1990s swing revival, *Down Beat*, February 1999

Brian Setzer has twice led rock revival movements. During the 1980s, he and the Stray Cats reinvigorated interest in rockabilly, a combination of rock, country, and R&B first popularized by Elvis Presley (1935–1977) in the 1950s. Then in the 1990s, his Brian Setzer Orchestra took the forefront in what became known as the swing revival (see sidebar). In neither case, however, did Setzer's music simply draft off the accomplishments of past artists: he has managed to create his own sound, one that is both nostalgic and contemporary.

The rockabilly rebel

Raised in Long Island, New York, Brian Setzer first became interested in music when at the age of six he discovered the Beatles. He begged his parents to give him a guitar, and learned to play, but by the time he was fourteen he had begun looking toward an older set of musical models.

Indeed, Setzer's new heroes such as Eddie Cochran (1938–1960; "Summertime Blues," "20 Flight Rock") had them-

Brian Setzer. (Ken Settle. Reproduced by permission.)

selves influenced the Beatles. Among his other favorites were Presley, Carl Perkins, Johnny Cash, Buddy Holly, and Gene Vincent, all of whom had contributed to the rockabilly style's melding of black and white musical styles—blues and country respectively.

Under the name of Rockabilly Rebel, Setzer began playing at bars on Long Island's south shore. Accompanying him were a variety of other musicians, including his brother at one point. In time he settled on a trio that included himself on guitar, Leon Drucker (a.k.a. Lee Rocker) on bass, and Jim McDonnell (a.k.a. Slim Jim Phantom) on drums.

In their choices of instruments the group members, who initially called themselves the Tom Cats, were faithful to their rockabilly roots. Rocker played a standup acoustic bass, rather than the electric model typical of rock musicians. And because the stage at one bar was too small for a regular drum set, Slim Jim had to make do with just a bass, snare, and cymbal—a minimalist kit appropriate for a group that harkened back to rock's earliest years.

Superstars outside America

America in 1980, however, was not particularly interested in a rockabilly revival. But a chance meeting with British bartender Tony Bidgood led Setzer to the realization that they would find a much more willing audience in England. Therefore the four—Bidgood had agreed to manage them—took off for London.

Their first months in England were hard ones for the Stray Cats, as they now called themselves. They slept in an all-night movie theatre whose admission price was cheaper than a hotel room, and spent the days pounding the pavement for a gig. In time they got one, and soon their shows attracted the attention of established musicians such as the Rolling Stones, Robert Plant of Led Zeppelin, and Dave Edmunds.

Edmunds, though hardly a household name, is known as a "musician's musician" for his work in Rockpile, a rockabilly-influenced group. He had turned to producing, and worked with the Cats after they signed with Arista Records. What followed were two British releases that made the Cats superstars in Western Europe and Japan, where they were greeted with a fervor unmatched since the Beatles arrived there fifteen years earlier. Yet they remained unknowns in their homeland.

All that changed after the Cats opened for the Stones in 1981, and landed a spot on ABC's shortlived variety show *Fridays*. The enthusiastic response led to a U.S. recording contract with EMI, which compiled the best from the first two British albums on *Built For Speed* (1982).

"It was nice while it lasted..."

For the next two years, the Stray Cats were everywhere on U.S. radio, with hits that included "Rock This Town," "Stray Cat Strut," and—from *Rant 'n Rave with the Stray Cats* (1983)—"Sexy and

Brian Setzer leads his orchestra as they play on the final day of Woodstock '99 in Rome, New York. (AP/Wide World Photos. Reproduced by permission.)

Seventeen." At a time when music was turning toward the glitzy pop of groups such as Culture Club, the Cats offered a refreshingly basic brand of music. Few groups directly emulated their rockabilly style, but they encouraged a return to musical basics that paved the way for the two greatest bands of the mid- to late 1980s: **U2** and **R.E.M.** (see entries).

The 1984 single "I Won't Stand in Your Way" seemed to herald a shift in style for the Cats; then, in the fall of 1984, Setzer abruptly announced the end of the Stray Cats. Later he explained to *Rolling Stone* that rockabilly had become just another marketing gimmick: "When I saw string basses and bowling shirts in the windows at Macy's, I thought, 'Well, it was nice while it lasted....'"

World's first guitar-led swing band

While his former bandmates went on to other projects, Setzer released two solo albums that enjoyed huge critical praise but made little commercial impact. He also played Cochran in the 1987 film *La Bamba*, and periodically reunited with the other Stray Cats. At the same time, however, he began returning to a style of music that had interested him from boyhood, one even older than rockabilly: swing.

Swing Revival Bands

Among the biggest bands to emerge during the swing revival heyday of 1997 to 1999 were: Royal Crown Revue, Big Bad Voodoo Daddy, Cherry Poppin' Daddies, and the Squirrel Nut Zippers.

Consisting of vocalist Eddie Nichols and a six-piece instrumental ensemble, Royal Crown Revue (RCR) got its start in Los Angeles in 1989. Like Brian Setzer, members of RCR started out playing rockabilly before turning to swing; in fact, they preceded Setzer by two years with *The Kings of Gangster Bop* (1992). The album's success led to a deal with Warner Brothers, which released *Mugzy's Move* (1997) and *The Contender* (1998).

Big Bad Voodoo Daddy (BBVD) also come from southern California, where they started playing together in 1992. They got their big break after appearing in *Swingers* (1996), whose soundtrack included "You and Me and the Bottle Makes Three Tonight (Baby)." Coolsville Records later signed them and released *Big Bad Voodoo Daddy* (1998), which stayed on the charts for a year. In 1999, BBVD played the halftime show at the Superbowl and released *This Beautiful Life*.

Another "Daddy" band from the West Coast is the Cherry Poppin' Daddies. More punkish than the others, they first hit it big with *Zoot Suit Riot: The Swinging Hits* (1997), which contains songs from their first three albums. In 2000 the Daddies released *Soul Caddy*.

Unlike the others, Squirrel Nut Zippers come from North Carolina, where the group had its beginnings with vocalists Jim Mathus and Katharine Whalen. Named after an old-fashioned brand of chewy sweet, the Zippers play in a crazy swing-influenced style that they call "hot music," which they showcased in the 1997 radio hit "Hell." Albums include *The Inevitable* (1995), *Hot* (1997), and *Bedlam Ballroom* (2000).

Popularized by artists that included Cab Calloway, Duke Ellington, Count Basie, Glenn Miller, and Benny Goodman, swing was the music of the 1940s. Characteristics of swing include a powerful horn-driven sound and a beat, sometimes cool and sometimes frantic, that went with dance styles such as the jitterbug and Lindy hop.

As a child, Setzer had won many awards playing the euphonium, a tuba-like instrument, and after jamming with a group of horn players in 1993, he began forming a swing band. The result was the Brian Setzer Orchestra (BSO), a seventeen-piece combo that included five saxophones, four trumpets, four trombones, a piano, bass, and drums. At the head was Setzer with his guitar, a major departure from swing bands, which had usually been led by woodwind or horn players.

At the crest of a wave

The group's self-titled debut, released in 1994, led to a deal with Interscope Records, and between the release of *Guitar Slinger* (1996) and *The Dirty Boogie* (1998), something big happened:

a swing revival, spurred in part by the 1996 film *Swingers*. Suddenly swing was popular, not only as a musical style, but as a lifestyle, complete with zoot suits, cigars, martinis, and expressions such as "you're so money, baby!"

> **"Setzer has had the last laugh as, millions of album sales and numerous soldout concerts later, his prescient view on rock 'n' swing was indeed the Next Big Thing."**

Swing, which flourished during the period from 1997 to 1999—when the BSO played at Woodstock—merged well with the ska revival spawned by groups such as **No Doubt, The Mighty Mighty Bosstones** (see entries), and Sublime. But swing was its own style—and Setzer, as Ed Enright wrote in the jazz magazine *Down Beat*, "reign[ed] as the new King of Swing."

By the time of *Vavoom!* (2000) the craze had peaked, but Setzer remained true to his style. And as John Lappen wrote in the *Hollywood Reporter*, "Setzer has had the last laugh as, millions of album sales and numerous soldout concerts later, his prescient [forward-looking] view on rock 'n' swing was indeed the Next Big Thing."

Setzer and his wife, Christine, have two children, Cody and Dane, and he collects old cars, including a 1932 Ford that he and a friend rebuilt.

Selected Awards

(With Brian Setzer Orchestra), Grammy Award, Best Pop Performance by a Duo or Group with Vocal, for "Jump Jive An' Wail," 1999.

(With Brian Setzer Orchestra), Grammy Award, Best Pop Instrumental Performance, for "Sleepwalk," 1999.

Multi-platinum certification (2 million sales), *The Dirty Boogie,* 1999.

(With Brian Setzer Orchestra), Grammy Award, Best Pop Instrumental Performance, for "Caravan," 2001.

Selected Discography

(With Stray Cats) *Built for Speed* (EMI America), 1982.

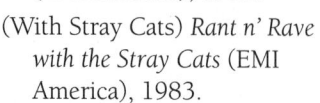

(With Stray Cats) *Rant n' Rave with the Stray Cats* (EMI America), 1983.

The Knife Feels Like Justice (Razor & Tie), 1986.

Live Nude Guitars (EMI America), 1988.

(With Stray Cats) *Blast Off* (EMI America), 1989.

(With Stray Cats) *Choo Choo Hot Fish* (JRS), 1994.

(With Brian Setzer Orchestra) *The Brian Setzer Orchestra* (Hollywood), 1994.

(With Brian Setzer Orchestra) *Guitar Slinger* (Interscope), 1996.

(With Brian Setzer Orchestra) *The Dirty Boogie* (Interscope), 1998.

(With Brian Setzer Orchestra) *Vavoom!* (Interscope), 2000.

Further Reading

Dunn, Jancee. "Brian Setzer: Reflections on the Year of Swing." *Rolling Stone,* December 29, 1998.

Enright, Ed. "New Swing King." *Down Beat,* February 1999, p. 20.

Helland, Dave. "Jazz Goes Pop." *Down Beat,* February 1999, p. 28.

Lappen, John. "Brian Setzer Orchestra." *Hollywood Reporter,* August 7, 2000, p. 8.

Morden, Darryl. "Brian Setzer." *Hollywood Reporter,* August 16, 1999, p. 27.

Contact Information

Interscope Records
70R Woodland Ave.
San Rafael, CA 94901

Web Sites

Brian Setzer.com. http://www.briansetzer.com (accessed on January 22, 2001).

SISQO

American R&B and hip-hop artist
Born Mark Andrews on November 9, 1978, in Baltimore, Maryland

> "[Sisqo] compares himself to an exciting movie: 'I don't want to be corny. I want to be something good to look at. I hate to go to the movies and I'm all pumped, then the movie is whack'.... In all his dazzling splendor, Sisqo is anything but whack."
>
> —*Jet*, August 7, 2000

Sisqo. (AP/Wide World Photos. Reproduced by permission.)

A fan of Michael Jackson as a child, Sisqo at age sixteen co-founded Baltimore-based R&B group Dru Hill. Four years and two albums later, group members began releasing solo albums, starting with Sisqo's *Unleash the Dragon* (1999) and its sexy hit single "Thong Song." Judging by his solo debut, the singer will be a tough act to follow.

"I'm working a little something"

Mark Andrews acquired the Spanish-sounding nickname of "Sisqo" due to his mother's Puerto Rican heritage. In his neighborhood, he later told *Jet*, "If you had [wavy] hair like mine as a kid, you looked Puerto Rican. They used to tease me and call me that name...."

He was also physically small: as an adult, Sisqo stands five feet, five inches tall and weighs less than 150 pounds. Yet his size did not stop him from being a favorite with the ladies: "... I'm working a little something," he told *Jet*. "I used to get the girls before I was famous, but ... not for the way I look.... My person-

Sisqo collects an armful of awards at the 2000 Billboard Music Awards thanks to the "Thong Song." (AP/Wide World Photos. Reproduced by permission.)

ality is so bright, it'll make up for anything else I don't have, like height."

From the beginning, he was fascinated by music. When Jackson was all the rage during the mid-1980s, Sisqo pasted glitter onto his feet to look like his hero—"But the hard glue almost ripped my little toes right off," he explained to *People*.

Dru Hill gets Sisqo noticed

Sisqo, who got his start singing each Sunday in his church choir, grew up partly in his parents' middle-class neighborhood, and partly at his godmother's house "in the ghetto," as he told *People*. "Basically I'm from the hood. You can be from the hood but not of the hood."

> "Basically I'm from the hood. You can be from the hood but not of the hood."

Yet during his teens he got thrown in jail three times, and by the age of fifteen he had a baby girl, Shaione. "There was a blur in my life because so much was happening," he later explained in *Jet*. "I didn't have a record deal, and I was trying to get signed. I was working three jobs. I know how it feels to struggle."

In 1995 he had formed Dru Hill (named for their neighborhood of Druid Hill Park) with high-school friends James "Woody" Green, Tamir "Nokio"

Sisqo

Ruffin, and Larry "Jazz" Anthony, Jr. The group began singing in a local fudge shop, and soon won a number of talent shows. They even went to a competition at Harlem's historic Apollo Theatre, and though they did not win, their appearance there led to a contract with Island Records on its Def Jam label.

Dru World Order

With a sound that has been compared to that of Boyz II Men, Dru Hill sold more than a million copies of their debut album, and a million more of the hit single "In My Bed." Another hit followed with "Tell Me," which hit the Top 5 in 1997.

> "My music ain't whack. I got my pop songs, I got my hood songs. I'm touching everybody right now."

The group's sophomore album sold twice as many copies as its predecessor. Therefore in 1999 the four young men resolved to cash in on their commercial potential by forming Dru World Order, a joint company that would manage both solo and group efforts. *Unleash the Dragon* followed soon afterward, launching one of the hugest hits of 2000 with "Thong Song."

The music and the look

Though he is a talented performer with an ability to create exciting music, part of Sisqo's appeal lies in his extraordinary appearance: hence a writer for *Jet* observed that "His silver, spray-painted hair, multiple body-piercings and tattoos, and brightly colored outfits make him difficult to ignore."

Even in high school, Sisqo dyed his hair, but during 2000 he introduced the spray-painted platinum look. Displaying both a good sense of humor and a head for numbers, he quickly calculated in an interview with *Rolling Stone* that he had spent 6,750 minutes spray-painting his hair over the course of the year.

Fortunately, Sisqo discontinued the spray-painting; and in any case, his appeal owes more to his music than to his admittedly flamboyant appearance. Hence the *Jet* writer went on to note that "he knows how to electrify an audience with his high-powered performances that include smooth dance moves . . . laced with a hard, hip-hop edge."

Venturing out of music and into acting, Sisqo took a role on the big screen in "Get Over It" (2001), and was in talks to develop a starring role on a television series. He also hosted the popular dance show *Sisqo's Shakedown* on MTV during the channel's 2000 summer season. It is always music and singing that remain at the forefront, though.

Again displaying his easygoing humor, Sisqo told *Rolling Stone,* "Basically, it's like [professional] wrestling has been the blueprint for my solo career. Every time I go onstage, I think like I'm [professional wrestlers] Stone Cold or the Rock. . . . I have my signature sayings and my signature look." As for his critics, he said, "if you hating on me right now, you just hating 'cause you feel like hating. Because it's like, God's blessed me. My music ain't whack. I got my pop songs, I got my hood songs. I'm touching everybody right now."

Selected Awards

MTV Video Music Award, Best Hip-hop Video, for "Thong Song," 2000.

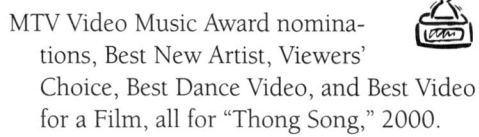

MTV Video Music Award nominations, Best New Artist, Viewers' Choice, Best Dance Video, and Best Video for a Film, all for "Thong Song," 2000.

Multi-platinum certification (4 million sales), *Unleash the Dragon,* 2000.

Platinum certification, "Incomplete" (single), 2000.

Grammy Award nomination, Best New Artist, 2001.

Grammy Award nomination, Best R&B Album, for *Unleash the Dragon,* 2001.

Grammy Award nomination, Best Male R&B Vocal Performance, for "Thong Song," 2001.

(With two cowriters) Grammy Award nomination, Best R&B Song (Songwriter), for "Thong Song," 2001.

Selected Discography

(With Dru Hill) *Dru Hill* (Island), 1996.

(With Dru Hill) *Enter the Dru* (Island), 1998.

Unleash the Dragon (Def Jam), 2000.

Return of Dragon (Def Jam), 2001.

Further Reading

"Breakthroughs 2000: Sisqo, Singer." *People,* December 25, 2000–January 1, 2001, p. 136.

Eliscu, Jenny. "Q & A: Sisqo." *Rolling Stone,* March 30, 2000, p. 28.

"Sisqo: Why He's Become Music's Main Attraction." *Jet,* August 7, 2000, p. 60.

Stein, Joel. "Sisqo." *Time,* April 3, 2000, p. 87.

Udovitch, Mim. "People of the Year: Sisqo." *Rolling Stone,* December 14–21, 2000, p. 147.

Contact Information

Island/Def Jam Records
825 8th Ave.
New York, NY 10019

Web Sites

Sisqo (official site). http://www.sisqo.com (accessed on January 24, 2001).

Sisqo Fan Page. http://music.acmecity.com/pitch/347/ (accessed on January 24, 2001).

Sisqo Online. http://www.geocities.com/sisqo_online (accessed on January 24, 2001).

Sister Hazel

American rock and roll band

Formed 1994 in Gainesville, Florida

> "When you go into a town and play for four people, the next time you . . . tell them to bring their friends, and you have eight people. After a few months, there are a thousand. We always worked at it like that."
>
> –Ken Block, *Billboard*, July 12, 1997

Named after a minister in their hometown of Gainesville, Florida, Sister Hazel has a sound that calls to mind a number of influences. Certainly they recall the glory days of southern rock (see sidebar), but they reflect the impact of other musical trends as well, including the various styles labeled as "alternative" in the 1990s. At heart, however, is something unique to Sister Hazel, a feel-good sound that carried their single "All for You" into the Top 10 in 1997. Further success followed with "Happy," and in 2000 *Fortress* showed the band exploring a more hard-edged variety of rock.

"Ken can sing"

Lead singer Ken Block (born November 23, 1966) grew up in a musical family: his father had a degree in music, and the Blocks would often get together with friends and relatives for singalongs and storytelling in Gainesville or St. Augustine Beach, Florida. From the age of twelve, Block was performing in front of others with a guitar, and in high school he played for a band composed of boys older than he was.

Southern Rock

Some bands today—among them Sister Hazel and the Black Crowes—might be described as "southern rock," at least in part. But the term doesn't begin to describe most bands from the South: one would hardly describe Georgia's **R.E.M.**, not to mention Florida's **Limp Bizkit** (see entries) as "southern rock." In fact even Sister Hazel and the Black Crowes, which both reflect non-southern influences as well, are only echoes of "southern rock" as it existed in its 1970s heyday.

It can be argued that southern rock was an outgrowth of the larger "back to the earth" movement that characterized lifestyles and music in the early 1970s—a turn from psychedelia to simpler ways. The southern sound had its beginnings with the Allman Brothers of Macon, Georgia, who introduced listeners to a breezy, laid-back version of rock in songs such as "Melissa" and "Ramblin' Man."

Next to pick up the southern torch was Jacksonville, Florida's Lynyrd Skynyrd, known for such classics as "Free Bird" and "Sweet Home Alabama." Both bands lost members tragically—Duane Allman died in a 1971 motorcycle accident, and several members of Lynyrd Skynyrd perished in a 1977 plane crash—but by then the bluesy style known as southern rock had exploded throughout Dixie, as the South is often called.

Among the southern-rock bands that made it big during the 1970s were the Atlanta Rhythm Section, Blackfoot, Black Oak Arkansas, Little Feat, Marshall Tucker Band, Molly Hatchet, the Outlaws, and Wet Willie. The sound can still be enjoyed on greatest-hits compilations, but with the coming of new wave and other styles in the 1980s, southern rock itself faded from the popular music scene.

"One day the lead singer was late to practice," he recalled on Sister Hazel's Web site, "and these girls that were hanging out kept saying, 'Ken can sing, Ken can sing,' so I stepped up and did until the other guy got there. I was scared to death because . . . they were the 'hot band' at school. Well, the next day they canned the other guy. I felt really bad for him, but I've been a lead singer ever since."

A flyer on a university campus

Block began writing songs at age fifteen, and recorded some of these with Scorcher and Redline, two Florida bands with which he played in his late twenties. By 1994, however, he was ready to start an outfit in which he could function as primary singer and songwriter, and Sister Hazel was born.

He first recruited backup singer and rhythm guitarist Andrew Copeland (born March 21, 1968), and together they placed flyers around the University of Florida campus in Gainesville looking for other members. One of the musicians who answered their ad was bassist Jeff Beres (born February 23, 1971), then studying archi-

Sister Hazel hold a special performance at Shands Children's Hospital in Gainesville, Florida, in 1999. Lead singer Ken Block's younger brother was once a patient at Shands. (AP/Wide World Photos. Reproduced by permission.)

tecture. Around that time, they were joined by lead guitarist Ryan Newell (born December 8, 1971), who has said that the course of his life was set after he performed Chuck Berry's "Johnny B. Goode" in a fifth-grade talent contest.

Last to arrive was drummer Mark Trojanowski (born January 21, 1970), who had been playing for one of oldest and most distinguished names in show business: the Guy Lombardo Orchestra. Founded in 1919 by bandleader Guy Lombardo (1902–1977), the orchestra had a number of hits during the 1920s, and later their New Years' broadcasts became a national tradition. But by the time Trojanowski played for them, the orchestra was performing on cruise ships, and he was ready to do something more creative. Then, in the summer of 1995, he received a tape of a Florida band looking for a drummer, and by July he had joined Sister Hazel.

Two independent releases

The tape Trojanowski heard was the group's self-titled debut album, of which Sister Hazel managed to sell 11,000 copies without any sort of distribution agreement. "Gainesville is a great place to start out as a band," Block later told *Billboard*. "It's a solid, original music scene, and the bands network between each other regardless of what kind of music they play. I guess we all realized that if we all got behind the wagon and pushed, we'd get . . . a lot further than if we had just one person out front pulling."

The band maintained a rough schedule of tour dates, constantly building and maintaining a following. "We thought," Block recalled, "'if we get a major-label deal, that's great, but in the meantime we'll build a market through concentric circles"—that is, circles around circles—"further and further from our home . . . and create a fan base."

A major-label deal is exactly what happened with . . . *Somewhere More Familiar*, released on the independent Autonomous label in 1996. The album's strong sales attracted the attention of Universal Records, which signed Sister Hazel and re-released *Somewhere* in 1997. Label executives briefly considered having the group re-record the album, but decided instead to simply remix the tracks so as not to alter a sound that Universal's former president Dan Glass called "lighting in a bottle."

Back into the studio

The next few years were a whirlwind for Sister Hazel, who spent still more hours on the road. "We were listening to [*American Top 40* host] Casey Kasem on the radio," Block told *Billboard*, "and we were at No. 18, and there are nine of us crammed into the back of a Ryder truck. 'If people only knew,' I was thinking."

Copeland got exposure of a different kind when in June 1999 he appeared on the TV game show *The Price is Right*. He was in Los Angeles with the other group members recording what would become *Fortress*, and attended a taping of the show. Sitting in the audience, he heard the magic words: "Come on down!" He won a Ford Escort, which he gave to his father.

> "Gainesville's a solid, original music scene, and the bands network between each other regardless of what kind of music they play. I guess we all realized that if we all got behind the wagon and pushed, we'd get . . . a lot further than if we had just one person out front pulling."

Back in the recording studio, the group worked on the album, which included a contribution by Emily Saliers of the **Indigo Girls** (see entry) on "Champagne High." *Fortress*'s release would mean still more months of touring, which would take them away from loved ones. (Block and his wife had a baby boy in August 2000, and Beres got married a month later.) Still, the road beckoned; and for a band such as Sister Hazel—as loyal to its fans as the fans are to the group—the real strength of the music can be found in live performances.

Selected Awards

Platinum certification, . . . *Somewhere More Familiar*, 1997.

Selected Discography

Sister Hazel (Soul Trax), 1995.
. . . *Somewhere More Familiar* (Autonomous), 1996; reissued by Universal, 1997.
Fortress (Universal), 2000.

Further Reading

Pedersen, Erik. "Sister Hazel." *Hollywood Reporter,* August 24, 2000, p. 16.

Reece, Doug. "Universal's Sister Hazel Getting 'More Familiar.'" *Billboard,* July 12, 1997, p. 13.

"Sister Hazel, Come on Down!" *PR Newswire,* June 10, 1997.

Stewart, Alison. "Blue Skies Again." *Rolling Stone,* February 23, 1999.

Contact Information

Sixthman Artist Management Company
83 Walton Street
2nd Floor
Atlanta, GA 30303

Web Sites

Sister Hazel (official site). http://www.sisterhazel.com (accessed on January 12, 2001).

Sister Hazel Link Page. http://www.cosmo.com/sisterhazelhome.html (accessed on January 12, 2001).

Smash Mouth

American alternative pop/rock band
Formed 1994 in San Jose, California

Combining elements of 1960s psychedelia, lounge-variety jazz, ska, and even a little hip-hop, Smash Mouth's song "Walkin' on the Sun" was one of the great soundtracks to the summer of 1997. Much of the remainder of their debut album, *Fush Yu Mang,* suggested a heavy skate-punk influence, and their cover of the 1970s hit "Why Can't We Be Friends" by funk band War showed yet another side to Smash Mouth.

Despite this diversity of styles, critics still wondered if Smash Mouth had what it took to do it again—which they did with 1999's *Astro Lounge.* The latter sold more than 3 million copies, more than their debut, and yielded another big hit with "All Star."

Elvis fan turned rapper and rocker

One of the most distinctive things about Smash Mouth's "look" is its beefy lead singer, Steve Harwell (born 1967?) He has a strong presence that comes across in videos, and it is easy to see that he is the source for much of the band's humor. As a child, Harwell was a big Elvis Presley fan, and every Thanksgiving

"It's California goulash. Use it, walk the dog to it, mow the lawn to it, dance to it. Forget about it by winter. It's that kinda album."

–Steve Harwell, describing *Astro Lounge* in *Melody Maker,* July 31, 1999

Smash Mouth. (Corbis Corporation. Reproduced by permission.)

forced his family to sit through his performances of "Hound Dog" and other classics by The King.

In junior high, Harwell discovered reggae, a style of music from the Caribbean, as well as rap and heavy metal. For a time he and drummer Kevin Coleman jammed together in a garage band, but after high school Harwell took a gig with a rap outfit called F.O.S. When his recording deal fell through, however, he returned to his California home and hooked up with Coleman again.

Through a manager, the two met guitarist Greg Camp and bassist Paul De Lisle. Calling themselves Smash Mouth, they made a demo in Camp's apartment. Producer Eric Valentine, who had also worked with **Third Eye Blind** (see entry) was impressed enough to work with them in the studio on a demo that included the song "Nervous in the Alley." The latter in turn became a favorite on a local radio station, KOME, and on the strength of its airplay Smash Mouth was able to sign a lucrative contract with Interscope Records.

That word from *Scarface*

The 1982 film *Scarface*, starring Al Pacino, seems to have attracted the attention of several rock groups. This is especially the case with regard to the use of a certain four-letter word by Pacino's character, gangster Tony Montana. The name of **Blink-182** (see entry) refers to the number of times Montana uses the word; likewise the title of *Fush Yu Mang* is based on Tony's slurred use of the same term.

The video of "Walkin' on the Sun" went into regular rotation on MTV and VH1, and soon the song caught on with radio as well. Meanwhile Smash Mouth went on the road to promote the album, for instance by opening for **U2** (see entry) on its *Popmart* tour. They further increased their exposure with the "Why Can't We Be Friends" video, which Neva Chonin in *Rolling Stone* described as "featur[ing] Harwell executing classic Presley hip-swivels as he leads an army of white cops, black B-boys and miniskirted go-go girls in a dance down a suburban street."

Overgrown children

Smash Mouth's mixture of styles, in particular its homage (tribute) to the 1960s in "Walkin' on the Sun," called to mind **Beck** (see entry). But Beck's music is much smoother, whereas Smash Mouth's style incorporates thrash-metal and skate-punk elements. The latter is not just a part of their music but of their life as well, since several band members are avid skateboarders.

They are also big pranksters, overgrown children who do things such as shoot off fireworks from a moving vehicle—as Harwell did from the group's tour bus in Louisville, Kentucky, in the summer of 1999. They nearly got arrested, he told Chonin: "We got pulled over by about fifteen cops. Oh, they were [mad]. We all jumped in our bunks and pretended we were sleeping. They called the dogs out. We thought, '. . . We're going to jail.'" As it turned out, however, one of the policemen was a big fan of the group.

"It was great," Harwell said, "finally, a fan who could really help us." He let them go, and the group went on their way.

More than a one-album group

Not everyone has been amused by Smash Mouth—particularly the critics who confidently proclaimed that they would never be heard from again after *Fush Yu Mang*. As though to defy them, Smash Mouth scored an even bigger commercial triumph with *Astro Lounge*. "They hate it," Camp said, laughing, in an interview with *Melody Maker*. "They're almost hurt by it." Said De Lisle, "This guy was absolutely appalled at us the other day, 'cause we'd 'done an album full of songs you could play on the radio.' Ummm, yeah. That's our job."

"[I]n America," De Lisle observed, "people are just disgusted at how shamelessly we want to make great pop records. It's like, 'So, when you make those hamburgers you actually want people to eat them?' 'When you make that car you actually want people to drive it?' There was just no way on earth we can deny our influences, and they're all pop. If anything, the last LP had one good song on it. *Astro Lounge* is sixteen good songs. It's music for everyone. . . ."

The freedom that comes from success

Their earlier success had freed them to lavish attention on their followup, Harwell told *Melody Maker*: "It was the freedom only hard cash could buy. So we decided to slam everything we've ever loved in and just make a fab pop album for summer, the kinda album that has everything you ever wanted in one go."

Around the time the group released *Astro Lounge*, Coleman left Smash Mouth, and thereafter they used various drummers on tour without adding a permanent one to the lineup. In 2000 they released *The East Bay Sessions*, which contained early songs. Smash Mouth, whose "Can't Get Enough of You Baby" had appeared in the movie *Can't Hardly Wait* (1998), continued to contribute to a number of soundtracks in 2000, including *The Grinch*.

Selected Awards

Multi-platinum certification (2 million sales), *Fush Yu Mang*, 1999.
Grammy Award nomination, Best Pop Performance by a Duo or Group with Vocal, for "All Star," 2000.
Multi-platinum certification (3 million sales), *Astro Lounge*, 2000.

Selected Discography

Fush Yu Mang (Interscope), 1997.
Astro Lounge (Interscope), 1999.
East Bay Sessions (Red Clay), 1999.

Further Reading

Chonin, Neva. "Ska Punks Smash Mouth Party All the Way to the Top." *Rolling Stone,* February 19, 1998, p. 24.
Chonin, Neva. "Q&A: Steve Harwell of Smash Mouth." *Rolling Stone,* August 5, 1999, p. 27.
Lorenz, Christian. "Smash Mouth's All Star Performance." *Music & Media,* July 24, 1999, p. 1.

"Mighty Mouth." *Entertainment Weekly,* September 24, 1999, p. 144.

Sweet, Stephen. "'Boarding School." *Melody Maker,* July 31, 1999, p. 14.

Contact Information

Interscope Records
70R Woodland Ave.
San Rafael, CA 94901

Web Sites

Official Smash Mouth Club. http://clubs.yahoo.com/clubs/smashmouthoutloud?s (accessed on December 18, 2000).

Smash Guy's Smash Mouth Lounge. http://www.angelfire.com/on2/Radio/index.htm (accessed on December 22, 2000).

Smash Mouth (official site). http://www.smashmouth.com (accessed on December 18, 2000).

"Smash Mouth." *Top3.net.* http://www.top3.net/smash_mouth/ (accessed on December 18, 2000).

Smashing Pumpkins

American alternative rock band
Formed 1989 in Chicago, Illinois

Both musically and personally, the Smashing Pumpkins are a complex band. Singer and guitarist Billy Corgan's lyrics are filled with observations on life and the nature of the universe, and the music provided by guitarist James Iha, bassist D'Arcy Wretzky, and drummer Jimmy Chamberlin has often been described as lush. Equally challenging are their personal lives: drug problems forced Chamberlin to take a long break from the band, and may have played a role in D'Arcy's 1999 departure. A year later, the group called it quits, leading behind a musical legacy that can only be described as "smashing."

In fact the first word of the group's name is an adjective, meaning "stunning"—not, as is popularly supposed, a verb meaning "destroying." The name, like much else about the group, is the creation of Corgan (born March 17, 1967). At six feet, four inches, with a shaved head, Corgan is one of the most distinctive-looking rock stars around, but when he was growing up in suburban Chicago, Illinois, standing out in the crowd was not a good thing. As reported in *Chicago* magazine, school jocks singled him

> "I'm not saying I'm the one to bring (rock) back from the dead. I'm just saying I still believe in rock and roll...."
>
> –Billy Corgan, *Rolling Stone*, March 16, 2000

Billy Corgan. (Archive Photos. Reproduced by permission.)

The Pumpkins perform on the *Late Show with David Letterman* in 1998. (AP/Wide World Photos. Reproduced by permission.)

out as a "geek," but as Corgan defiantly promised a teacher, "Give me ten years and I'll be at the top."

Shuffled between parents and later a caring stepmother, who raised him and his physically disabled brother without the help of his father, Corgan was a lonely child. He found comfort in music, especially Black Sabbath, and eventually dedicated himself to relentlessly practicing the guitar. He formed his first band, the Marked (named because Corgan and another member had prominent birthmarks), when he was nineteen. But after the Marked went nowhere, he hooked up with Iha (born March 26, 1968) and later D'Arcy (born May 1, 1968). By 1988 they had hired Chamberlin (born June 10, 1967) as their drummer.

In retrospect it might seem that Smashing Pumpkins rode the alternative-rock wave created by Nirvana in 1991, but in fact Nirvana's success actually took attention away from *Gish* (1991), the Pumpkins' debut album. During the next few years, Corgan battled depression and Chamberlin drugs while Iha and D'Arcy, who were romantically linked for a time, went through a painful breakup. But *Siamese Dream* (1993) proved the group's breakthrough, and two years later they released their hugely popular two-disc CD, *Mellon Collie and the Infinite Sadness*.

What Is It About Rock Stars and Drugs?

Jimmy Chamberlin and D'Arcy Wretzky, both formerly of Smashing Pumpkins, have had problems with drugs, as have a whole range of artists from **Mary J. Blige** to members of the **Red Hot Chili Peppers** (see entries). The suicide of Nirvana's Kurt Cobain can be linked to heroin abuse, and heroin claimed the life of Sublime's Bradley Nowell before the group ever hit it big.

Nor is the problem a new one. The list of classic rock groups that lost a member to death as a result of drinking and/or drugs is a long one, and includes the Rolling Stones, the Who, Led Zeppelin, the Sex Pistols, and AC/DC. Then there were the three great artists claimed by substance abuse over a period of a few months in 1970 and 1971: Janis Joplin, Jimi Hendrix, and Jim Morrison of the Doors.

Further back, 1950s rock pioneer Chuck Berry was arrested for marijuana possession—and still further back were the jazz musicians of the 1940s who also smoked pot. Nor was marijuana the only drug used by classic jazz artists: Billie Holliday (see sidebar with **Macy Gray** entry) and Charlie Parker, among others, were heroin users.

Is there a necessary connection between drugs and music—in other words, does a person need to have a drug problem to be a great artist? The answer is *absolutely not!* If anything, drugs get in the way of creativity.

The connection between drugs and music probably comes from the tough schedule that characterizes a musician's life. Being a rock star is hardly an enviable job: they spend endless hours practicing, and endless days and nights touring, playing the same songs over and over in city after city. When the day is done—often in the wee hours of the morning—drugs and drink often seem like an easy way to relax. But the promise of release through substances is an empty one, and those who have kicked the habit (or better yet, never got involved with drugs) have found much greater and more lasting peace—and often rediscover the sheer joy of making music itself.

Spurred by hits such as "1979" and "Tonight, Tonight," *Mellon Collie* went on to sell more than 8 million copies. But 1996 brought a number of misfortunes to Smashing Pumpkins. First a fan was killed in a mosh-pit incident at a Dublin, Ireland, concert; then in July Jonathan Melvoin died of a heroin overdose while touring with the group as keyboardist. (**See original entry on Smashing Pumpkins in** *Parents Aren't Supposed to Like It,* Volume 1, p. 163.)

The departure and return of Chamberlin

Chamberlin, who had been using heroin with Melvoin, was arrested on drug charges late in 1996, and by the end of the year Smashing Pumpkins had replaced him with former Filter drummer Matt Walker. The remaining group

The Talking Heads, circa 1978. (Corbis Corporation. Reproduced by permission.)

Talking Heads

If only on a superficial level, the similarities between the lineup of Talking Heads and Smashing Pumpkins are striking: an artistically dominant singer/guitarist (David Byrne/Billy Corgan); a lead guitarist (Jerry Harrison, also a keyboardist/James Iha); a female bass

members went on to win several awards, including their first Grammy, and in 1997 *Rolling Stone* named them "Best Band."

After the incident in Ireland, Smashing Pumpkins had publicly spoken out against moshing—violent and unruly dancing, usually at very close quarters in an area known as a mosh pit. Now they also issued a number of public statements about Chamberlin in particular, drug use in general.

But after Walker decided to form his own band at the end of 1997, the group found itself once again without a drummer. They recorded *Adore* (1998), their first studio album in three years, with a variety of drummers, but in April 1999 they announced the return of Chamberlin.

During his two years away from the band, Chamberlin had gone through a great deal of soul-searching—and had kicked drugs. "We did one of those get-acquainted jams on the first day," Iha told *Rolling Stone*. "We all looked at each other and went, 'Yeah, that's exactly the way it used to sound.'"

player (Tina Weymouth/D'Arcy Wretzky and later Melissa Auf Der Maur); and a drummer (Chris Frantz/Jimmy Chamberlin). The bass player and one of the male members in both groups were also romantically involved; but whereas Iha and Wretzky broke up, Weymouth and Frantz are married with two teenage sons.

Coming out of the mid-1970s early punk scene, the Talking Heads came into their own working with producer Brian Eno on a series of memorable albums: *More Songs About Buildings and Food* (1978), *Fear of Music* (1979), and *Remain in Light* (1980). At a time when disco and lighthearted pop dominated the airwaves, the Talking Heads' sound—in hits such as "Take Me to the River," "Life During Wartime," and "Once in a Lifetime"—offered Byrne's haunting voice and the irresistible rhythms and instrumentation of Harrison, Weymouth, and Frantz.

The group had its biggest hit with "Burning Down the House" from *Speaking In Tongues* (1983), and also charted with *Little Creatures* (1985). Since 1992 they have been largely inactive, though in 1996 the other three members regrouped without Byrne to make an album.

Weymouth and Frantz have focused their energies on the Tom Tom Club, a rhythm and funk ensemble responsible for dance hits such as "Genius of Love" and "Wordy Rappinghood." Harrison has had his solo albums, and Byrne has created several works, most notably *My Life in the Bush of Ghosts* (1981), a collaboration with Eno. To say that it introduced the world to sampling—the use of other, older recordings in a new one (see entry on **Puff Daddy**)—hardly does justice to *Bush of Ghosts,* one of the strangest, most disturbing albums in music history.

The end of Smashing Pumpkins

When Iha released a solo album, *Let It Come Down,* in 1998, it was the first of many signs that Smashing Pumpkins were on their way to a breakup. *Adore* sold poorly, and *MACHINA/The Machines of God* (1999) did even worse; then, soon after Chamberlin rejoined the band, D'Arcy quit. The remaining group members refused to discuss her reasons, but when she was arrested in January 2000 on charges of purchasing crack cocaine, it seemed apparent that drugs played a role.

By the end of 1999, former **Hole** (see entry) bassist Melissa Auf Der Maur had taken D'Arcy's place, but problems continued. The group had taken on Sharon Osbourne, wife of former Black Sabbath singer **Ozzy Osbourne** (see entry), as manager, but she quit after just three months, issuing a statement that she had left "due to medical reasons . . . Billy Corgan was making me sick!" She and Corgan traded barbs in the press, Osbourne calling him "a control freak" and Corgan referring to her as "a dishonorable woman."

Then in May 2000, the Pumpkins made it official: they were calling it quits after a series of concerts around the world, concluding with two farewell shows in their hometown of Chicago on November 29 and December 2, 2000. They had made the decision to split up, Corgan told *Rolling Stone,* before recording *MACHINA.* "If you listen to the record or look at the artwork," he said, "it's screaming that this is the last record, the last slide down the mountain."

Selected Awards

MTV Video Music Awards, Video of the Year and Best Alternative Video, for "Tonight, Tonight," 1996.

Multi-platinum certification (4 million sales), *Siamese Dream,* 1996.

Grammy Award, Best Hard Rock Performance, for "Bullet with Butterfly Wings," 1997.

Multi-platinum certification (8 million sales), *Mellon Collie and the Infinite Sadness,* 1997.

Grammy Award, Best Hard Rock Performance, for "The End Is the Beginning Is the End," 1998.

Platinum certification, *Adore,* 1998.

Grammy Award nomination, Best Alternative Music Performance, for *Adore,* 1999.

Selected Discography

Gish (Caroline), 1991.
Siamese Dream (Virgin), 1993.
Pisces Iscariot (rarities and B-sides; Virgin), 1994.
Mellon Collie and the Infinite Sadness (Virgin), 1995.
The Aeroplane Flies High (five-CD set of B-sides and previously unreleased material; Virgin), 1996.
Adore (Virgin), 1998.
MACHINA/The Machines of God (Virgin), 2000.

Further Reading

Fricke, David. "Prisoners of Rock & Roll: Smashing Pumpkins." *Rolling Stone,* March 16, 2000, p. 50.

Kot, Greg. "Smashing Pumpkins Storytellers." *Rolling Stone,* November 23, 2000, p. 109.

Kot, Greg. "Pumpkins Break Up." *Rolling Stone,* July 6-20, 2000, p. 63.

Kurson, Robert. "Billy: A Rock Opera." *Chicago,* June 2000, p. 104.

Muret, Don. "Pumpkins to Have Last Smash at Chicago Venues." *Amusement Business,* November 13, 2000, p. 8.

Contact Information

Smashing Pumpkins
8380 Melrose Avenue
Suite 210
Los Angeles, CA 90025

Web Sites

The Pumpkin Palace. http://www.geocities.com/SunsetStrip/7371/pumpkpal.html (accessed on January 8, 2001).

Smashing Pumpkins (official site). http://www.smashingpumpkins.com (accessed on January 8, 2001).

Smashing Pumpkins Net. http://www.smashingpumpkins.net (accessed on January 8, 2001).

Starla.org: Celestial Smashing Pumpkins Sites. http://www.starla.org (accessed on January 8, 2001).

WILL SMITH

American hip-hop and pop artist

Born Willard Christopher Smith on September 25, 1968, in Philadelphia, Pennsylvania

From fame as "the Fresh Prince" to the smash successes of his solo career a decade later, Will Smith has demonstrated again and again that nice guys can rap. He has also proved his ability as an actor, starring in a variety of blockbuster motion pictures. In either career, Smith would be judged a success by anyone's standards, but as a committed family man, he has made it clear that he judges success according to things that last.

Son of Will, an Air Force veteran, and Caroline Smith, who worked for the school board in their hometown of Philadelphia, Smith grew up in a home that placed a high value on education. At seventeen he earned a scholarship to study computer engineering at one of the nation's most prestigious schools, M.I.T. (Massachusetts Institute of Technology)—but turned it down to become a rapper.

At age twelve, Smith had joined Jeff Townes to form DJ Jazzy Jeff and the Fresh Prince, and by 1986 they had a record deal. *Rock the House* (1987) gave them moderate success, but their breakthrough came with *He's the DJ, I'm the Rapper* (1988). The

> "The important thing about being on stage is sharing joy. And I have more joy in my life now than I've ever had, which means I'll have that much more to share with an audience."
>
> -Will Smith, *Rolling Stone*, December 10, 1998

Will Smith. (Archive Photos. Reproduced by permission.)

latter included "Parents Just Don't Understand," which won them a Grammy, as well as the first-ever MTV Video Music Award in the rap category.

Their success faltered on *And In This Corner* ... (1989), but the duo gained another smash hit—and another Grammy—with "Summertime" from *Homebase* (1991). By then Smith, who had no previous acting experience, had starred on the NBC situation comedy *Fresh Prince of Bel Air,* and had gone on to big-screen success in *Six Degrees of Separation* (1993). Also in 1993, the duo issued what turned out to be their final album, *Code Red,* and in the mid-1990s Smith appeared in the box-office smashes *Independence Day* (1996) and *Men in Black* (1997). **(See original entry on DJ Jazzy Jeff and the Fresh Prince in Parents Aren't Supposed to Like It, Volume 2, p. 326.)**

First solo Grammy

Smith's theme song for *Men in Black* hit No. 1 in the summer of 1997, and in November he released *Big Willie Style,* which contained the hits "Just the Two of Us" and "Gettin' Jiggy Wit It" in addition to "Men in Black." The album would eventually sell over 9 million copies, and in 1998 "Men in Black" earned Smith his first solo Grammy.

Smith had married Sheree Zampino in 1992, and the two had a son, Willard Smith III or Trey, in 1993 before divorcing. Five years later, as he accepted an MTV Video Music Award for "Just the Two of Us" in September 1998, he had Trey standing beside him, and told the audience, "It's really a song about the other side of divorce ... so I really want to thank my wife, and actually, I want to thank my ex-wife for both of them being mature enough to make the situation turn out on the positive, happy side."

Marriage to Jada Pinkett

The wife he referred to was actress Jada Pinkett, whom he had first met when she auditioned for a part on *Fresh Prince of Bel Air.* Though there was a strong initial attraction, as the couple later told Nancy Collins of *Rolling Stone,* it was years before friendship turned to romantic involvement, and finally—on New Year's Eve 1997—marriage. A son, Jaden, was born in July 1998. (Daughter, Willow, was born in 2000.)

Amid the fast life of Hollywood and the music world, the Smiths presented an image of marital happiness, symbolized in the wedding itself: "When the two married ... in Baltimore, Pinkett's hometown, they gave each other away, walking arm in arm up the aisle—a symbol of the equality of their relationship." Collins went on to observe, "If Pinkett believes this will be her only marriage, Smith says he knows it will be his last."

More successes

Another motion-picture success followed for Smith in November 1998 with *Enemy of the State* as another hit, "Miami," climbed the charts. At the end of the year he racked up a host of awards for *Big Willie Style,* and in 1999 "Gettin' Jiggy Wit It" earned him his second solo Grammy.

Though *Wild Wild West* (1999), in which Smith co-starred with Kevin

Kline, did not prove a success, his theme song from the film hit No. 1 that summer. In November, Smith released *Willennium*, which sold 2 million copies in the first two months. He starred with Matt Damon in *The Legend of Bagger Vance,* released in November 2000, and in 2001 appeared as legendary boxer Muhammad Ali in *Ali.*

Selected Awards

Grammy Award, Best Rap Solo Performance, for "Men in Black," 1998.

MTV Video Music Awards, Best Male Video (for "Just the Two of Us") and Best Rap Video (for "Gettin' Jiggy Wit It"), 1998.

Grammy Award, Best Rap Performance, for "Gettin' Jiggy Wit It," 1999.

American Music Awards, Favorite Soul/R&B Album, Favorite Pop/Rock Album (both for *Big Willie Style*), and Favorite Soul/R&B Male Artist, 1999.

MTV Video Music Award, Best Male Video, for "Miami," 1999.

American Music Award, Favorite Male Artist, 2000.

Multi-platinum certification (9 million sales), *Big Willie Style,* 2000.

Selected Discography

Big Willie Style (Columbia), 1997.
(With others) *Wild Wild West* (soundtrack; Interscope), 1999.
Willennium (Columbia), 1999.

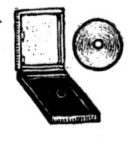

Further Reading

Brown, Corie. "The 'Wild' Bunch." *Newsweek,* July 5, 1999, p. 56.

Collins, Nancy. "Will Smith." *Rolling Stone,* December 10, 1998, p. 62.

Marron, Maggie. *Will Smith: From Rap Star to Mega Star.* New York: Warner Books, 2000.

McCracken, Kristin. *Will Smith.* New York: Children's Press, 2000.

Rodriguez, K. S. *Will Smith: From Fresh Prince to King of Cool.* New York: HarperCollins, 1998.

"Will Smith Balances Acting, Rap, and Family Life with Jada Pinkett Smith." *Jet,* March 29, 1999, p. 58.

Contact Information

Sony Music Entertainment Corporation
550 Madison Avenue
Sixth Floor
New York, NY 10022

Web Sites

The Will Smith Fan Site. http://www.musicfanclubs.org/willsmith/ (accessed on November 9, 2000).

"Will Smith at Sony Music." *Sony Music.* http://www.sonymusic.com/artists/WillSmith/main.html (accessed on November 9, 2000).

WillSmith.com (official site). http://www.willsmith.com (accessed on November 9, 2000).

SNOOP DOGG

American rap artist

Born Cordazar Calvin Broadus on October 20, 1972, in Long Beach, California

> "Getting to the top and staying sane on the way up is about the toughest game you can play. You've got to keep your wits sharp, twenty-four seven, or you're going to find out real quick what they mean when they say, 'It's lonely at the top.'"
>
> –Snoop Dogg, *Jet*, May 22, 2000

Standing six feet, five inches tall, Snoop Dogg got himself noticed in the world of rap long before he released *Doggystyle* in 1993. The latter became the fastest-selling debut album in pop history, and though it pushed Snoop to new levels of fame, the mid-1990s saw an increase of troubles for the gangsta rapper. By the latter part of the decade he had married and settled down, shortened his name, and matured, presenting himself in *The Last Meal* (2000) as a sort of rap godfather.

Calvin Broadus got his nickname from the famous cartoon dog from the *Peanuts* comic strip. Growing up in Long Beach, California, he became involved in the Cripps street gang, and spent time in jail. Fortunately for Snoop, however, he could rap, and that may have saved his life. He later told a reporter that of some twenty-eight boys on his football team from elementary school, twelve were dead, seven in prison, and three hooked on drugs. Only two—he and rapper/producer Warren G (born Warren Griffin III)—had become successes.

Snoop Dogg. (Ken Settle. Reproduced by permission.)

George Clinton

Snoop, **Dr. Dre**, and **Busta Rhymes** (see entries) have all been identified as inheritors of George Clinton. The latter, originator of a wacked-out but laid-back style of funk, virtually created the soundtrack for the childhood of many a future rapper growing up in the 1970s and 1980s.

Clinton came along in the late 1960s, at a time when Detroit's Motown label was turning out tame, by-the-numbers hits. Beginning with *The Clones of Dr. Funkenstein* (1975), Clinton turned R&B inside out with his masterfully layered funk backbeats and wild lyrics, and transformed the musical landscape with off-the-wall hits such as "Flashlight" (1977).

He headed up an assortment of bands—sometimes Parliament, sometimes Funkadelic, and sometimes just George Clinton—that included an array of performers, among them bassist Bootsy Collins. But Clinton was always the center of the show. What came to be known as the P-funk style (which included outlandishly spacey costumes and sunglasses) emanated from Clinton, who rivalled soul master James Brown (see sidebar with **Mystikal** entry) as the godfather of a whole musical genre.

Clinton's first career as P-funk pioneer peaked in 1982 with the monster hit "Atomic Dog." There-

George Clinton. (AP/Wide World Photos. Reproduced by permission.)

after he continued to put out albums and produced records for a number of performers—including the **Red Hot Chili Peppers** (see entry)—but he got little airplay.

With the rise of rap in the late 1980s, however, there emerged a whole generation of young artists who acknowledged Clinton as one of their great musical influences. "Atomic Dog" became one of the most-often sampled tracks in rap, and by the 1990s Clinton had returned to the limelight with songs such as "If Anybody Gets Funk Up (It's Gonna Be You)."

Warren G passed a tape of Snoop to his cousin **Dr. Dre** (see entry), who was impressed enough to include Snoop on his classic "Nuthin' But a 'G' Thang" from *The Chronic* (1992). With his effortless rap style, Snoop nearly stole the show from Dre, and soon the whole music world was talking about Snoop Doggy Dogg. As a result, *Doggystyle* became the first album to debut at No. 1 on the *Billboard* charts.

"(My children) need a fulltime father, and no matter what else I may decide to do or not do, that's one job I'll never take for granted. It's the number-one priority in my life."

The album appeared on Death Row, flagship label of gangsta rap, and soon Snoop became associated with the violence that surrounded the label and its controversial founder, Suge Knight (for more about Knight and Death Row, see Dr. Dre entry). In 1993, Snoop drove a vehicle from which his bodyguard fired shots, fatally wounding twenty-two-year old Phillip Woldemariam. Defended by Johnny Cochran—famous for helping football star O. J. Simpson beat a murder charge in 1995—Snoop and the bodyguard were acquitted of criminal charges in 1996. (**See original entry on Snoop Dogg in** *Parents Aren't Supposed to Like It,* **Volume 2, p. 418.**)

Moving from Death Row to Priority

Even with *Tha Doggfather* (1996), his second major release, Snoop showed signs of turning from his gangsta ways. Then in 1998 he announced that he was leaving Death Row Records, telling a reporter "I definitely feel my life is in danger if I stay. . . ." He then joined No Limit, a label run by rapper/producer Master P (Percy Miller).

Announcing that it was "time to do something different," Snoop dropped the "Doggy" from his name when he issued *Da Game Is to Be Sold, Not to Be Told* (1998). He followed up with a string of releases, among them *Top Dogg* in 1999, and in 2000 *Dead Man Walkin'* (consisting of tracks from the Death Row years); the collaboration *Snoop Dogg Presents Tha Eastsidaz;* and *The Last Meal.* Produced in part by Dre, *Meal* earned praise from Kathryn Farr of *Rolling Stone,* who called it his best album since *Doggystyle.*

"God's got a reason"

Working as he has with a number of lesser-known performers—including Long Beach homeboys Tha Eastsidaz—Snoop has taken on the role of a godfather or perhaps just plain father, helping younger artists come up through the ranks. Fatherhood comes naturally to Snoop, who with his wife, Shante Taylor, has two sons, Corde (born 1994) and Cordell or "Little Snoop" (born 1997), and a daughter, Cori (born 1999).

"Becoming a father made me settled down, go out a lot less and stay out of trouble," he told *Jet.* "[My children] need a fulltime father, and no matter what else I may decide to do or not do, that's one job I'll never take for granted. It's the number-one priority in my life." Of his wife, with whom he was involved for seven years before marrying her in 1997, he said, "Before I ever knew I loved her, or ever thought about asking her to be my wife, Shante was my friend, my number-one homegirl, and the one person I trusted with my deepest and darkest secrets."

As with Dre, also a family man, this is hardly what one would expect of a gangsta rapper, but again like Dre, Snoop has grown and changed through his experiences. "I paid the price to get myself free," he wrote in his 1998 autobiography, *Tha Doggfather: The Times, Trials, and Hardcore Truths of Snoop Dogg,* "from drugs and violence, from incarceration and intoxication and from fear and death of every description. . . . The truth is, there's nothing about my life I would change. . . . I know God's got a reason for everything he does."

Selected Awards

MTV Video Music Award, Best Rap Video, for "Doggy Dogg World," 1994.

Multi-platinum certification (4 million sales), *Doggystyle,* 1994.

American Music Award, Favorite Male Rap or Hip-hop Artist, 1995.

Multi-platinum certification (2 million sales), *Tha Doggfather,* 1997.

Multi-platinum certification (2 million sales), *Da Game Is to Be Sold, Not to Be Told,* 1998.

(With Dr. Dre) Grammy Award nomination, Best Rap Performance by a Duo or Group, for "Still Dre," 2000.

(With Dr. Dre) Grammy Award nomination, Best Rap Performance by a Duo or Group, for "The Next Episode," 2001.

Selected Discography

Doggystyle (Death Row), 1993.
Tha Doggfather (Death Row), 1996.
Da Game Is to Be Sold, Not to Be Told (No Limit/Priority), 1998.
Top Dogg (No Limit/Priority), 1999.
Dead Man Walkin' (previously unreleased material; No Limit/Priority), 2000.
The Last Meal (No Limit/Priority), 2000.

Further Reading

Christian, Margena A. "Rap Star Snoop Dogg Talks About Fame, Fatherhood, and Family." *Jet,* May 22, 2000, p. 58.

Farr, Kathryn. "The Last Meal." *Rolling Stone,* January 18, 2001, p. 56.

Perkins, William. "The Doggfather: The Times, Trials, and Hardcore Truths of Snoop Dogg." *Black Issues Book Review,* May/June 2000, p. 26.

Snoop Dogg with Davin Seay. *Tha Doggfather: The Times, Trials, and Hardcore Truths of Snoop Dogg.* New York: William Morrow, 1999.

Contact Information

Priority Records
6430 Sunset Boulevard
Los Angeles, CA 90028

Web Sites

Big Snoop Dogg (official site). http://www.bigsnoopdog.com (accessed on January 8, 2001).

Snoop-Dogg.com. http://www.snoop-dogg.com (accessed on January 8, 2001).

Snoops Dogghouse. http://www.snoopsdogghouse.com (accessed on January 8, 2001).

Britney Spears

American pop singer

Born Britney Jean Spears on December 2, 1981, in Kentwood, Louisiana

> "I will practice and practice a move in front of a mirror, over and over again ... ten, twenty, one hundred times until I'm happy with it. ... I'm my own worst critic."
>
> —Britney Spears, *Los Angeles Times*, July 27, 2000

With her sexy dance numbers and provocative lyrics, Britney Spears has been accused of using something more than her talent to sell records. Certainly Spears's looks and naughty-but-nice image have attracted a male audience in addition to her principal fan base of teenage and preteen girls. Likewise it is obvious that the people managing her career have used these assets to get her into the spotlight, but it is equally clear that Spears has worked hard to get to the top.

The mouseketeer

Jamie Spears, a building contractor, and his wife, Lynne, an elementary school teacher, raised three children in their Kentwood, Louisiana, home. The family still lives in their old house, and both parents still work, despite the enormous financial success of their middle child, Britney.

Her parents began grooming her for stardom from early childhood, and at age eight, Spears auditioned for a part on Disney's *Mickey Mouse Club Show*. Turned down because she was too young, she attended the Off-Broadway Dance Center and the Professional Performing Arts School in New York City. By the age of ten, she had a role in the off-Broadway stage production *Ruthless*. (The Broadway theatre district in New York City is the Hollywood of live theatre; "off Broadway" refers to theatres and shows that are less prestigious, and sometimes more experimental, than those on Broadway.)

She also appeared in a number of commercials; then at age eleven, Spears was accepted by the *Mickey Mouse Club,* and began work at Disney headquarters in Orlando, Florida. After two years with Disney, she returned to her hometown, where she played on the basketball team in high school. Meanwhile, she and her parents began looking for a record deal.

Into the limelight

In late 1997, the fifteen-year-old Spears signed with Jive Records. She and producers Eric Foster and Max Martin, who had worked with **Whitney Houston** and **The Backstreet Boys** (see entries) respectively, began work on her debut album in 1998. They released her first single, " . . . Baby One More Time," in October of that year, and by January it had hit the No. 1 position.

The album by the same name debuted at No. 1, and within six weeks had sold 2 million copies. In the spring and summer of 1999, Spears had two more hits with "Sometimes" and "(You Drive Me) Crazy," and early in 2000, "From the Bottom of My Broken Heart" hit the charts.

Britney Spears wows the crowd with a live performance on the *Today* Show. (David Atlas. Reproduced by permission.)

Nominated for two Grammy Awards in February 2000, Spears announced a tour with boy band LFO in March and April. In March, she had to have four stitches in her head after a piece of equipment fell on her while she was shooting a

Milli Vanilli at the 1990 Grammys. (AP/Wide World Photos. Reproduced by permission.)

The "Kiss of Death" Award?

Nominated for the Best New Artist Grammy in 2000, Britney Spears lost to pop rival **Christina Aguilera** (see entry). But perhaps Spears should have thanked her lucky stars, since the Best New Artist Award has been nicknamed "the kiss of death." Since it first appeared in 1961, more than a few people who received the award have never been heard from again.

Many Best New Artist recipients had explosive debut releases, but never managed to do it a second time. Such was the case with the Starland Vocal Band (1977), Debby Boone (1978), A Taste of Honey (1979), Christopher Cross (1980), and Arrested Development (1993). At least these names are identifiable; by contrast, one wonders how many people could name hits by the Swingle Sisters (1964). However, almost everyone can identify Milli Vanilli (1990): the duo had their award revoked after it was revealed that they did not sing a single note on their album.

The "kiss of death" reputation is, of course, simply a superstition. After all, no one would call Tom Jones (1966), Crosby, Stills & Nash (1970), or the Carpenters (1971) one-hit wonders. The same holds true for **Mariah Carey** (1991; see entry), Toni Braxton (1994), Sheryl Crow (1995; see sidebar with **Sarah McLachlan** entry), and **LeAnn Rimes** (see entry). For a complete list of "Best New Artist" winners through the years, visit *Rock on the Net* via the Web at www.rockonthenet.com/grammy/newartist.htm.

Parents Aren't Supposed to Like It

video, but she went on the road, performing elaborate dance numbers that drew as much attention as her songs.

Over-the-top sexuality

Oops . . . I Did It Again, Spears's second album, appeared in May 2000, almost simultaneously with the book *Britney Spears: Heart to Heart,* which she cowrote with her mother. *Oops* sold more than 1.3 million copies in its first week, breaking a record previously set by **Mariah Carey** (see entry) for the highest first-week sales by a female solo artist. In June, the town of Kentwood opened a Britney Spears Museum.

Spears had two hit singles in the summer of 2000, the title track of *Oops* and "Lucky." She closed out the season with a sexually charged performance at the MTV Video Music Awards in September by stripping practically to a bra and panties as she sang a cover of the Rolling Stones' 1965 hit "(I Can't Get No) Satisfaction," followed by "Oops! . . . I Did It Again."

This was just one example of the over-the-top sexuality in Spears's stage shows, as well as in videos such as " . . . Baby One More Time," where she appeared as a naughty Catholic schoolgirl. These images contrasted sharply with Spears's claims to be a devout Christian (her family is Baptist) leading a wholesome lifestyle, but she maintains that she never intended to project a sexual image. "And then everyone was, 'Oh my God. Oh, she's so sexy,'" she told Isaac Guzman in the *Los Angeles Times.* "And I was like, 'Oh, well thank you. Gosh.'"

A young girl at heart

Spears herself has had little to do with shaping her career. Virtually all of her songs—including one from *Oops* cowritten by **Shania Twain** (see entry)—are written for her. In fact there are very few teen-pop stars (see sidebar with **Hanson** entry) who exercise much control over their songs, their image, or their futures.

"And then everyone was, 'Oh my God. Oh, she's so sexy.' And I was like, 'Oh, well thank you. Gosh.'"

"Despite all the trappings of stardom," Guzman noted, "Spears does project an appealing naïveté [innocence]. She's at her most animated when hugging little girls at her pre-show 'meet and greet' or exclaiming over the tropical-flavored snow cones being served backstage. 'You've got to try one of these!' she shouts at me at the end of our interview. It's the first and only time I see her express any genuine enthusiasm when not in the spotlight."

After closing out 2000 with another top-ten hit, "Stronger," Spears began 2001 with a rousing performance at the Super Bowl in January. As has often been the case, she caused a stir with her apparel, in this case a tube sock—which she wore on her arm. The socks, long out of style in America, were making a comeback in Europe and Japan, and thus Spears was at the crest of a new fashion wave. Though she failed to win a Grammy in February (she received two nominations), Spears signed a multimillion-dollar with Pepsi-Cola. Her first Pepsi commercial aired during the broadcast of the Academy Awards ceremony in March 2001.

Selected Awards

MTV Europe Awards, Best Female Artist, Best Pop Artist, Best Breakthrough, and Best Song (". . . Baby One More Time"), 1999.

Grammy Award nominations, Best New Artist and Best Female Vocal Performance (for " . . . Baby One More Time"), 2000.

American Music Award, Favorite New Artist, 2000.

Multi-platinum certification (12 million sales), . . . Baby One More Time, 2000.

Multi-platinum certification (6 million sales), Oops! . . . I Did It Again, 2000.

Grammy Award nomination, Best Female Pop Vocal Performance, for "Oops! . . . I Did It Again," 2001.

Grammy Award nomination, Best Pop Vocal Album, for Oops! . . . I Did It Again, 2001.

Selected Discography

. . . Baby One More Time (Jive), 1999.

Oops! . . . I Did It Again (Jive), 2000.

Further Reading

Anderman, Joan. "Britney Speaks: Oops! . . . She Said It Again." *Boston Globe,* August 25, 2000, p. C-13.

Burr, Ramiro. "Britney Spears Sets the Record Straight." *Houston Chronicle,* July 20, 2000, p. G-4.

Guzman, Isaac. "Cover Story: Britney Blossoms." *Los Angeles Times,* July 27, 2000, p. 6.

Johns, Michael-Anne. *Britney Spears.* Kansas City, Missouri: Andrews & McMeel, 1999.

Spears, Britney, Lynne Spears, and Sheryl Berk, *Britney Spears: Heart to Heart.* New York: Three Rivers, 1999.

Talmadge, Morgan. *Britney Spears.* New York: Children's Press, 2000.

Contact Information

Jive Records Corporation
137–139 W. 25th St.
New York, NY 10001

Web Sites

"Britney.com." *Jive Records.* http://www.peeps.com/britney/home.html (accessed on September 19, 2000).

BritneySpears.org. http://www.britneyspears.org (accessed on September 19, 2000).

The Official Britney Spears Website. http://www.officialbritney.com (accessed on September 19, 2000).

Sting

British alternative pop/rock, and world music artist

Born Gordon Matthew Sumner on October 2, 1951, in Wallsend, England

Like a handful of artists from **Dr. Dre** to **Brian Setzer** (see entries), Sting has had more than one career: first as bassist and vocalist for the Police, one of the most influential bands of the late 1970s and early 1980s, then as a hugely popular solo artist from the mid-1980s onward. And, in a situation that offers parallels with that of **Santana** (see entry), his hit album *Brand New Day* (1999) proved that it is possible for an established artist to build a new following with a young audience.

Sumner, Copeland, and Summers

Born Gordon Sumner, Sting got his nickname because he often wore a gold-striped sweater that friends said made him look like a bumblebee. He made a living variously as a ditch-digger and a schoolteacher, but he also played bass in jazz clubs, and together with a young American drummer named Stewart Copeland, he decided to form a band.

In time Sting and Copeland found Andy Summers, who had played with a number of bands in the 1960s, including Eric Bur-

"I'm most happy at the moment because... I've made a record that's nothing like anything that's out there. To come out of left field is thrilling to me."

—Sting on *Brand New Day* and "Desert Rose," *Rolling Stone*, November 23, 2000

Sting. (Liaison Agency. Reproduced by permission.)

don and the Animals. Indeed, though they came to the forefront in the punk movement of the late 1970s, the Police—whose name came from the fact that Copeland's father worked for the U.S. Central Intelligence Agency (CIA)—were always more musically talented and experienced than most punk groups.

Without a full-length LP to their credit, the group toured the United States in a rented van during the summer of 1978 to promote their single "Roxanne." It appeared on *Outlandos d'Amour,* released that fall, and after the song's re-release in America during the spring of 1979, it became a hit. Yet though the Police soon became popular in Britain, major U.S. success still eluded them.

The Police take the world

Fall 1979 brought a second album, *Regatta de Blanc,* and another single, "Message in a Bottle." At that point Copeland's brother Miles, the group's manager, took a rather unusual strategy for a band still struggling to gain an audience outside of England: he sent them on a world tour that took them to countries such as India and Egypt, which are rarely visited by rock bands from the West.

In fact the non-Western character of the tour suited the Police, whose next album, *Zenyatta Mondata* (1980), reflected Middle Eastern as well as Caribbean influences. The album also gave them their breakthrough in the United States, where both "De Do Do Do, De Da Da Da" and "Don't Stand So Close to Me" reached the Top 10. By the beginning of 1981, the Police had established themselves as superstars, and when they released *Ghost in the Machine* that fall, it shot to No. 2 in the United States.

A single from *Ghost,* "Every Little Thing She Does Is Magic," became their biggest hit yet, but much greater success would follow with *Synchronicity* in the summer of 1983. The album, which spent a staggering seventeen weeks at No. 1 on the U.S. charts, spawned one of the biggest hit songs in history, "Every Breath You Take," which stayed in the number-one position for eight weeks.

Quitting at the height of success

The album yielded more hits with "Wrapped Around Your Finger" and "King of Pain," keeping the Police on the radio well into 1984. But after completing a tour that year, the group members—whose fights with one another had become legendary—decided to take a break. In fact the break never ended; what resulted instead was the splintering of the Police into three solo careers, of which Sting's was by far the most successful.

Meanwhile Sting and his former bandmates played with the idea of a reunion, and finally entered the studio in 1986 to record a few new songs for a greatest hits album. But working together again only reminded everyone of the tensions that had pulled them apart, and all that resulted from the sessions was a new version of "Don't Stand So Close to Me."

In fact the Police would reunite for just one more "concert": an impromptu jam session at Sting's wedding to actress and producer Trudie Styler in 1992.

Sting has long dedicated himself to issues such as human rights and the environment. Pictured here, Sting is wearing a sash from a decoration presented to him on January 15, 2001, by the government of Chile for his promotion of human rights. (AP/Wide World Photos. Reproduced by permission.)

They had sold millions of albums, and during the late 1990s their ska-influenced sound would reverberate through that of groups such as **No Doubt** (see entry), but when Joseph Tirella of *People* asked Sting if the Police would ever do a reunion tour, he said, " . . . I don't think so. We haven't tried anything like that, which is why our legend is intact; we haven't tried to cash in on it."

Jazz and world music characterize solo work

In June 1985, Sting released his first full-fledged solo LP, *The Dream of the Blue Turtles*, which revealed the jazzy style that would characterize much of his solo work. "If You Love Somebody Set Them Free" reached the Top 3, and the album spawned further hits with "Fortress Around Your Heart," "Love Is the Seventh Wave," and "Russians." Two years later, *Nothing Like the Sun* (1987) yielded the Top 10 singles "We'll Be Together" and "Be Still My Beating Heart."

In line with his interest in world music, Sting in 1988 recorded *Nada Como El Sol*, a version of *Nothing Like the Sun* consisting of songs in Spanish and Portuguese. He hit the Top 10 with "All This Time" from *Soul Cages* (1991); enjoyed critical acclaim for *Ten Summoner's Tales* (1993); and a 1994 collaboration with Rod Stewart and Bryan Adams gave him his first number-one hit since the Police years, "All For Love."

In addition to several Grammys with the Police, Sting won an astounding nine such awards in the period from 1985 to 2000, and accumulated an almost equal number of Grammy nominations. Yet *Mercury Falling* (1996) sold far fewer copies than *Tales,* and it seemed that for all his recent successes, Sting was poised to begin a long, slow decline.

A brand new day for Sting

The first sign that Sting might still be relevant to young listeners came in 1997, when **Puff Daddy** (see entry) sampled "Every Breath You Take" for his number-one hit "I'll Be Missing You." Puffy also worked with Sting on a remake of "Roxanne," which hit the R&B charts in December 1997—during the same week that also found Sting and Toby Keith on the country Top 10 with "I'm So Happy I Can't Stop Crying."

But the biggest surprise came with *Brand New Day,* released in September 1999. The album included appearances with Stevie Wonder (see sidebar with **Jamiroquai** entry), James Taylor, and jazz artist Branford Marsalis. Yet the collaboration that got the most attention was with someone most Western listeners had never heard of: Algerian superstar Cheb Mami, who contributed vocals in Arabic on "Desert Rose," a top-ten hit.

Sting, who is the father of six children—two from an earlier marriage, and four more with Trudie (the last born in 1996)—thus had an opportunity to see his music embraced by listeners his children's age. Once upon a time, he was an angry young man whose music helped define an era; then he became the soft-rock favorite of aging baby boomers—and then, on the brink of fifty, he proved that he had much more artistic life left. "[I]n the wake of his alleged slump," wrote Gerri Hirshey in *Rolling Stone,* "the artist is enjoying his last laugh. It is a gentle one, and not at all bitter."

Selected Awards

Grammy Award, Song of the Year (Songwriter), for "Every Breath You Take," 1984.
Grammy Award, Best Male Pop Vocal Performance, for *Bring on the Night,* 1988.
Grammy Award, Best Rock Song (Songwriter), for "Soul Cages," 1992.
Grammy Award, Best Male Pop Vocal Performance, for "If I Ever Lose My Faith in You," 1994.
Grammy Award, Best Male Pop Vocal Performance, for "Brand New Day," 2000.
Grammy Award, Best Pop Album, for *Brand New Day,* 2000.
Multi-platinum certification (2 million sales), *Brand New Day,* 2000.
Grammy Award, Best Male Pop Vocal Performance, for "She Walks This Earth (Soberana Rosa)," 2001.

Selected Discography

(With the Police) *Outlandos d'Amour* (A & M), 1978.
(With the Police) *Regatta de Blanc* (A & M), 1979.
(With the Police) *Zenyatta Mondata* (A & M), 1980.

(With the Police) *Ghost In the Machine* (A & M), 1981.
(With the Police) *Synchronicity* (A & M), 1983.
The Dream of the Blue Turtles (A & M), 1985.
Nothing Like the Sun (A & M), 1987.
Soul Cages (A & M), 1991
Ten Summoner's Tales (A & M), 1993.
Mercury Falling (A & M), 1996.
Brand New Day (A & M), 1999.

Further Reading

Clarkson, Wensley. *Sting: The Secret Life of Gordon Sumner.* New York: Thunder's Mouth Press, 1996.

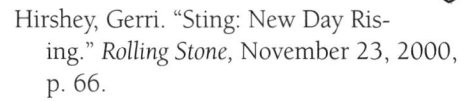

Hirshey, Gerri. "Sting: New Day Rising." *Rolling Stone,* November 23, 2000, p. 66.

Tirella, Joseph V. "Talking With . . . Sting." *People,* October 4, 1999, p. 48.

White, Timothy. "Sting's French Sojourn Yields 'Brand New Day.'" *Billboard,* September 18, 1999, p. 5.

Wild, David. "People of the Year: Sting." *Rolling Stone,* December 14–21, 2000, p. 84.

Contact Information

A & M Records, Inc.
P.O. Box 118
Hollywood, CA 90078

Web Sites

Stingchronicity. http://www.stingchronicity.co.uk/ (accessed on January 23, 2001).

Synchronosite. http://www.geocities.com/BourbonStreet/5646/ (accessed on January 23, 2001).

Unofficial Homepage of the Police and Sting. http://www.cris.com/~donsden/ (accessed on January 23, 2001).

Sugar Ray

American alternative pop/rock band
Formed 1992 in Newport Beach, California

> "... We're not trying to be anybody's lifestyle.... I believe there's a niche [place] for bands like us, bands that have a good time and are just happy to be here."
> –Mark McGrath, *Rolling Stone*, February 18, 1999

Sugar Ray. (Corbis Corporation. Reproduced by permission.)

Listening to Sugar Ray's explosive 1997 hit "Fly," an easygoing combination of hip-hop and alternative pop with just a hint of the Caribbean, it is hard to believe that the group started out playing speed-metal. But that is not the only thing about Sugar Ray that is not quite as it seems.

Frontman Mark McGrath works hard to project the image of an ignorant, fun-loving jock—obnoxious but magnetic, and hard to dislike. In reality he is thoughtful, intelligent, and prone to laughing at himself. And though he beats critics to the punch by insisting that the band is not very good, millions of Sugar Ray fans would beg to differ.

McGrath's ability to charm

"The charisma was always there," McGrath's mother told *Rolling Stone*. "He was one of those children who, when you went to a restaurant, would be visiting four tables away and charming the adults." McGrath (born March 15, 1970) has described his early years as happy ones: "I didn't have a dramatic childhood," he told *Melody Maker,* "and I still love my parents, and I was raised in a nice place, Newport Beach, California."

By all accounts, however, the experience of his parents' divorce when he was twelve was a painful one. For a year and a half, he could not even bear to tell his friend Joseph McGinty Nichols, nicknamed McG, who later directed most of Sugar Ray's videos. "I was afraid he wouldn't like me anymore," McGrath later admitted. "That's how fragile my mind was." Despite the divorce, however, both his father and mother remained heavily involved in McGrath's life, and this gave him the encouragement he needed to rebound in high school, where he excelled as a basketball player.

"Animal House without college"

At the University of Southern California (USC), McGrath met guitarist Rodney Sheppard (born November 25, 1967), bassist Murphy Karges (born June 20, 1968), and drummer Stan Frazier (born April 23, 1969). Together they formed Sugar Ray, naming themselves after boxer Sugar Ray Leonard, and moved into a house together. For two years, the band played its brand of thrash-metal around southern California, eventually attracting enough attention to get a contract with Atlantic Records in 1994.

The group's debut, *Lemonade and Brownies* (1995), showed the influence of the **Red Hot Chili Peppers** (see entry), who combined punk and rap influences. Touring in support of the album, Sugar Ray opened for another rap-metal group, **KoRN** (see entry), as well as rappers Cypress Hill. Also during the tour, the group hired Craig "DJ Homicide" Bullock (born December 17, 1972) to work the turntables, and eventually he became the group's fifth member.

They were having plenty of fun—McGrath has described life at the house they shared as "*Animal House* with no college"—but Sugar Ray's debut attracted virtually no attention. Undaunted, they rented a studio in a run-down part of New York City in 1996 and recorded *Floored* (1997). The title described their feelings after completing the album, but it could just as easily have expressed their reaction when "Fly" shot to No. 1 in the summer of 1997.

More than fifteen minutes of fame

Sugar Ray's success with its second album owed little to the critics, most of whom panned them. In the view of many observers, their "fifteen minutes of fame"—an expression drawn from American artist Andy Warhol's (1928?–1987) statement that "In the future, everyone will be famous for fifteen minutes"—were almost over.

> "... we know where we want to be. We want to be in your radio speaker. We're not the kind of people who are going to rail against the only hit we've ever had."

The title of Sugar Ray's followup in January 1999 even played on the "fifteen minutes" theme: *14:59*. But by March, the song "Every Morning" had hit the number-one position. In August, Sugar Ray again made the Top 10, this time with "Someday," and played at Woodstock '99.

The Sugar Ray sound

Both of the first two hits from *14:59* followed the pattern of "Fly," which had been established as the Sugar Ray sound—even though Sugar Ray had started out playing a very different brand of music. Chris Mundy of *Rolling Stone* wrote that "no fewer than five songs on *14:59*" had used "Fly" as their model.

At first, McGrath had reacted strongly to what became Sugar Ray's sound: after he first heard "Fly," he later said, he quit the band for five days. But with success had come acceptance: "We certainly didn't set out to make fifteen 'Fly's,'" he told Mundy, "but we know where we want to be. We want to be in your radio speaker. We're not the kind of people who are going to rail against the only hit we've ever had." Yet on "Falls Apart," a top-ten hit in February 2000, the band returned to a somewhat edgier guitar sound, which it combined with DJ Homicide's work on the turntables.

Not just McGrath's backup band

As with many another group, the news about Sugar Ray tends to focus on its frontman: as Karges told Mundy, "We're a band, and sometimes we're portrayed like we're Mark and a backup group." Sheppard agreed, noting that "Everything stems from the song. It wouldn't matter what Mark looked like if there wasn't a song to back it." Frazier, too, complained that "We've worked really hard to get a plateau of success, and then Mark is out there saying, 'Ah, we're terrible musicians.'"

In fact this has a great deal to do with McGrath's humor, which has been described as self-effacing or self-deprecating—in other words, he makes fun of himself. Describing his future plans, McGrath told Mundy that he had considered acting, "but I'm not a very good actor, man. I went to a [TV show] *Party of Five* audition and ran out of there . . . I was so scared."

"Mark's public persona [image] is sort of like a pinup, pretty-boy . . . and he's actually the antithesis [opposite] of that," McG explained. "He's well-schooled and savvy . . . a very shy, very humble guy." Describing the group, McGrath said, "We're not trying to start a revolution. We never claimed to be anything but what we are." And that, concluded Mundy, sums up both McGrath and the band: "maddening, likable, insecure, yet smart enough to beat himself up before anyone else has the chance."

Selected Awards

Multi-platinum certification (2 million sales), *Floored,* 1998.
MTV Video Music Award nomination, Best Group Video, for "Every Morning," 1999.
Multi-platinum certification (3 million sales), *14:59,* 2000.

Selected Discography

Lemonade and Brownies (Lava/Atlantic), 1995.
Floored (Lava/Atlantic), 1997.
14:59 (Lava/Atlantic), 1999.
Sugar Ray (Lava/Atlantic), 2001.

Further Reading

Mundy, Chris. "Q&A: Mark McGrath of Sugar Ray." *Rolling Stone,* February 18, 1999, p. 27.

Mundy, Chris. "The Sweet Smell of Success: Sugar Ray." *Rolling Stone,* March 18, 1999, p. 48.

Swenson, Kyle. "Sugar Ray: Sweeter Shades of Tone." *Guitar Player,* May 1999, p. 29.

Watson, Ian. "Sugar and Spice . . . It's Not All Nice." *Melody Maker,* October 16, 1999, p. 17.

Contact Information

Sugar Ray
P.O. Box 46066
Los Angeles, CA 90046-0066

Web Sites

Sugar Ray (official site). http://www.sugar-ray.com (accessed on November 13, 2000).

"Sugar Ray." *Atlantic Records.* http://www.atlantic-records.com/frames/Artists_Music/main.html?artistID=69 (accessed on November 13, 2000).

Sugar Ray Fans. http://www.sugarrayfans.com (accessed on November 13, 2000).

Sugar Ray Online. http://www.sugarrayonline.com (accessed on November 13, 2000).

THIRD EYE BLIND

American alternative pop/rock band

Formed 1995 in San Francisco, California

> "Third Eye Blind's connection with our fans has been very direct, because it comes from playing live."
>
> —Stephan Jenkins, *Interview*, May 2000

Third Eye Blind. (Photo by Steve Granitz. WireImage.com. Reproduced by permission.)

Third Eye Blind was one of many acts that emerged on the national scene in 1997 (see sidebar), hitting the charts with "Semi-Charmed Life." The song was everywhere that summer, and with its upbeat, poppish sound, it seemed perfectly harmless—though in fact frontman Stephan Jenkins explained to MTV that it was "a song about a junkie's [heroin addict's] decline into speed addiction."

The dark side of "Semi-Charmed Life" was only one surprise where Third Eye Blind was concerned. Much more shocking, to critics who judged them a "one-hit wonder," was the string of hits that followed it, continuing with the release of *Blue* in 1999. Though Third Eye Blind had defied the odds and returned to the charts, new trouble loomed on the horizon with a lawsuit in 2000 that threatened to tear the group apart.

From literature to rock and roll

Born on September 27, 1968, to parents George, a political science professor at California's Stanford University, and Elizabeth Jenkins, a former administrator at the school, the future lead singer of Third Eye Blind seemed bound for something more serious than rock and roll. "Dad wanted me to become a professor or an environmentalist," Stephan Jenkins later explained to *People*. "He wanted me to make a direct, tangible [identifiable] impact on the world."

Jenkins studied literature at the University of California at Berkeley, and after graduating entered the San Francisco music scene. He performed with a hip-hop outfit before meeting guitarist Kevin Cadogan (born August 14, 1970), with whom he started writing songs. Together with bassist Arion Salazar (born August 9, 1972) and drummer Brad Hargraves (born July 30, 1972), they formed Third Eye Blind. The name refers to a concept in the Hindu religion, the idea of a spiritual "third eye" that sees things invisible to the two physical ones.

The Class of '97

Nineteen ninety-seven was a good year for music. Listed below are some of the performers featured in *Parents Aren't Supposed to Like It* who either enjoyed their first U.S. success in 1997, or released albums that greatly increased their exposure on the national stage:

Fiona Apple
Backstreet Boys
Busta Rhymes
Missy "Misdemeanor" Elliott
Hanson
Jamiroquai
Jewel
Matchbox Twenty
Puff Daddy
Radiohead
Sugar Ray
Third Eye Blind
The Wallflowers
Wu-Tang Clan

Third Eye Blind gets noticed

Times were hard in the early days of Third Eye Blind, as Jenkins explained when describing a typical meal during his post-college years: "In the morning you scrounge enough dimes to get coffee," he told *People*. "You put in thick cream and a lot of sugar, which gives you the calories you need to get to lunch. Then you show up at friends' houses around dinner."

The group's fortunes began to change in 1996, when it opened for Oasis in San Francisco. As interest increased, suddenly the group had a number of offers from record companies. They finally signed with Elektra, which released their debut album—produced by Jenkins—in March 1997. On the strength of "Semi-Charmed Life," the band played as opener for **U2** (see entry) and even the Rolling Stones before going on the road as a headlining act. Meanwhile, Jenkins emerged as a public star who was romantically linked with actress Charlize Theron.

The group closed out 1997 with another hit, "How's It Going to Be," which reached the Top 10 in January of the following year. By the end of 1998, Third Eye Blind had reached the number-one position again with "Jumper," which

Third Eye Blind

Third Eye Blind lead singer Stephan Jenkins fronts the band at the 2000 Radio Music Awards. (Archive Photos. Reproduced by permission.)

ber 1999 they released *Blue,* which yielded two more hits in 2000 with "Never Let You Go" and "Deep Inside You."

Conflicts outside and inside the band

In June 1998, the bassists for Third Eye Blind and Green Day had gotten into a fight after Salazar jumped onto a stage where Green Day was playing. It had started as a prank, but when security guards—not knowing who Salazar was—attacked him, he ended up hitting Mike Dirnt in the ensuing scuffle. "It's basically a joke that went way over the line," Jenkins told MTV, "and we definitely hope that Mike heals up." At the end of 1999, Third Eye Blind cancelled a Washington, D.C., New Year's concert with **Everclear** (see entry) and Fuel. None of the groups involved gave a reason for the cancellation.

Much worse than conflicts outside the band was a rupture within it, one that boiled over in June 2000. That was the month when Cadogan, having left Third Eye Blind to form a group called Cousin Kevin, filed a multi-million-dollar lawsuit against the band. According to Cadogan's lawyers, he was entitled to 50 percent of the royalties or payments from his songwriting efforts with Jenkins, but Jenkins had taken 100 percent. The case went to court in November 2000.

stayed at No. 1 for three weeks. All these songs, however, were from the group's first album, and thus critics could still say that they would be unable to make the charts with a followup. Then in Novem-

Selected Awards

Billboard Music Award, Best Modern Rock Track, for "Semi-Charmed Life," 1997.

American Music Award nominations, Favorite Pop/Rock New

Artist and Favorite Alternative Artist, 1998.

(Jenkins and Cadogan) California Music Award, Outstanding Songwriters, 2000.

Multi-platinum certification (4 million sales), *Third Eye Blind,* 2000.

Platinum certification, *Blue,* 2000.

Selected Discography

Third Eye Blind (Elektra), 1997.
Blue (Elektra), 1999.

Further Reading

Bozza, Anthony. "Q&A: Stephan Jenkins of Third Eye Blind." *Rolling Stone,* April 30, 1998, p. 35.

Helligar, Jeremy and Jennifer Longley. "The Eye Has It." *People,* October 12, 1998, p. 105.

Lee, Henry K. "Guitarist Sues His Former Band Members." *San Francisco Chronicle,* November 1, 2000, p. A-22.

Sarko, Anita. "Stephan Jenkins of Third Eye Blind." *Interview,* May 2000, p. 54.

Contact Information

Elektra Entertainment Group
75 Rockefeller Plaza
New York, NY 10019

Web Sites

The Third Eye. http://thethirdeye.hypermart.net (accessed on November 13, 2000).

Third Eye Blind (official site). http://www.3eb.com (accessed on November 13, 2000).

Third Eye Blinded. http://angelfire.com/de/3EBlinded/ (accessed on November 13, 2000).

The Village Church Yard. http://www.3eb.co.uk (accessed on November 13, 2000).

311

American rap-rock band
Formed 1991 in Omaha, Nebraska

> "... There has to be some correlation between your musical and lyrical content and how the people who are following you act. I just want to feel that my influence is positive."
>
> —Nick Hexum, *Rolling Stone*, December 9, 1999

Tim Mahoney, Nick Hexum, Chad Sexton, P-Nut, and S.A. Martinez. (Capricorn Records. Reproduced by permission.)

Coming from Omaha, Nebraska—not known for its musical activity—311 built a following, as lead singer and guitarist Nick Hexum has said, "One fan at a time." By relentless touring, the five-piece band established a fan base for their upbeat rock/ska/reggae/hip-hop sound, and they did so with a minimum of radio or video exposure.

With the success of their self-titled third album in 1995, 311 rose from the status of a marginal road band to an MTV favorite. "It's kind of funny," Hexum later told *Rolling Stone*. "We finally had gotten to a place where we really didn't need MTV and everything because we could make a living through touring. And I always kind of thought that when we didn't need them, they would come to the plate. And it happened."

Debate-team punk

In high school, Hexum (born April 12, 1970) was an unusual combination of bad boy and smart kid: he listened to punk rock, and often got into trouble, but he was also a member of the school debate team—and its jazz band. During the late 1980s, Hexum began playing in a number of groups with guitarist Tim Mahoney (born February 17, 1970); vocalist and deejay S. A. (Douglas) Martinez (born October 29, 1970); bassist P-Nut (Aaron Wills; born June 5, 1974); and drummer Chad Sexton (born September 17, 1970).

By 1991 they had formed 311, and they soon signed a deal with Capricorn, a small record label. What followed were some hard years of touring as the band set out on the road to conquer America from the ground up. In 1993, the year they debuted with *Music,* their RV and trailer caught fire on a Missouri highway, and virtually all their possessions burned up in the ensuing blaze.

Yet the members of 311 soldiered on, and during those hardest years of the early to mid-1990s they either opened for, or headlined with, other groups destined to make a name for themselves, including **KoRN, No Doubt,** and **Sugar Ray** (see entries). The title of *Grassroots* (1994) reflected their strategy of taking their music directly to the fans, but as with its predecessor, the album's sales hardly made a dint in the market.

The mainstream finds 311

All of that changed with *311* (1995), which sold more than 3 million copies and yielded an MTV hit with the video for "Down." Of that song, which a *Rolling Stone* journalist described as "a shout-out to [311's] grassroots fans," Hexum said, "Yeah, I had a good feeling about the song because it had that hook that I kept singing, and then everyone else started singing it. But it is ironic that it would be a grassroots message that would bring us to the mainstream."

The mainstream, however, was changing, as Hexum himself noted in a *Rolling Stone* interview: "When *Music* came out, everyone was still really into grunge, and now I think people are moving away from straight rock and getting into bands like No Doubt, Goldfinger, and KoRN. They are hybrid bands such as ourselves with either ska or hip-hop elements. I just think it's time that people are appreciating cross-genre stuff."

A range of influences

Among the musical influences cited by members of 311 are everything from Public Enemy and Ice Cube to **Beck,** the **Red Hot Chili Peppers** (see entries), the Clash, and the Smiths. Critics have also compared them to the **Beastie Boys** and **Rage Against the Machine** (see entries).

"I figure that if I sort of sensitized my brain to only natural highs, the experience of playing gigs would be more totally uplifting.... Now I can feel the energy and heat coming off the crowd."

With regard to Rage, however, Hexum told Wade Chamberlain in a 1995 interview with *Rational Alternative Digital,* "If you listen to [both bands'] albums side by side, you're gonna feel good after listening to our albums, and you're gonna feel pissed after listening to their albums. And we're very proud of that. I don't really get into the screaming part, the whole, 'you're gonna burn' over and over again."

311

Bands with Numbers in Their Names

U2 (see entry)
Three Dog Night
3 Doors Down
Third Eye Blind (see entry)
The Four Seasons
The Four Tops
Gang of Four
Ben Folds Five
Jackson 5
MC5
Pizzicato Five
L 7
7 Mary 3
10CC
Heaven 17
Matchbox Twenty (see entry)
20/20
.38 Special
UB40
Level 42
Black 47
The B-52s
54-40
Sham 69
The 77s
98 Degrees (see entry)
Haircut 100
112
Blink-182 (see entry)
311
10,000 Maniacs

The role of drugs

Certainly 311 takes a positive approach in their music, but one thing many listeners might find less positive is their outspoken approval of marijuana, symbolized by a sign on the door of their recording studio reading "Work-Free Drug Zone." (See sidebar, "What Is It About Musicians and Drugs?" with **Smashing Pumpkins** entry.)

As vocal as they are in support of pot, however, members of 311 have been just as strong in their disapproval of harder drugs such as cocaine. And, reported *Rolling Stone*'s Mark Binelli in late 1999, "Hexum has given up pot for 311's current theater tour. 'I figure that if I sort of sensitized my brain to only natural highs, the experience of playing gigs would be more totally uplifting, because there'd be nothing in the way,' he says. 'Now I can feel the energy and heat coming off the crowd.'"

Controlling their own destiny

The success of *311* resulted in still more touring, with the group only taking out time to record what became *Transistor* (1997). The latter, at seventy-four minutes, was about as long as a single CD can be.

"When a band has success like we did with our last album," Hexum told *Rolling Stone*, "they've earned the rights to call their own shots on their next record." This desire to control their own destiny would ultimately lead to a lawsuit against their record company, which the members of 311 maintained had failed to provide them with adequate marketing support.

In the meantime, 311 released a live album, and in 1999 opened for **KISS** (see entry). While on the road in 1999, they recorded *Soundsystem*. The latter, its name perhaps a reference to the fact that they were using portable recording equipment, found them returning to a straight hard-rock sound with less ska and reggae. Late in 2000, with their suit against Capricorn Records still pending, the members of 311 were busy recording a new album.

Selected Awards

Platinum certification, *Transistor*, 1997.

Multi-platinum certification (3 million sales), *311*, 1998.

Selected Discography

Music (Capricorn), 1993.
Grassroots (Capricorn), 1994.
311 (Capricorn), 1995.
Transistor (Capricorn), 1997.
311 Live (Capricorn), 1998.
Soundsystem (Capricorn), 1999.

Further Reading

Binelli, Mark. "311: Giving Rap Metal a Good Name." *Rolling Stone,* December 9, 1999, p. 31.

"Radio Heads." *Rolling Stone,* July 16, 1999.

Swenson, Kyle. "Amalgamated Metal." *Guitar Player,* November 1999, p. 64.

"311 Makes It Out of the Grass and Into the Green." *Rolling Stone,* October 24, 1999.

Vineyard, Jennifer. "311 Give Up the 411 on Next Album." *Rolling Stone,* October 20, 2000.

Vineyard, Jennifer and Troy J. Augusto. "311 File Suit Against Their Record Label." *Rolling Stone,* August 31, 2000.

Contact Information

The 311 Hive (fan club)
8904 Florence Dr.
Omaha, NE 68147

Web Sites

Enter Gate 311. http://www.valdosta.peachnet.edu/~mcreynol/threleven (accessed on January 12, 2001).

311 Music.com (official site). http://www.311music.com (accessed on January 12, 2001).

311 Page. http://www.duke.edu/~bak4/main.html (accessed on January 12, 2001).

TLC

American R&B and hip-hop trio
Formed 1991 in Atlanta, Georgia

> "The group has, since its start, been drawn to the outrageous...."
>
> —Christopher John Farley on TLC,
> *Time*, March 1, 1999

(L–R) T-Boz, Chilli, and Left Eye. (Photo by Steve Granitz. WireImage.com. Reproduced by permission.)

Certified in 1995 as the all-time biggest-selling female group in U.S. history, TLC was everywhere in the mid-1990s, thanks in large part to the monster hits "Waterfalls," "Creep," and "Red Light Special." These songs pushed sales of *CrazySexyCool* beyond the 11 million mark, but with the group's subsequent problems, it seemed unlikely TLC could top the charts again. They managed to do so with *Fanmail* (1999), but as members each moved in separate directions, the future of TLC remained open to question.

The name "TLC" is an acronym comprising the first letter of each group member's nickname: Tionne "T-Boz" Watkins (born April 26, 1970); Lisa "Left Eye" Lopes (born May 27, 1971); and Rozanda "Chilli" Thomas (born February 27, 1971). Watkins and Lopes met in Atlanta late in the 1980s, and Thomas joined shortly thereafter. Each brought something unique to the trio. Watkins, cool and sultry, has an R&B flair; Lopes, somewhat wild, is a straight-up rapper; and Thomas, a romantic, sings smoothly and sweetly.

Released in February 1991, their debut album, *Ooooooh... On the TLC Tip,* quickly spawned a top-ten hit with "Ain't 2

Proud 2 Beg." This they soon followed with "Baby, Baby, Baby" and "What About Your Friends," both of which also reached the Top 10. Another hit followed in 1993 with "Get It Up," from the *Poetic Justice* soundtrack.

Much greater successes followed in 1994 with *CrazySexyCool*, but there were also signs of trouble ahead for TLC. The always volatile Lopes was arrested for setting fire to the house of boyfriend Andre Rison, a football player with the Atlanta Falcons. In the fallout from this incident, Lopes found herself in debt to the tune of $3 million, and thus in 1995 TLC filed for bankruptcy.

On a more positive note, Thomas and Dallas Austin, who had produced both of TLC's albums, became parents of a baby boy in June 1997. But around the same time, the other members of TLC announced that they would not work with Austin due to financial disagreements. **(See original entry on TLC in *Parents Aren't Supposed to Like It*, Volume 3, p. 535.)**

Successes in the wake of *Fanmail*

During the time between albums, Watkins appeared in the film *Belly*, Thomas spent time with her child, and Lopes hosted *The Cut* on MTV. The group released *Fanmail* in February 1999, and soon had a number-one hit with "No Scrubs." More hits followed in 2000 with "Dear Lie" and "Unpretty."

TLC collected a string of awards and nominations through 1999 and 2000. Leading the list were two awards and five nominations at the 2000 Grammy ceremonies, where the group performed "Unpretty" and "No Scrubs." Also during the two-year period they received an American Music Award and nomination; an MTV Video Music Award and five nominations; three MTV Europe Music Award nominations; a Blockbuster Award; five *Soul Train* awards and a nomination; a Brit

---

Where Are They From? The Southeast

Eighteen artists and groups in *Parents Aren't Supposed to Like It*, volumes 4, 5, and 6, hail from the southeastern United States:

Florida
- Backstreet Boys (Orlando)
- Creed (Tallahassee)
- Gloria Estefan (Miami; born in Cuba)
- Enrique Iglesias (Miami; born in Spain)
- Limp Bizkit (Jacksonville)
- Marilyn Manson (Fort Lauderdale)
- Matchbox Twenty (Orlando)
- 'NSync (Orlando)
- Sister Hazel (Gainesville)

Georgia
- Collective Soul (Stockbridge)
- Indigo Girls (Decatur)
- R.E.M. (Athens)
- TLC (Atlanta)

Louisiana
- Mystikal (New Orleans)
- Britney Spears (Kentwood)

Mississippi
- Faith Hill
- LeAnn Rimes (also Texas)

South Carolina
- Hootie and the Blowfish

Award and nomination; a Teen Choice Award; a Kids' Choice Award nomination; and a VH1 Fashion Award nomination.

Going their separate ways?

Despite all these successes, there were signs that members of TLC might be going in their own directions. All of them have spoken out against one another—primarily with Thomas and Watkins on one side, and Lopes on the other—in magazines. Each had her own projects as well: motherhood for Thomas and solo efforts for Lopes and Watkins.

Lopes hit the charts in Britain with "Never Be the Same Again," a collaboration with Melanie C. of the Spice Girls, in March 2000. Later in the year, Watkins contributed "My Getaway" to the soundtrack of *Rugrats in Paris—The Movie*. In fact Watkins, who in December 1999 published a book of poetry called *Thoughts*, may be the busiest member of TLC.

Watkins's struggle with sickle-cell anemia

Watkins has long suffered from sickle-cell anemia, a hereditary disease in which red blood cells assume the shape of a sickle, thus making it difficult for them to move through the blood and deliver oxygen. African Americans are particularly susceptible to the disorder, which affects about one in every 600 black children born in the United States.

In 1996, Watkins became spokesperson for the Sickle Cell Disease Association of America (SCDAA), and in 1999 the group donated twenty-five cents from the sale of every concert ticket to the organization. "I feel very strongly about the need for people of child-bearing age who might have the sickle cell trait to be tested and counseled," Watkins told *Jet* in 1999.

In fact she herself became pregnant early in 2000, by rapper Mack 10, a.k.a. D'Mon Rolison. (The two married in August 2000.) Blood tests showed that her child would not be affected by the disease, but Watkins's pregnancy remained a high-risk one. In October she gave birth to a healthy baby girl named Chase.

Selected Awards

Grammy Award, Best R&B Album, for *CrazySexyCool*, 1995.
Grammy Award, Best R&B Performance by a Duo or Group with Vocal, for "Creep," 1995.
Multi-platinum certification (4 million sales) *Oooooooh . . . On the TLC Tip*, 1996.
MTV Video Music Award, Best Group Video, for "No Scrubs," 1999.
Multi-platinum certification (11 million sales) *CrazySexyCool*, 1999.
Grammy Award, Best R&B Performance by a Duo or Group, for "No Scrubs," 2000.
Grammy Award, Best R&B Album, *Fanmail*, 2000.
American Music Award, Favorite R&B Band/Duo/Group, 2000.
Multi-platinum certification (6 million sales) *Fanmail*, 2000.

Selected Discography

Oooooooh . . . On the TLC Tip (LaFace/Arista), 1991.
CrazySexyCool (LaFace/Arista), 1994.
Fanmail (LaFace/Arista), 1999.

Further Reading

Farley, Christopher John. "The Spicier Girls." *Time,* March 1, 1999, p. 70.

McDonald, Steven. "etc: TLC." *Harper's Bazaar,* April 1999, p. 129.

Rizzo, Monica. "TLC's T-Boz Shares a Diary of Her Pregnancy." *Us,* November 13, 2000, p. 30.

"T-Boz and R&B Group TLC Fight Sickle Cell Through Their Music." *Jet,* November 29, 1999, p. 30.

"TLC: Sexy Trio Back on Top After Bankruptcy." *Jet,* April 12, 1999, p. 60.

Contact Information

LaFace Records
3350 Peachtree Street
Suite 1500
Atlanta, GA 30326-1040

Web Sites

"TLC." *GetMusic.* http://www.getmusic.com/pop/tlc/ (accessed on December 18, 2000).

TLC!!!!!!! http://members.aol.com/Casey35142/TLCMAIN.html (accessed on December 18, 2000).

tlcfanmail.com (official site). http://fanasylum.com/tlc/main.html (accessed on December 18, 2000).

A Tribe Called Quest

American hip-hop group
Formed 1988 in Queens, New York
Disbanded 1998

> "[T]hey produced five albums which gave the hip-hop nation something to think about beyond misogyny and mindless gangsta poses."
>
> –Renee Graham, *Boston Globe*, November 2, 1999

A Tribe Called Quest, in foreground with award. (Archive Photos. Reproduced by permission.)

Though their decade-long run ended in 1998, A Tribe Called Quest will long be remembered as one of the most innovative, intelligent, and creative hip-hop groups of all time. Their first three albums are widely regarded as masterpieces, and some fans and critics maintain that *The Low End Theory* (1991) was the greatest hip-hop record ever. Pioneers of a new style that merged the cool tones of jazz with the hot beat of hip-hop, Tribe constructed their albums as layered masterworks—more like novels or movies than just collections of songs.

At the heart of their music were the lyrics themselves, noted for their philosophical content and their positive message. At a time when figures such as Tupac Shakur and The Notorious B.I.G. promoted anger and violence, Tribe offered something new. In the words of Renee Graham of the *Boston Globe*, writing after the group's breakup, they "gave the hip-hop nation something to think about beyond misogyny [hatred of women] and mindless gangsta poses."

A more intellectual approach

The trio known as A Tribe Called Quest consisted of vocalists Q-Tip (born Jonathan Davis on November 20, 1970) and Phife (born Malik Taylor on November 21, 1970), with Ali Shaheed Muhammad (born August 11, 1970) as DJ. After meeting in high school in Queens, New York, the three started performing together in 1988. They soon found themselves among a rising movement within the hip-hop genre.

This movement was the Native Tongues Posse, a collection of performers and groups, mostly from New York, who emphasized a more intellectual (that is, of the mind) approach to rap than was typical of earlier acts. Among the other members of the informal "posse" were De La Soul, Monie Love, and The Jungle Brothers; but it was Tribe that was destined to make the most impact.

The group had its debut with the 1989 single "Description of a Fool"; then in 1990 Q-Tip made a guest appearance on the hit "Groove Is in the Heart" by Deee-lite . Also in 1990 came the first of the group's highly acclaimed albums, *People's Instinctive Travels and the Paths of Rhythm*.

The first three albums

People's Instinctive Travels has been rightly called a concept album (see sidebar). The album is a musical work that is more than just a collection of songs; rather, the songs are arranged in such a way as to form a larger idea—in this case, the birth, growth, education, and healing of an individual.

Tribe vocalist Q-Tip. (Ken Settle. Reproduced by permission.)

> **"I knew people were sampling jazz musicians, but Q-Tip actually knew who Charles Mingus was."**

The group firmly established its blend of jazz and hip-hop in *The Low End Theory*, an album that showed Tribe's place in the past, present, and future of music. Jazz bassist Ron Carter played on one cut, and another sampled (used parts of) pieces by legendary trumpeter Miles Davis (1926–1991). Referring to one of the most creative and influential composers in the history of jazz, Carter later told *Spin* magazine, "I knew people were sampling jazz musicians, but Q-Tip

Sgt. Pepper and the Concept Album

The Beatles's 1967 release *Sgt. Pepper's Lonely Hearts Club Band* is widely regarded as the greatest rock recording of all time. It is also known as the first "concept album," a work in which the songs are arranged together in such a way as to form a larger idea. However, band members John Lennon (1940–1980), Paul McCartney (1942–), George Harrison (1943–), and Ringo Starr (1940–) laughed off the idea that *Sgt. Pepper* was really a concept album, because the "concept" was a loosely defined one. But it worked.

Later groups, from the Moody Blues (another band from the 1960s "British Invasion") to A Tribe Called Quest, have released their own "concept albums." Sometimes this emerges as a literal story or play, as in *Tommy* (1969) by the Who or Tribe's debut album, *People's Instinctive Travels*. Sometimes the "concept" is just a collection of related ideas, as in the Moody Blues's *A Question of Balance* (1970). Often a musical theme, or certain repeated sounds, help tie together the album, as was the case with Pink Floyd's *Dark Side of the Moon* (1973).

Part of *Sgt. Pepper*'s success can be attributed to the fact that the Beatles did not try too hard to make it a concept album: they just let the pieces come together without forcing them. Many of the songs seem to harken back to another time, an idea emphasized by the band members' costumes on the cover. (In fact the cover, with its array of faces, is almost as widely known as the album itself.) The album is further tied together by the "Sgt. Pepper" theme, which creates the impression that the entire collection of songs is a show put on by a fictional group, Sgt. Pepper's Lonely Hearts Club Band. Near the end of the album is a reprise or return to that theme, followed by "A Day in the Life," often cited by critics as the greatest song of the rock era.

---

actually knew who Charles Mingus [1922–1979] was."

The album also paid tribute to early rap greats such as the Last Poets; sampled a piece from the Chambers Brothers, a 1960s group that blended R&B with rock; and adapted the bass line from "Walk on the Wild Side" by punk pioneer Lou Reed. In 1999, *Spin* included *The Low End Theory*—a work that influenced later artists such as the Fugees and **Wu-Tang Clan** (see entries)—among its "90 Greatest Albums of the '90s."

Two years after *Theory*, Tribe released *Midnight Marauders,* an album built around the idea of a day in the life of the band. Weaving together the various cuts on the album is a futuristic-sounding female voice-over that provides a form of narration.

Embracing Islam

Many critics maintained that *Beats, Rhymes and Life* (1996) lacked the power of its three predecessors. Yet the album, with its message of individual responsibility, still provided a refreshing alternative to the glorification of sex, drugs, and violence that prevailed in much rap music at the time. By the mid-1990s, all three members of Tribe had embraced Islam, or the Muslim faith, which emphasizes devotion to God or Allah. Islam also strongly promotes clean living and observance of daily rituals such as prayers.

Though their shared Islamic faith helped bring them closer together, each group member was growing eager to break out on his own, and *The Love Movement* (1998) would be Tribe's last album. By that time Q-Tip—who changed his given name from Jonathan Davis to Kamal Fareed to reflect his newfound faith—had emerged as the band's frontman. He had further made a name for himself as producer on albums by artists such as **Busta Rhymes** and **Janet Jackson** (see entries), and late in 1999 he released the solo album *Amplified*.

Tribe members go their separate ways

The Q-Tip that emerged on *Amplified*, which yielded a hit single in "Vivrant Thing," was quite a different person from the one known to Tribe fans. His new music emphasized the sexuality that was typical of much hip-hop, and downplayed the intellectual qualities typical of Tribe's work.

Phife, too, went on to a solo career, while Ali joined a hip-hop supergroup of sorts, Lucy Pearl. The latter, which released its eponymous (self-titled) debut album in 2000, consisted of Raphael Saadiq, a former member of Tony! Toni! Tone!; Dawn Robinson of En Vogue; and Ali. Post-Tribe efforts, particularly those of Lucy Pearl, won critical acclaim; but in the eyes of many fans, the greatest music put out by Ali, Q-Tip, and Phife would always be that of Tribe itself.

What made Tribe special?

When Tribe was first starting out, Q-Tip told Dimitri Ehrlich of *Interview* magazine in 1998, "I was shocked that Run DMC was able to do more than singles; I didn't think hip-hop albums could happen. . . . Now it's just expanding every day. . . ."

"I definitely want to see (hip-hop) grow bigger and bigger, but the first thing people have to do is start being themselves. There are too many people duplicating the next man or woman. . . ."

Ehrlich commented that Tribe's albums "hold together as a whole, like classic rock albums," to which Phife said, "I guess one reason we're able to do things like that is because we listen to a lot of different music. Tip will listen to a Beatles album and the way they structure it as far as sequence and everything, and he'll apply it to his own music."

Asked about the future of hip-hop in the next decade, Phife told Ehrlich, "I definitely want to see it grow bigger and bigger, but the first thing people have to do is start being themselves. There are too many people duplicating the next man or woman. . . . If people keep biting each other, the music will just stay in one place, if not drop down. We definitely have to be ourselves, first and foremost."

Selected Awards

Platinum record certification, *The Low End Theory*, 1995.

Platinum record certification, *Midnight Marauders*, 1995.

Gold record certification, *People's Instinctive Travels and the Paths of Rhythm*, 1996.

Platinum record certification, *Beats, Rhymes & Life*, 1998.

Gold record certification, *The Love Movement*, 1998.

Grammy Award nomination, for *The Love Movement*, 1999.

Selected Discography

People's Instinctive Travels and the Paths of Rhythm (Jive), 1990.
The Low End Theory (Jive), 1991.
Midnight Marauders (Jive), 1993.
Beats, Rhymes & Life (Jive), 1996.
The Love Movement (Jive), 1998.

Further Reading

Ehrlich, Dimitri. "Blazing the Other Way." *Interview*, August 1998, p. 36.

Graham, Renee. "In Tribe, An Exploration of Hip-Hop's Potential." *Boston Globe*, November 2, 1999.

Sansevere, John R. and Erica Farber. *Post-Bop Hip-Hop: A Tribe Called Quest*. Racine, Wisconsin: Western Publishing Company, 1993.

Contact Information

Jive Records Corp.
137-139 W. 25th St.
New York, NY 10001

Web Sites

A Tribe Called Quest. http://www.hevanet.com/jonh/tribe (accessed on September 7, 2000).

A Tribe Called Quest at Jive Records (official site). http://www.peeps.com/tribe/index.shtml (accessed on September 7, 2000).

SHANIA TWAIN

Canadian country and pop singer

Born Eileen Regina Edwards on August 28, 1965, in Windsor, Ontario, Canada

Her songs bring together the polish of pop music and the down-home feel of country, a blend that has made Shania Twain one of the biggest stars in music. Twain has won a string of awards, including four Grammys, and her 1997 release *Come on Over* is one of the biggest-selling albums of all time. Nor have Twain's stunning good looks hurt her, as her videos attract almost as much attention as her songs.

Twain's happy marriage to music producer Robert John "Mutt" Lange, sixteen years her senior, seems like the stuff of storybooks. The couple even live in a castle of sorts, or a "mini-castle" as Twain has called it: in the late 1990s, the two purchased a chateau or mansion in Switzerland. But her early life was hardly enviable: raised in poverty, she lost both her parents at age twenty-one, and had to support her three younger siblings. Thus it is with good reason that Shania Twain has been called "the Cinderella of country music."

"On my way"

—Translation of the Ojibwa Indian name *Shania*, adopted by Twain in 1990

Shania Twain. (AP/Wide World Photos. Reproduced by permission.)

Growing up the hard way

"We were really poor," Twain told Brian Johnson of the Canadian magazine *Maclean's*, recalling her childhood, "although I never considered it that bad. We would go for days with just bread and milk and sugar—heat it up in a pot. I'd judge other kids' wealth by their lunches. If a kid had [store-bought] baked goods, that was like, oh, they must be rich."

Eileen Regina Edwards, the second of three daughters of Sharon and Clarence Edwards, was born in the Canadian city of Windsor, Ontario. Her parents divorced when she was still a small child, and her mother moved the family to the remote town of Timmins, some 500 miles (800 kilometers) north of the U.S. border.

There her mother married Jerry Twain, a Native American of the Ojibwa nation. Jerry adopted all three of Sharon's daughters, and he and Sharon had two more sons. Jerry had a hard time supporting the family on his income as a lumberman, but he refused to go on welfare, and the Twains struggled to get by.

Supporting a family

From the time she was three, young Eileen would sing along to music at a jukebox in a local diner. Her younger sister Carrie-Ann later recalled, "Shania would always be singing, even just walking down the street. I'd be embarrassed."

By the time she was eight, she was already earning money as a singer in a local club, and as a teenager, Eileen's work as a singer increased. Sometimes she had to walk home alone late at night, and on those occasions, she would carry a rock in her pocket in case anyone tried to hurt her. Not all her work was behind a microphone: for several summers, she worked with her father and his crew, and during this time she learned to use an axe and chain saw. She also helped take care of the three younger children, since her older sister had left home long before.

As hard as Eileen's life was, it was about to get harder. In 1987, when she was twenty-one years old, her mother and stepfather were killed in a car crash. Suddenly she was left all alone to take care of her siblings, so to earn an income she went to work as a singer.

On her way to the top

Eileen landed a job at Deerhurst, an expensive resort in Huntsville, Ontario. In addition to singing, she played an Indian in a show that dramatized the area's past. With her good looks and talent, she soon attracted attention, but she was initially shy about her appearance—something that would come as a surprise to the many fans who later watched her videos.

By 1990, Eileen's situation had eased considerably: her younger siblings were now old enough to support themselves, and she got a contract to record an album. It was then that she changed her name to Shania (pronounced shuh-NY-uh), which in the Ojibwa language means "On my way."

Producer, cowriter, friend, and husband

Twain's early work attracted little attention from American audiences, but that too was about to change. In 1993, she got a call from R.J. "Mutt" Lange, who had seen the video of her song "What Made You Say That" from her self-titled debut album. He had already established a solid track record as producer for rock acts such as AC/DC, the Cars, Def Leppard, Foreigner, and Bryan Adams, but Twain later said she had no idea who he was at the time.

Over the course of many months, the two talked on the phone, becoming friends and writing songs that would appear on her 1995 blockbuster *The Woman in Me*. Soon friendship turned to something much more, and in December 1993, Twain and Lange were married.

With Lange's help, Twain got a contract with Mercury Records' Nashville division and recorded *The Woman in Me*. The album consisted almost entirely of songs by Twain and Lange, and Lange's production style showed evidence of a strong rock and pop influence. Not only were the drum beats more pronounced and the guitar licks more dominant than in most country music, but the songs themselves had a catchy, upbeat style familiar to Top 40 audiences.

Country and controversy

During the early 1990s, country music was coming back into style with a larger audience, expanding its boundaries and enjoying the kind of record sales that country music pioneers such as Hank Williams (1923–1953) or Patsy Cline (1932–1963; see sidebar in **LeAnn Rimes** entry) could hardly have imagined. In part this was because new country stars such as Twain and **Garth Brooks** (see entry) were broadening their approach, bringing elements of pop and rock into their music.

This did not sit well with old-school country fans. Nor did the fact that Twain sold 11 million albums without touring: normally singers have to put in long hours on the road, promoting their albums with a grueling series of concert dates, but Twain shot to the top of the charts without leaving her home. In many people's minds, she was an overnight success who had not paid her dues.

In fact Twain was, to borrow an old expression, "An overnight success that took thirty years." She had paid her dues, playing bars and clubs and concerts—only she had done it all before she was famous. Nor could anyone look at her early life and claim that her road to success had been an easy one.

A new record—and new sales records

In 1996, Twain recorded the single "God Bless the Child," and donated all the proceeds to two charities: Kids Cafe/Second Harvest Food Bank in the United States, and the Canadian Living Foundation in her home country, both of which provide meals to underprivileged children. As a child, Twain told *Redbook,* "I was that hungry kid. My goal is to save kids the humiliation, the anguish of feeling inferior."

Come on Over, which she backed up with a long-awaited tour, yielded eight hit singles, including "You're Still the One" and "That Don't Impress Me Much." Twain became the first woman ever to have two albums in a row that sold more than 10 million copies in the United States, and worldwide the album sold more than 26 million copies. As of mid-2000, *Come on Over* was tied with *The Beatles* (sometimes known as "The White Album," 1968) and *The Bodyguard* soundtrack by **Whitney Houston** (see entry) as the eighth best-selling record of all time.

"I was that hungry kid. My goal is to save kids the humiliation, the anguish of feeling inferior."

Fans of Twain had expected a new album, her first in more than three years, by Christmas 2000; but in December of that year Twain announced that they would have to wait a little longer. She was indeed working on a new album, she said, but she wanted to focus on crafting the songs, rather than rush to get a CD to the stores by Christmas. In April 2001, she and Lange announced that they had something much more important than an album in the works: their first child, with a due date some time in the summer.

Selected Awards

(With R. J. "Mutt" Lange, producer), Grammy Award, Best Country Album, for *The Woman in Me,* 1995.

Multi-platinum certification (11 million sales), *The Woman in Me,* 1998.

(With R. J. "Mutt" Lange, cowriter), Grammy Award, Best Country Song, for "You're Still the One," 1998.

Grammy Award, Best Female Country Vocal Performance, for "You're Still the One," 1998.

Platinum certification, *Shania Twain,* 1999.

(With R. J. "Mutt" Lange, cowriter), Grammy Award, Best Country Song, for "Come on Over," 1999.

Grammy Award, Best Female Country Vocal Performance, for "Man! I Feel Like a Woman!," 1999.

Multi-platinum certification (17 million sales), *Come on Over,* 2000.

Best Female Artist and Best Female Country Artist, American Music Awards, 2000.

Entertainer of the Year, Country Music Awards, 2000.

Selected Discography

Shania Twain (Mercury Nashville), 1993.
The Woman in Me (Mercury Nashville), 1995.
Come on Over (Mercury Nashville), 1997.

Further Reading

Buchalter, Gail. "Now I Know I Can't Fix Everything" (interview). *Parade,* July 21, 1996, p. 8.

Gray, Scott. *On Her Way: The Shania Twain Story.* New York: Ballantine Books, 1998.

Handelman, David. "She's Still the One." *Redbook,* December 1999, p. 114.

Hedegaard, Erik. "Shania Twain" (interview and cover story). *Rolling Stone,* September 3, 1998, p. 52.

Johns, Michael-Anne. *Shania Twain.* Kansas City, Missouri: Andrews McMeel Publishing, 1999.

Johnson, Brian. "Cinderella of Country: Shania Twain." *Maclean's,* December 18, 1995, p. 50.

Keeley, Jennifer. *Women Pop Stars.* San Diego, California: Lucent Books, 2001.

Contact Information

Mercury Nashville Records
66 Music Square West
Nashville, TN 37203

Web Sites

"Shania Twain." *Mercury Records.* http://www.mercurynashville.com/shaniatwain/welcome.html (accessed on September 8, 2000).

Shania Twain Online Fan Club. http://www.shania.org (accessed on September 8, 2000).

Shania Twain Supersite. http://www.shania.com (accessed on September 8, 2000).

U2

Irish alternative rock band
Formed 1976 in Dublin, Ireland

> "The way you write music is at once humdrum ... and at the same time you're waiting for a miracle, or else it's just the sum of the parts. And yesterday we got this great gift of this melody...."
>
> –Bono, on writing songs for *All That You Can't Leave Behind*, *Rolling Stone*, August 17, 2000

(L–R) The Edge, Larry Mullen, Bono, and Adam Clayton. (AP/Wide World Photos. Reproduced by permission.)

Rather than simply settle into rock-star semi-retirement after their monster hit *The Joshua Tree* (1987), the members of U2 did a surprising thing: they reinvented themselves. The 1990s saw a series of releases that combined electronic sounds with the powerful guitars and rhythm section that had propelled U2 to the top. Results were mixed, and critics wondered how the group would handle the role of rock's elder statesman. In 2000, a new album and some inspired activism on the part of frontman Bono suggested the future of U2.

In 1976, drummer Larry Mullen (born October 31, 1961) formed a band at his high school in Dublin, Ireland, recruiting vocalist and guitarist Bono (Paul Hewson; born May 10, 1960); guitarist The Edge (David Evans; born August 8, 1961); and bassist Adam Clayton (born March 13, 1960). They soon attracted attention in their homeland, but remained unknown in the United States when Island Records signed them in the late 1970s.

Boy (1980) included a minor hit, "I Will Follow," and *October* (1981) introduced such memorable tracks as "Gloria" and "I Through a Brick Through a Window." But it was *War* (1983), with "New Years Day" (their first Top 40 hit) and "Sunday Bloody Sunday," that really showed what the group could do. *The Unforgettable Fire* (1984) propelled them to superstardom with their tribute to Martin Luther King, Jr., "Pride (In the Name of Love)"; yet nothing prepared them or the world for the explosive success of *The Joshua Tree*.

The album yielded two number-one hits, "With or Without You" and "I Still Haven't Found What I'm Looking For," as well as additional hits in "Where the Streets Have No Name" and "In God's Country." Yet in the eyes of many critics and some fans, the group faltered on the double album *Rattle and Hum* (1988), which was accompanied by a film of the same title.

U2 entered the 1990s with an entirely different sound on *Achtung Baby* (1991), which yielded the hits "Mysterious Ways" and "One." The group continued to explore new musical territory in *Zooropa* (1993), but sales were lower than for any studio effort since *October*. The mid-1990s saw the band again reinventing themselves with *Original Soundtrack, Vol. 1* (1995), released under the name "The Passengers" with Brian Eno; a collaboration by Mullen and Clayton on *Mission: Impossible Soundtrack* (1996); and the next group album, *Pop,* in the following year. **(See original entry on U2 in *Parents Aren't Supposed to Like It,* Volume 1, p. 190.)**

Selecting from a hundred songs

The idea behind *Pop* was to make fun of the commercialism of rock music, but with a PopMart tour sponsored by Pepsi and other corporations, it was a little hard for some people to see the joke. Still, *Pop* and its accompanying tour were commercial successes, as was a greatest hits package, *U2 The Best of 1980–1990* (1998). Also in 1998, Bono cowrote the screenplay for *The Million Dollar Hotel,* a film starring Mel Gibson. Released in 2000, *Hotel* included seven new songs by U2.

October 2000 saw the release of *All That You Can't Leave Behind* and its accompanying single, "Beautiful Day." The latter hit the Top 40, and in November U2's album topped the U.S. *Billboard* charts. As for the music, it represented countless hours in the studio as U2 experimented with different sounds. The Edge told Chris Heath of *Rolling Stone* that the group had tried about a hundred songs before selecting the ones that appeared on the album, but their efforts were rewarded in a release that showed U2 still capable of the artistic mastery displayed on earlier classics.

The year of Jubilee

In the *All That You Can't Leave Behind* sessions, the group had recorded a song variously called "Stir My Soul" and "Jubilee." The track did not make it onto the album, but Bono remained intrigued with the idea of jubilee—an Old Testament practice whereby every forty-nine years, debts were forgiven and slaves freed. "It was a time of grace," he told *Rolling Stone.* "Beautiful idea, really."

Bono put this concept into action with his efforts toward Third World debt relief. (The term Third World dates back to the Cold War [1945–1991], when there were three groups of countries: the United States and its allies; the Soviet Union and its allies; and the rest of the world. The latter, called the Third World, consisted primarily of poor countries in Africa, Asia, and Latin America.) He was certainly not the first rock star to become politically active, but Bono set himself apart: rather than simply latch on to a few slogans and let himself get carried away by emotion, he devoted himself to serious study.

"There are people much better qualified to do this than me. But as it happens, we live in this culture where people think pop stars and film stars are more important than nurses and firemen. I'm prepared to work with that. But I'm as skeptical as anyone would be about celebrities and causes. . . ."

"Sadly," he joked with Susan Dominus of the *New York Times,* "I do my homework. I've got a soft spot for the boring minutiae [details]. I read the Charter of the United Nations before meeting with [UN Secretary-General] Kofi Annan. I read the Meltzer Report, and then I'll read C. Fred Bergsten's defense of institutions like the World Bank and the IMF [International Monetary Fund]. It's embarrassing to admit."

Bono has met with powerful figures ranging from Pope John Paul II to U.S. Senator Jesse Helms, who he said "felt it as a burden on a spiritual level" to do something for poor countries in Africa. Reflecting on his role as advocate for Third World debt relief in the *New York Times,* Bono said, "There are people much better qualified to do this than me. But as it happens, we live in this culture where people think pop stars and film stars are more important than nurses and firemen. I'm prepared to work with that. But I'm as skeptical as anyone would be about celebrities and causes. . . ."

By the end of 2000, "Beautiful Day" had hit the Top 10, and in February 2001 U2 performed the song at the Grammy Awards ceremonies. They did not just come to the ceremonies to perform, however: the group walked away with three Grammys, all for "Beautiful Day." The following month saw a new hit, "Walk On," climbing the Top 40 charts, and in June, Bono gave the commencement (graduation) speech at Harvard University.

Selected Awards

Grammy Award, Best Rock Performance by a Duo or Group with Vocal, for *Achtung Baby,* 1993.

Grammy Award, Best Alternative Music Album, for *Zooropa,* 1994.

Multi-platinum certification (10 million sales), *The Joshua Tree,* 1995.

Multi-platinum certification (5 million sales), *Rattle and Hum,* 1995.

Multi-platinum certification (4 million sales), *War,* 1995.

Multi-platinum certification (8 million sales), *Achtung Baby,* 1997.

Grammy Award nomination, Best Rock Album, for *Pop,* 1998.

Grammy Awards, Record of the Year, Best Rock Performance by a Duo or Group with Vocal, and Song of the Year, all for "Beautiful Day," 2001.

Selected Discography

Achtung Baby (Island), 1991.
Zooropa (Island), 1993.
Pop (Island), 1997.
All That You Can't Leave Behind (Island), 2000.

Further Reading

Dominus, Susan. "Questions for Bono: Relief Pitcher." *New York Times Magazine,* October 8, 2000, p. 27.

Fox, Darrin. "Basic Instincts." *Guitar Player,* January 2001, p. 100.

Heath, Chris. "U2: 'It's About Self-Respect.'" *Rolling Stone,* August 17, 2000, p. 43.

Mundy, Chris. "People of the Year: U2." *Rolling Stone,* December 14-21, 2000, p. 96.

Sawyers, June Skinner. *The Complete Guide to Celtic Music: From the Highland Bagpipe and Riverdance to U2 and Enya.* London: Aurum, 2000.

Stokes, Niall. *Into the Heart: The Stories Behind Every U2 Song.* New York: Thunder's Mouth Press, 1997.

Contact Information

Principle Management
30-32 Sir John Rogersons Quay
Dublin 2
Ireland

Web Sites

In the Name of Love U2 Fanzine. http://www.geocities.com/inthenameofloveu2fanzine/ (accessed on December 18, 2000).

U2.com (official site). http://www.u2.com (accessed on December 18, 2000).

U2 Online. http://www.u2-online.de/ (accessed on December 18, 2000).

U2 World. http://hem.passagen.se/u2world/index2.htm (accessed on December 18, 2000).

THE WALLFLOWERS

American alternative rock band
Formed 1990 in Los Angeles, California

> "I just have to believe that there are people who don't care where I grew up or how I grew up or what my parents were like."
>
> –Jakob Dylan, *Rolling Stone*, October 26, 2000

First row (sitting), L–R: Michael Ward, Rami Jaffee. Second row, L–R: Mario Calire, Greg Richling, Jakob Dylan. (Archive Photos. Reproduced by permission.)

Part of the Wallflowers' story is the fact that frontman Jakob Dylan's father is one of the most influential figures in the history of music (see sidebar on Bob Dylan with **Beck** entry). But that is far from the whole story: Jakob has never tried to coast off of Bob's fame, and *Bringing Down the Horse* (1996) became a huge hit on its own merits. The group followed their smash success with years of relentless touring, and finally in October 2000 released a followup, *Breach,* which included the hit "Sleepwalker."

Jakob (born December 9, 1969) briefly attended art school in New York City before realizing that he wanted to be a musician himself. During this time he wrote his first song, "6th Avenue Heartache." In 1989 he formed a band with himself on vocals and guitar, Rami Jaffee (born 1969) on keyboard, Tobi Miller on guitar, Barrie Maguire on bass, and Peter Janowitz on drums. Originally called the Apples, they renamed themselves after a photographer made a passing comment while shooting pictures of the band lined up against a wall.

The group paid their dues playing at small clubs in Los Angeles, including a longstanding gig at Canter's Delicatessen, and eventually they hooked up with manager Andrew Slater, whose other clients would include **Fiona Apple** and **Macy Gray** (see entries). Slater helped them get a deal with Virgin Records, but despite critical praise, *The Wallflowers* (1992) sold poorly. Eventually Dylan realized that the Wallflowers and Virgin were not a good fit, and he parted ways with the label.

During those difficult days of the early to mid-1990s, Dylan saw the entire band—except for Jaffee—depart as well. He then formed a new ensemble with Michael Ward (born 1967) on guitar; high-school friend Greg Richling (born 1970) on bass; and Matt Chamberlain on drums. (After the recording of *Bringing Down the Horse*, Dylan replaced Chamberlain with Mario Calire, born June 24, 1973.)

Starting practically from scratch, the band recorded a demo that included "6th Avenue Heartache," and on the strength of it Slater was able to get a deal with Interscope Records. As "6th Avenue Heartache" shot to the Top 10 in late 1996, a surprising thing happened: after years of plugging away in obscurity, the Wallflowers were suddenly the "new" sensation. **(See original entry on the Wallflowers in *Parents Aren't Supposed to Like It*, Volume 1, p. 199.)**

Playing every city there is to play

Bringing Down the Horse yielded three more hits: "One Headlight," which reached the Top 5 in 1997; "The Difference"; and the top-ten "Three Marlenas," which hit the charts in 1998, nearly two years after the album's release. The group also received numerous awards and nominations in 1997 and 1998. Some of them had more to do with Dylan's good looks than with the music—*People* named him "Sexiest Rock Star" in 1997, for instance—but two Grammys and a nomination in 1998 showed just how far the Wallflowers had come.

> "Almost every day off we had, we booked a gig somewhere on our own. We would drive way out of the tour route to do our own gigs. We played every city there is to play, shook every hand there is to shake."

Meanwhile the group played a seemingly endless series of engagements—275 shows in 1997 alone. On tour with the **Counting Crows** (see entry), Calire told *Rolling Stone,* "almost every day off we had, we booked a gig somewhere on our own. We would drive way out of the tour route to do our own gigs. We played every city there is to play, shook every hand there is to shake."

Out of the shadow

After two and a half years, the Wallflowers needed a break. Dylan took five months off with his wife, Paige, and their three sons, the last of whom was born in September 1999. Then, having rested, he was ready to start recording. Therefore, as David Fricke wrote in *Rolling Stone,* he "rented a small house in Los Angeles, outfitted it as a demo studio, and put in workingman's hours, eight to five, trying to find a new, clear voice in his writing."

Joe Strummer, Topper Headon, Paul Simonon, and Mick Jones. (Corbis Corporation. Reproduced by permission.)

The Clash

Jakob Dylan has cited the Clash's *London Calling* (1979) as his favorite album, and he is far from the only artist influenced by this powerful British band. The punkish, stripped-down sound of

Breach, which includes a guest spot by Elvis Costello, shows that the Wallflowers' musical range and sense of humor have expanded greatly. Fricke described the video of "Sleepwalker" as "a parody of pop-music videos in which Jakob vogues his way through a succession of exaggerated pained-artist, babe-magnet scenarios."

Having established a name for himself as a musician, Dylan is much more inclined to discuss his father, though still in a veiled fashion. Fricke wrote that "Jakob smiles—broadly—when asked how it might be for his sons if they, in turn, follow him into the family business. 'I don't think it's comparable [to following Bob], let's put it that way,' he says with a rich laugh. 'I anticipate that working within my shadow is not going to be that big of an issue.'"

Selected Awards

MTV Video Music Award nominations, Viewer's Choice, Best Group, and Best New Artist, 1997.
Multi-platinum certification (4 million sales), *Bringing Down the Horse,* 1997.
Grammy Awards, Best Rock Performance by a Duo or Group with Vocal; and (Dylan only) Best Rock Song (Songwriter), for "One Headlight," 1998.

Parents Aren't Supposed to Like It

Blink-182, Everclear, and Green Day suggests a Clash influence, as does the reggae-rock sound of **Smash Mouth** and **Sugar Ray.** And the radical politics of **Rage Against the Machine** certainly calls to mind that of the group that billed itself as "the only band that matters."

Formed in 1976, the Clash emerged on the scene at the same time as the Sex Pistols, but with their reggae and ska influences, they were never just punk rockers. Also, they were much better musicians than most punk bands, as they proved on their explosive debut album in 1977. Soon after *The Clash,* the band's lineup solidified: Joe Strummer (born John Mellor) on vocals and rhythm guitar; Mick Jones on lead guitar and vocals; Paul Simonon on bass; and Nicky "Topper" Headon on drums.

The band went through growing pains with *Give 'Em Enough Rope* (1978), but in the following year released one of the great recordings of all time: *London Calling,* a double album that included the track "Train in Vain," their first hit. They followed this with the bizarre *Sandinista!,* released in late 1980, which was one of the few triple studio albums in history.

Ironically, the album that brought the group mainstream success, *Combat Rock* (1982)—which yielded the hits "Rock the Casbah" and "Should I Stay or Should I Go?"—would be their last. Strummer and Jones came to a parting of the ways, and with a new lineup Strummer released *Cut the Crap* (1985), a disappointing record that hardly deserved to be called a Clash album. Jones went on to continued success with his own band, Big Audio Dynamite. Strummer, after disbanding the Clash for good in 1985, made several solo albums and soundtracks.

Grammy Award nomination, Best Rock Song, for "The Difference," 1998.

American Music Award nominations, Favorite Band Rock/Pop, Favorite New Artist, and Favorite Album Rock/Pop, 1998.

Selected Discography

The Wallflowers (Virgin), 1992.
Bringing Down the Horse (Interscope), 1996.
Breach (Interscope), 2000.

Further Reading

Bozza, Anthony. "Wallflower in Bloom." *Us,* November 6, 2000, p. 58.

Fricke, David. "The Confessions of Jakob Dylan: A Wallflower's Coming Out." *Rolling Stone,* October 26, 2000, p. 44.

Swartley, Ariel. "Overcoming Success." *New York Times Upfront,* November 27, 2000, p. 24.

Wild, David. "Q&A: Jakob Dylan." *Rolling Stone,* January 22, 1998, p. 24.

Contact Information

Interscope Records
70R Woodland Ave.
San Rafael, CA 94901

Web Sites

Fork in the Road. http://www.geocities.com/SunsetStrip/Lounge/3922/ (accessed on December 22, 2000).

The Wallflowers (official site). http://www.the-wallflowers.com (accessed on December 22, 2000).

The Wallflowers Network. http://www.the-wallflowers.net (accessed on December 22, 2000).

Wu-Tang Clan

American rap group
Formed 1991 in Staten Island, New York

The Wu-Tang Clan is known for a hard-driving brand of hip-hop, characterized by lyrics that are sometimes angry, sometimes humorous. Their music is a mix of highly complicated rhymes, rhythms, and instrumentation; in fact, there is little about this nine-man ensemble that is *not* complicated.

The members of Wu-Tang put out a seemingly limitless number of solo albums while maintaining their affiliation with the larger unit. That unit is held together in part by a shared philosophy, as complex as their music, that brings together Chinese martial arts, Islam, and chess.

A group of individuals

Early in the 1990s, eight young MCs—Masta Killa, a.k.a. Elgin Turner, joined later—formed a group in Staten Island, New York. Each of them had begun work in the music business as individuals, and each had experienced frustrations in trying to land a major record deal. Therefore they decided to come together as one without losing their individual identities as performers.

> "The Wu, you see, is not so much a (nine)-member rap group from Staten Island as it is a chaotic way of life."
>
> —Anthony Bozza, *Rolling Stone*, November 26, 1998

Method Man of Wu-Tang Clan. (Photo by Steve Granitz. WireImage.com. Reproduced by permission.)

Symbolic of that identity were the names each member had chosen for himself, names they would continue to use as members of Wu-Tang. There was Prince Rakeem or The RZA (a.k.a. Robert Diggs; born January 12, 1968); his cousin Genius or GZA (Gary Grice); Method Man (Clifford Smith); U-God (Lamont Hawkins); Inspektah Deck (Jason Hunter); Raekwon (Corey Woods); Ghostface Killa (Dennis Coles); and Ol' Dirty Bastard or ODB (Russell Jones).

A plan and a philosophy

From the beginning, The RZA (he went by the name Prince Rakeem at the time) had a strategy in mind: he put together a business plan, and together the group members established Wu-Tang Records. Pooling their modest resources, they were able to finance the production of a single called "Protect Ya Neck." Initially they printed only 500 copies, but as the record (it was on vinyl, not a CD) circulated among college radio disk jockeys, Wu-Tang rapidly attracted notice.

The group's name is taken from the mythology of the Shaolin kung-fu masters from medieval China, who spoke of a "liquid sword" called Wu-Tang that could slay all their enemies.

The single also got the attention of executives at Loud Records, who in 1993 released *Enter the Wu-Tang (36 Chambers)*. The album exposed listeners to a new sound in rap, somewhere between the threatening style of gangsta artists such as Tupac Shakur on the one hand, and the gentler jazz-influenced sounds of **A Tribe Called Quest** (see entry) on the other.

Enter the Wu-Tang also presented the quirky Wu-Tang philosophy. The group's name is taken from the mythology of the Shaolin kung-fu masters from medieval China, who spoke of a "liquid sword" called Wu-Tang that could slay all their enemies. Group members espoused the belief systems that went with the study of martial arts, particularly an emphasis on self-control and inner harmony, and frequently quoted from ancient Chinese texts such as the *The Art of War* by Sun-tzu (300s B.C.) In addition, most members adopted the Muslim faith. Finally, Wu-Tang members regarded the game of chess as a semi-spiritual exercise, and all became avid players.

Group and solo hits

The album spawned a hit single, "C.R.E.A.M. (Cash Rules Everything Around Me"), and *Enter the Wu-Tang* went on to enormous commercial and critical success. Around this time, group members began bombarding the listening public with solo album after solo album. Among the most widely acclaimed of these were *Only Built for Cuban Linx . . .* (1995) by Raekwon; *Liquid Swords* (1995) by Genius; and Ghostface Killa's *Ironman* (1996).

The group's follow-up album, *Wu-Tang Forever* (1997), likewise got the attention of fans, selling more than 4 million copies and earning a Grammy nomination. The nomination was a particular triumph: just a few years before, it would have been hard to imagine a group such as Wu-Tang, with its hardcore lyrics and music, enjoying this sort

The Wu-Tang Clan perform at the BET (Black Entertainment Television) Harlem Block Party in September 2000. (AP/Wide World Photos. Reproduced by permission.)

of recognition from the musical mainstream. But critics disliked *Wu-Tang Forever,* a double-CD effort that many said would have been much better if the best tracks had been released on a single CD.

More problems followed. Wu-Tang abruptly dropped out of a tour with **Rage Against the Machine** (see entry) in the summer of 1997, and though they gave no reason for their action, many observers believed it had something to do with charges that several group members had beaten a record company employee. Over the next few months, Raekwon, Genius, Inspektah Deck, and Method Man all had their scrapes with the law; but none compared to the troubled record of ODB.

ODB's troubles

During a two-year period beginning in November 1997, ODB was in and out of court on a series of charges, from not paying child support to drunken and disorderly behavior to attempted murder. He was acquitted on the last charge, but after skipping a court appearance in November 1999, he was sentenced to one year in a drug-rehabilitation facility, along with three years' probation.

On March 2, 1998, there was a brief break in the almost continuous stream of bad news relating to ODB. Leaving the group's recording studio, he saw a four-year-old girl trapped under a car that had hit her, and he and several others rushed to her assistance, lifting the car off of her. Later, he visited her in the hospital.

Time magazine proclaimed him "Citizen of the Week" for his actions, but it also reported the other newsworthy event in ODB's life that week, which occurred at the Grammy Awards on March 4. The Best Rap Recording Grammy had gone to **Puff Daddy** (see entry) rather than Wu-Tang, and in protest ODB rushed the stage. "Puffy is good," he announced to the stunned audience, "but Wu-Tang is the best!" He later apologized for his behavior.

Wu-Tang rolls on

Despite their challenges, Wu-Tang rolled on, releasing *Swarm 1* (1998) and *Wu-Chronicles* (1999), both compilations of various band members' works. Then there were the solo albums: in October 1998, *Rolling Stone* reported that as many as twenty-four new releases from various band members would appear in the next eighteen months.

"The Wu, you see," wrote Anthony Bozza in *Rolling Stone*, "is not so much a ten-member rap group from Staten Island"—Bozza was mistakenly adding Cappadonna, a rapper who has sometimes performed with the group, to the lineup—"as it is a chaotic [dizzying] way of life. Wu-Tangers release solo albums on a distracting array of different labels; then there's Wu Wear, their national clothing line (with its own store), and the usual video shoots, recording sessions, and shows. Most of the Clan's members have children, and all of them make time for their families. Life is hectic."

Wu-Tang went on tour in 2000, and Jim Harrington of the *Contra Costa Times* called theirs "the best hip-hop tour of the summer." After seeing their show at the Maritime Hall in San Francisco, he observed that "The scariest part of the show" was the fact that ODB, still under detention in a drug-rehabilitation facility, "wasn't even in the house. . . . When he gets out and gets back fully in the fold, things could get really out of control for the Wu-Tang Clan."

In October 2000, ODB escaped from rehab. With the police hot on his trail, he even dared to appear on stage with the rest of the group, and vowed that he would "live on birdseed," if necessary, to elude the law. Instead of sticking to his promise, however, he showed up at a Philadelphia McDonald's, and was promptly arrested by a policewoman who spotted him signing autographs. Meanwhile, the group released *The W,* and the Wu-Tang gang rolled on.

Selected Awards

Platinum certification, *Enter the Wu-Tang (36 Chambers),* 1995.
Multi-platinum certification (4 million sales), *Wu-Tang Forever,* 1997.
Grammy nomination, Best Rap Recording, for *Wu-Tang Forever,* 1997.
Platinum certification, *The W,* 2000.

Parents Aren't Supposed to Like It

Selected Discography

Enter the Wu-Tang (36 Chambers) (Loud), 1993.
Wu-Tang Forever (Loud), 1997.
Swarm 1 (Loud), 1998.
Wu-Chronicles (Wu-Tang Records), 1999.
The W (Wu-Tang Records), 2000.

Further Reading

Bozza, Anthony. "Wu-Tang Clan Works the Phones." *Rolling Stone,* November 26, 1998, p. 87.

Breithaupt, Jeff. "Wu-Tang Clan, You Da Man!" *National Post,* April 29, 2000, p. 3.

"Citizen of the Week." *Time,* March 9, 1998, p. 53.

Diehl, Matt. "Wu World Order." *Rolling Stone,* October 15, 1998, p. 23.

Harrington, Jim. "Wu-Tang Clan Woos Adoring Audience." *Contra Costa Times* (Walnut Creek, CA), August 14, 2000, p. D-2.

Morris, Chris. "Hot Rap Act Wu-Tang Clan Runs into Troubled Waters." *Billboard,* September 20, 1997, p. 1.

Contact Information

Priority Records
6430 Sunset Boulevard
Los Angeles, CA 90028

Web Sites

Wu-Tang.com (official site). http://www.wu-tang.com (accessed on February 6, 2001).

Wu-Tang.net. http://www.wu-tang.net/ (accessed on September 7, 2000).

Web Sites

Listed are Web sites about recording or various aspects of the music industry. Included are short annotations, or explanatory notes, for each. Please note: Readers should be reminded that Internet addresses are subject to change.

All Music Guide. http://allmusic.com (accessed on February 1, 2001). A highly useful general site, with information on genres and artists, as well as a glossary of a music terms.

Altculture. http://www.altculture.com (accessed on February 9, 2001). A helpful encyclopedia of popular culture.

Billboard. http://www.billboard.com (accessed on February 1, 2001). One of the leading industry publications, home of the famous *Billboard* charts.

CD Now. http://www.cdnow.com (accessed on February 1, 2001). This is a commercial site—-in other words, it exists for the purpose of selling albums—-but it is also a highly valuable resource, providing users with the opportunity to hear short segments from literally thousands of songs.

Grammy Awards. http://www.grammy.com (accessed on February 9, 2001). Web site of the National Academy of Recording Arts and Sciences, and of its prestigious awards.

Record Labels on the Web. http://www.rlabels.com (accessed on February 8, 2001). More than five thousand links to record-label Web pages, as well as information on the music business. (Some of the language is R-rated, but the content is valuable.)

Recording Industry Association of America (RIAA). http://www.riaa.org (accessed on February 1, 2001). Home of the organization that certifies gold and platinum records, with a searchable database of gold and platinum awards.

Rock on the Net. http://www.rockonthenet.com (accessed on February 1, 2001). A very user-friendly site with in-depth biographical information on more than a hundred artists, as well as databases on topics such as awards and artists' birthdays.

Rolling Stone. http://www.rollingstone.com (accessed on February 1, 2001). The most popular publication on rock and pop music. Most notable is a database containing a vast array of information on virtually every artist from the 1950s to today.

Soul Train. http://www.soultraintv.com (accessed on February 1, 2001). Home of the famous TV show and its awards.

The Source. http://www.thesource.com (accessed on February 1, 2001). The leading rap music publication, complete with articles, artist information, and sound and video clips.

Spin. http://www.spin.com (accessed on February 1, 2001). An interesting alternative to *Rolling Stone.* Spin is much smaller, and appears monthly instead of weekly, but its journalists tend to be less predictable than those of its major competitor.

Wall of Sound. http://wallofsound.go.com (accessed on February 9, 2001). A good general site in a vein similar to *All Music Guide,* but this one is less like an encyclopedia and more like a commercial site. Includes video and sound clips that change regularly.

INDEX

Italic type indicates volume numbers; **boldface** type indicates entries featured in *Parents Aren't Supposed to Like It*, Volumes 4, 5, and 6 and their page numbers; (ill.) indicates photographs.

A

A & M Records *1:* 169; *3:* 449, 549, 550, 563, 628, 629
Aaliyah *4:* 128; *5:* 224, 225, 226, 226 (ill.)
Aaliyah 5: 226
Abbey Road 6: 356
Abbott, Darrell "Dimebag" *3:* 491
Abbott, Jacqueline *2:* 225
Abbott, Vinnie Paul *3:* 490, 491
Abbruzzese, Dave *6:* 332
Abraxas 6: 370
Abruzzese, Dave *1:* 116
Abu-Jamal, Mumia *6:* 352
Achtung Baby 6: 443
"Adagio for Strings" *6:* 342
Adams, Bryan *6:* 414

Adams, Victoria *5:* 171
"Addiction" *6:* 302
"Adia" *5:* 283
"A.D.I.D.A.S." *5:* 242
Adler, Steven *3:* 474, 475
Adore 6: 396, 397
The Adventures of Joe Dirt 5: 233
Aerosmith *2:* 309, 404; *3:* 466, 468; *5:* 232 (ill.), 251; *6:* 303 (ill.)
Afghan Whigs *1:* 7-10
African art forms *2:* 304
African-American art forms *2:* 303
Afrika Bambaataa *2:* 304, 308
Afros *2:* 408
After 7 *3:* 508

Aftermath Entertainment (label) *2:* 331, 335, 336
Age Ain't Nothing But a Number 5: 226
Aguilera, Christina *4:* **1** (ill.), **1-4**, 3 (ill.), 40, 55, 103, 130, 133; *6:* 314, 408
AIDS (Acquired Immune Deficiency Syndrome) *2:* 339, 341, 413; *4:* 124; *5:* 207–208, 283
"Ain't 2 Proud 2 Beg" *6:* 428–429
Ajile *2:* 315
Aladdin Sane 2: 219, 232
Alanis Unplugged 5: 161
Alaska musicians *6:* 322

xlv

Albarn, Damon 2:227 (ill.), 228-229
Albert, Nate 5: 292, 293
Albini, Steve 1: 50, 98; 2: 239, 240
Alexakis, Art 4: 141 (ill.), 141–144, 143 (ill.)
Ali 6: 401
Alice in Chains 1: 11 (ill.), 12-15; 3: 469
Alice Cooper-The Nightmare 5: 270
"Alison" 2: 242
Alive! (KISS) 5: 237
"Alive" (Pearl Jam) 1: 116; 6: 332
Alive III (KISS) 5: 238
"All For Love" 6: 414
"All Along the Watchtower" 5: 246
"All By Myself" 4: 109
All for You (Jackson) 5: 208
"All for You" (Sister Hazel) 6: 384
"All Hail the Queen" 6: 345
"All I Have to Give" 4: 16
"All I Wanna Do" 5: 284
"All Star" 6: 389
All That Glitters 4: 62, 86
"All That I Can Say" 4: 36
All That You Can't Leave Behind 6: 443
"All the Man I Need" 5: 192
"All the Small Things" 4: 40
All the Way...A Decade of Song 4: 110
"All This Time" 6: 413
Allen, Johnny Ray 3: 603, 604
Allison, Luther 5: 249
Allman Brothers 6: 385
Allman, Greg 6: 385
Alternative metal music 6: 327
Alternative and pop rock 1: 1-6
Alternative Tentacles (record label) 1: 3
"Always Be My Baby" 4: 61, 85
Amadee, Steve 3: 603
Ambient/house 2: 279, 295
Ament, Jeff 1: 116; 6: 331, 333
American Bandstand (TV show) 3: 581
American Civil Liberties Union 1: 79
"American Pie" 4: 50, 77
American Records 3: 471, 494

"American Woman" 5: 247–248
Americana 6: 318, 319
Amnesiac 6: 349
Amnesty International's Conspiracy of Hope Tour 1: 192
Amor Prohibido 5: 265
Amos, Myra Ellen (see Tori Amos)
Amos, Tori 3: 613, 617, 618 (ills.), 619-620
Amplified 6: 435
Anarchy 4: 57
Anastasio, Trey 3: 588, 589
And In This Corner... 6: 400
And Justice for All 5: 288
And Out Come the Wolves 1: 147
And Then There Was X 4: 120
Anderson, Andy 2: 250
Anderson, Brett 2: 222, 254, 270-272
Anderson, Ian 6: 329
Anderson, Kevin 2: 419
Anderson, Laurie 3: 656
Anderson, Pamela 4: 86, 110; 5: 255
Anderson, Paul Thomas 4: 12
Anderson, Roberta Joan. See Mitchell, Joni
Andrews, Mark. See Sisqo
Androgyny 2: 222, 232, 270, 271; 4: 85
"Angel" 5: 283
Angel Eyes 5: 267
Angelil, Rene 4: 107, 108, 109
"Animal" 6: 332
Animalize 5: 237
"Annabella" 4: 144
"Another Brick in the Wall" 4: 77
Anselmo, Philip 3: 490, 491
Anthony, Larry "Jazz" 6: 382
Anthony, Marc 4: 2, **5–9**, 7 (ill.), 55; 5: 266
Anthrax 2: 395
Anti-Semitism 2: 363
Antichrist Superstar 5: 270
Antifolk movement 1: 25
Anuthatantrum 4: 85
"Any Time, Any Place" 5: 207
"Anything But Down" 5: 284
"Anything for You" 4: 138
Appel, Mike 3: 598, 599
Apple, Fiona 3: 613; **4:** 10 (ill.), **10–13**, 55; 6: 421
The Apples 6: 446–447
Aquemini 5: 298

Araya, Tom 3: 493 (ill.), 494
Archer, Michael D'Angelo. See D'Angelo
Arden, Sharon. See Osbourne, Sharon
Are You Experienced? 5: 246
Are You Gonna Go My Way? 5: 247
"Are You That Somebody?" 5: 226
Arista 3: 456
Arm, Mark 1: 118
Armstrong, Billy Joe 1: 60 (ill.), 61 (ill.), 62-64, 146; 4: 41
Armstrong, Dido. See Dido
Armstrong, Rollo 4: 132
Armstrong, Tim 1: 145 (ill.)
Arrested Development 2: 307, 312 (ill.), 313, 314 (ill.), 315-316; 5: 188; 6: 408
The Art of War 6: 452; 4: 45
Art-rock 1: 123, 165; 3: 654
"Arthurs, Paul 'Bonehead'" 2: 266
Artist Formerly Known As Prince (see Prince)
Arvizu, Reginald "Fieldy" 5: 240, 240 (ill.), 258
"As Long as You Love Me" 4: 15
As the World Turns 5: 179
Asleep at the Wheel 4: 49
Astro Lounge 6: 389, 391
Asuo, Kewsi 2: 315
At Your Best 5: 226
Athens, Georgia 1: 4, 154
Atlanta Rhythm Section 6: 385
Atlantic Records 3: 553, 573, 618
ATLiens 5: 298
"Atomic Dog" 6: 403
The Attractions 2: 243, 245, 246
Audio Adrenaline 4: 100
Auf der Maur, Melissa 5: 183 (ill.), 184, 185; 6: 397
August and Everything After 4: 75, 76
Austin, Dallas 6: 429
Austin, Thomas 6: 429
Austin Powers: The Spy Who Shagged me 5: 247
Australia 1: 160
Autobahn 2: 278, 288
Automatic Dlamini 2: 257
Automatic for the People 1: 157; 6: 361

Avant-garde music 2: 221, 222, 231; 3: 655
Avery, Eric 1: 76
AWOL 2: 292
Axis: Bold as Love 5: 246
Azor, Hurby "Luvbug" 2: 411

B

Babes in Toyland 1: 5, 16 (ill.), 17-19
Babes in Toyland: The Making and Selling of a Rock and Roll Band 1: 18
"Baby, Baby, Baby" 6: 429
Baby One More Time 6: 407, 409
Babyface 2: 277; 3: 503, 506 (ill.) 507-510, 517, 536
Bacharach, Burt 2: 220, 245; 5: 194
The Bachelor 4: 62
"Back and Forth" 5: 226
Back to the earth movement 6: 385
Back to the Future 6: 357
"Back 2 Good" 5: 280
Backbeat (film) 1: 49
Backstreet Boys **4: 14 (ill.), 14–18**, 16 (ill.), 40; 5: 258; 6: 313, 421, 429
"Bad, Bad Leroy Brown" 5: 230
Bad Boy Entertainment 6: 341
Bad Boy Records 2: 310, 427, 428
Bad Radio 1: 116, 117
Badmotorfinger 1: 175
Baez, Joan 3: 439, 440; 5: 201
Bagpipes 5: 242
"Bailamos" 4: 5; 5: 196, 197
Bair, Bret 6: 328
Baker, Anita 4: 34, 61
Ballard, Glen 3: 613, 640; 4: 96
Ballew, Chris 1: 127
Balzary, Michael. *See* Flea
Bamonte, Perry 2: 250
The Band 3: 603
Band Aid 1: 191
Band-Aid Boys 4: 44
Band of Gypsys 5: 246
Barber, Samuel 6: 342
Barenaked Ladies 1: 20 (ill.), 21-23; 4: 19 (ill.), **19–22**, 21 (ill.); 6: 322
Bark at the Moon 6: 324
Barker, Travis 4: 38 (ill.), 38–42

Barnwell, Timothy 2: 313
Barrett, Dicky 1: 5; 5: 291 (ill.), 292–294
Barron, Chris 3: 594-596
Barry, Hank 5: 289 (ill.)
Bartos, Karl 2: 288
Basic Instinct 6: 337
Bass, Lance 6: 313 (ill.), 314–315
Bassett, Angela 4: 34
Batman and Robin 4: 45
The Battle of Los Angeles 6: 351, 353
"Bawitdaba" 5: 231
Bayyan, Khalis 2: 345
B-Boy DJs 2: 304, 306
B-Boy label 2: 318
"Be Careful with My Heart" 5: 276
"Be Happy" 4: 34
Be My Baby 4: 105
"Be Still My Beating Heart" 6: 413
Be With You 5: 197
The Beach Boys 4: 20
The Beacon Street Collection 6: 311
Beastie Boys 1: 26; 2: 309; 4: 23 (ill.), **23–27**, 24 (ill.), 55; 5: 213
The Beatles 2: 220, 221, 237, 239,266, 267, 275; 3: 540, 613; 4: 11, 98; 6: 311, 356, 374–375
  folk rock and 5: 201
  long songs by 4: 77
  movies by 4: 70
  number one hits by 4: 59
The Beatles (White album) 6: 349, 440
Beats, Rhymes and Life 6: 434–435
Beauford, Carter 3: 585; 4: 93, 94
"Beautiful Day" 6: 443, 444
"The Beautiful People" 5: 271
Beautiful South 2: 223 (ill.) 224 (ill.) 225-226
"Beauty and the Beast" 4: 108
Beavis and Butthead 1:16, 18, 132
"Because of Love" 5: 207
"Because of You" 6: 306
"Because You Loved Me" 4: 109
Beck 1: 3, 24 (ill.), 25-26, 27 (ill.), 28-29; 3: 550; 4: 28 (ill.), **28–32**; 5: 188, 241; 6: 390
Bedford-Stuyvesant, New York 2: 387; 3: 631
Bedlam Ballroom 6: 377
Bee Gees 2: 276
Before These Crowded Streets 4: 96
Behind the Music 4: 51
Behler, Chuck 3: 483
Belew, Adrian 5: 217
Bell, Frank 2: 250
Bell, Marc 1: 141
Bell, Ricky 3: 517
Bellmark 3: 532
Belly (Band) 6: 348
Belly (Movie) 4: 120; 6: 429
Ben Folds Five 3: 613
The Bends 6: 349
Benjamin, Andre "Dre" 5: 298, 298 (ill.)
Bennett, Tony 2: 244
Bennett, Veronica "Ronnie" 4: 105
Bennett, William 1: 79
Benson, Al 3: 502
Benson, Brendan 3: 613
Benson, Ray 4: 49
"Bent" 5: 281
Beres, Jeff 6: 385–386, 386 (ill.), 387
Berkowitz, Daisy 5: 270
Berlin, Germany 1: 72; 2: 232
Berlin, Steve 3: 580
Berry, Bill 1: 154, 156; 6: 360 (ill.), 360–363
Berry, Chuck 2: 244, 275; 3: 539 (ill.), 540, 541; 5: 170; 6: 395
The Best of Grandmaster Flash 6: 341
Best New Artist Award 6: 408
BET Harlem Block Party 4: 35 (ill.)
"Beth" 5: 237
Bettie Serveert 1: 30 (ill.), 31-32
Beverly Hills 90210 1: 58
B52s 2: 292
B.I.B. 5: 224
Bidgood, Tony 6: 375
Bier, Stephen, Jr.. *See* Gacy, Madonna Wayne
Big Audio Dynamite 6: 449
Big Bad Voodoo Daddy 6: 377
Big Bank Hank (Henry Jackson) 2: 306
Big Daddy Kane 2: 307

Big Head Todd and the Monsters 3: 550
The Big Lebowski 6: 357
Big Night 4: 7
Big Willie Style 6: 400
"Big Yellow Taxi" 5: 208, 221
Bigger and Deffer 5: 261
Biggie Smalls (see Notorious B.I.G.)
Bill and Ted's Bogus Journey (film) 3: 483
"Bills, Bills, Bills" 4: 103
Billy Joel 4: 50
Bim Skala Bim 1: 185
Bin Hassan, Umar 2: 305
Bittan, Roy 3: 598, 601
Bivins, Michael 3: 517, 519
Bizzy Bone 4: 43–47, 45 (ill.)
Bjelland, Kat 1: 16 (ill.), 17-19
Bjork 2: 222, 300; 3: 613, 621 (ill.), 622 (ill.), 623-625
Black, Chris 5: 204
"Black Balloon" 5: 162
Black and Blue 4: 17
"Black Cat" 5: 207
"Black Chick, White Guy" 5: 233
Black Crowes 3: 541, 542, 545 (ill.), 546 (ill.), 547, 550; 6: 385
"Black Hole Sun" 1: 176
Black Love 1: 9
"Black Magic Woman" 6: 370
Black Men United Choir 4: 89
Black Oak Arkansas 6: 385
Black Panthers 2: 393, 425
Black Reign 6: 344, 345
Black Rock Coalition 3: 480
Black Sabbath 3: 465, 466; 6: 321, 322, 324 (ill.), 394
Black-on-black violence 2: 318, 372
Blackfoot 6: 385
Blackie O 1: 187
Blades, Ruben 2: 245
Blair, Barry 4: 100
The Blasters 3: 580
Bleach 1: 95
Blender 4: 66, 67
Blige, Mary J. 2: 307; 4: 33 (ill.), **33–37**, 35 (ill.), 55, 155; 5: 253
Blink-182 4: **38** (ill.), **38–42**, 133; 5: 241; 6: 390, 449
Blink Soon 4: 39
Blizzard of Oz 6: 323
Block, Ken 6: 384–388, 386 (ill.)

Blonde on Blonde 4: 31
Blondie 1: 139; 2: 277, 308
Blood of Abraham 2: 341
Blood on the Tracks 4: 31
Blood Sugar Sex Magik 6: 355, 356
Bloom 4: 100
Blow, Kurtis 2: 309, 404
"Blowin' in the Wind" 4: 31
Blue (Rimes) (Album) 6: 364, 366
"Blue" (Rimes) (Song) 6: 365
Blue (Sugar Ray) 6: 422
Blue Beat 1: 184
Blue Cheer 3: 466
Blue Flames 3: 502
Blues 2: 304; 5: 250
Blues Band 3: 549
Blues Brothers 2000 5: 251
Blues Traveler 3: 541, 542, 548 (ill.), 549-551; 5: 172, 251
Blunted on Reality 5: 180
Blur 2: 221, 222, 227 (ill.), 228 (ill.), 229, 255, 268
BMI New Music Showcase 3: 557
Boarder Baby Project 3: 509
Body Count 2: 366, 369, 370
The Bodyguard 6: 440; 5: 191, 192
Bolan, Marc 2: 272
The Bomb Squad 4: 55
Bones Thugs-N-Harmony 2: 307; 4: **43–47**, 45 (ill.), 61; 5: 230
Bones, Jimmie 5: 232
Bonet, Lisa 3: 630-632; 5: 247
Bono 1: 190 (ill.), 191-195; 4: 155; 6: 353, 442 (ill.), 442–445
Booga Basement 2: 345
Boogie Down Productions 2: 309, 317 (ill.) 318-320, 399, 407
Booker T. and the MGs 2: 276
Boomtown Rats 4: 72
Boone, Debby 6: 408
Bootleg albums 4: 95–96; 6: 332–333
Boquist, Dave 3: 592
Boquist, Jim 3: 592
Borland, Wes 5: 257, 258 (ill.)
Born Again 5: 255
Born into the '90s 5: 225
Born on a Pirate Ship 4: 20
The Bosstones. See Mighty Mighty Bosstones

Bostaph, Paul 3: 495
"Both Sides Now" 5: 221
Bottrell, Bill 3: 628
Bow, Clara 5: 185
Bowie, David 1: 6, 71, 72, 91; 2: 219 (ill.), 222, 230 (ill.), 231 (ill.), 232-236, 239, 271, 400; 3: 614, 655; 6: 342
Bowie, David, with Nine Inch Nails 1: 91; 2: 231 (ill.), 231
Bowman, Fallon 5: 185
Bowman, Steve 3: 557; 4: 75, 76
Boxley, James Hank 2: 393
Boy 6: 443
A Boy Named Goo 1: 58; 5: 160
The Boys 3: 507
"The Boys Are Back in Town" 4: 72
Boyz in the Hood (film and song) 2: 332, 339, 361, 362
Boyz II Men 3: 503, 511 (ill.) 512–514; 4: 61; 6: 305, 306
Bradley, Owen 3: 636
Brand New Day 6: 411, 414
Braxton, Toni 6: 408
Breach 6: 446, 448
Break A Dawn 3: 526
Break the Cycle 4: 128
"Break Stuff" 5: 243
Breakdancing 2: 277; 5: 230
"Breakdown" 4: 46
"Breathe" (F. Hill) 5: 176
"Breathe" (Prodigy) 5: 213
"Breathless" 4: 69
Brian Setzer Orchestra 5: 291; 6: 374, 377–378
"Brian Wilson" 4: 20
Bridewell, Tim 5: 292
"Bridge Over Troubled Water" 5: 201
Bridge School benefit concerts 1: 207
Brill, Dmitry 2: 283-285
"Bring It All to Me" 6: 316
Bringing Down the Horse 6: 446, 447
Bringing It All Back Home 4: 31
Bringing Out the Dead 4: 7
Brion, Jon 3: 613
Bristol (England) Sound 2: 299-301
Brit Pop 2: 219-222, 238, 255
British Invasion 3: 543
British new wave music 1: 154; 2: 253
British press 1: 39

Parents Aren't Supposed to Like It

Britney Spears: Heart to Heart 6: 409
Britney Spears Museum 6: 409
Britton, Akissi 5: 255
Broadus, Cordazar Calvin. *See* Snoop Dogg.
"Broadway" 5: 162
Brockenborough, Dennis 5: 292
Brodsky Quartet 2: 245
"Broken Home" 6: 330
Brooks, Garth 4: 48 (ill.), 48–53, 51 (ill.), 82, 112, 154; 5: 237
Broomfield, Nick 5: 184
The Brown Album 1: 133
Brown, Andre 2: 331
Brown, Bobby 3: 503, 516 (ill.) 517–519; 5: 192, 193
Brown, Charles 4: 55
Brown, James 2: 276, 304; 3: 502, 503; 4: 30, 55, 77; 5: 297, 297 (ill.)
Brown Mark 3: 529
Brown, Melanie 5: 171
"Brown, Rex "Rocker"" 3: 491
Brown Sugar 4: 90, 91
Brown, Vincent 2: 382, 383
"Brown-Eyed Girl" 4: 72
Brownleewe, Matt 5: 216
"Bruise Violet" 1: 18
Brutal Truth 3: 468
Bryan, Mark 3: 572; 5: 187 (ill.), 187–190
Bryson, David 3: 556; 4: 75, 75 (ill.)
Bryson, Peabo 4: 108
BTNH Resurrection 4: 46
Buchanan, Wallis 5: 210
Buchignani, Paul 1: 9
Buck, Peter 1: 154; 6: 360 (ill.), 360–363
Buckley, Jeff 3: 441 (ill.), 442, 443 (ill.), 444-445
Buckley, Tim 3: 442
Buckner, Dave 6: 327 (ill.), 327–330
Budd, Harold 2: 297
Buddhism 2: 231; 4: 26
The Buddy Holly Story 4: 70
Buffalo Springfield 1: 204; 5: 293
"Building a Mystery" 5: 283
Built For Speed 6: 375
Bullet 2: 427
"Bullet in the Head" 1: 135
Bulletproof 2: 414

Bullock, Craig "DJ Homicide" 6: 416 (ill.), 417–419
"Bulls on Parade" 6: 352
Bulworth 4: 119
"Bump N' Grind" 5: 225
Bumstead records 3: 635
Bunton, Emma 5: 171
Burdon, Eric 6: 411–413
Burnett, Chester Arthur 5: 250
"Burning Down the House" 6: 397
Burr, Gary 5: 176
Burrell, Stanley Kirk (see Hammer)
Burroughs, William S. 6: 329
Burton, Cliff 3: 486, 487; 5: 288
Burton, James 2: 244
Burton, Tim "Johnny Vegas" 5: 292
Busby, Jheryl 3: 513
Bush 2: 222, 237 (ill.), 238 (ill.), 239–240
Bush, Dave 2: 256
Bush, George H. 2: 340
Bush, George W. 5: 275
Busta Rhymes 4: 54 (ill.), 54–58, 56 (ill.), 119, 128; 5: 208; 6: 342, 421
Bustin' Records (label) 2: 350, 352, 353
Busy Bee 2: 372
Butcher Brothers 1: 188
Butler, Bernard 2: 270, 272
Butler, Terry "Geezer" 6: 322, 324 (ill.)
Butterfly 4: 61
Butthole Surfers 1: 3, 33 (ill.), 34 (ill.), 35-36
The Buzzcocks 1: 139; 2: 253
"Bye Bye Bye" 6: 316
The Byrds 2: 221; 3: 543
Byrne, David 6: 396, 397

C

Cadogan, Kevin 6: 420 (ill.), 421–423
Cage, Nicolas 4: 7; 5: 161
Caine, Michael 2: 272
Cajun music 2: 243
Cale, John 3: 654, 656
Calhoun, William 3: 480
California Boys Choir 5: 245
"California Girls" 4: 20
California musicians 5: 241
Californication 6: 355, 358
Calire, Mario 1: 200; 6: 447

Calleja, Joe. *See* Joe C.
Cameron, James 4: 109
Cameron, Matt 1: 118, 172, 173
Camp, Greg 6: 389 (ill.), 390–392
Campbell, Beck David. *See* Beck
Campbell, Sterling 1: 170
Campbell, Tevin 3: 503, 520 (ill.) 521–523; 6: 337
"Can't Forget You" 4: 138
"Can't Get Enough of You Baby" 6: 391
Can't Hardly Wait 6: 391
"Can't Let Go" 4: 60
Can't Take Me Home 6: 337, 338
Canadian Living Foundation 6: 439
Cantrell, Jerry 1: 11 (ill.), 12, 14
Capitol Records 3: 484
Cappadonna 6: 454
Captain Beefheart 2: 222
Carey, Mariah 2: 277; 3: 513; 4: 46, 55, 59 (ill.), 59–63, 85, 86, 138; 6: 306, 408
Carlos Santana and Buddy Miles Live! 6: 370
Caroline Records 1: 163
The Carpenters 6: 408
Carr, Eric 5: 237, 237–238
Carrey, Jim 5: 185
The Cars 2: 277
Carter, Nick Gene 4: 14 (ill.), 14–18, 16 (ill.)
Carter, Ron 6: 433
Cartoons 4: 128
Cash, Johnny 1: 194
Cash Money Click 5: 204
The Castilles 3: 597
Castro, Fidel 4: 137; 5: 202
Cauty, Jimmy 2: 295, 296
Cave, Nick 2: 222
CBGB's 1: 139
CBS/Columbia Records 3: 598
Cease, Jeff 3: 546
Celebrity 6: 316
Celebrity Skin 5: 183, 184–185
Celine Dion 4: 108
The Cell 5: 267
Censorship and freedom of speech issues 1: 62, 76, 79; 2: 310, 361, 368, 369, 394-395, 399; 3: 655–656; 6: 352
Chamberlin, Jimmy 1: 164 (ill.), 165, 167; 6: 393–398

Index xlix

"Champagne High" 6: 387
"A Change Will Do You Good" 5: 284
Chant Plamondon 4: 108
Chapel Hill, North Carolina 1: 4
Chapman, Tracy 3:439 (ill.), 441, 442, 446 (ill.), 447-450
Charles, Ray 3: 501 (ill.), 502
Charlie's Angels 4: 105
The Chase 6: 357; 4: 50
Chasez, J.C. 4: 2; 6: 313 (ill.), 314
Cheap Trick 2: 277
Check Your Head 4: 25
Cheeba, Eddie 2: 304
Chemical Brothers 2: 278, 280-282
Cher 4: 61
Cherone, Gary 3: 468
Cherry, Nenah 2: 300
Cherry Poppin' Daddies 6: 377
Chic 2: 276, 308
Chicago, Illinois 1: 165, 188
Childress, Ross 3: 553; 4: 65
Chilli. *See* Thomas, Rozanda.
Chiong, Roddy 5: 217
Chipperfield, Sheila 2: 256
Chisholm, Melanie 5: 171
Chocolate Starfish & the Hot Dog Flavored Water 5: 259
Choice 6: 337
Christian music 4: 79, 100
Christian Right 2: 292, 293
Christianity 2: 291
Christianne F 2: 233
Christina Aguilera 4: 2
Christmas 4: 155
The Chronic 2: 336; 4: 123; 6: 404
Chronic Town 6: 361
Chrysler Corporation 3: 600
Chuck D 1: 27; 2: 305, 362, 374, 392 (ill.), 394-396, 408; 4: 55; 5: 231
Church Boy 4: 154
Church of Satan 5: 270
Cinderella 5: 193
"Cinnamon Girl" 1: 204
Circus 5: 247
City of Angels 5: 161
City Spud 6: 302
Civil rights movement 3: 439
Claanad 4: 72
Clapton, Eric 4: 36; 5: 250; 6: 370
Clarke, Gilby 3: 477
Clash of the Titans tour 1: 13

The Clash 1: 1, 60, 139, 154; 2: 219, 225, 308; 5: 292, 293; 6: 448 (ill.), 448-449
Classical music 2: 245
Claypool, Les 1: 130 (ill.), 131-133
Clayton, Adam 1: 190, 191, 192 (ill.); 6: 442 (ill.), 442-445
Clearmountain, Bob 3: 476
Clearwater Project 5: 222
Clemmons, Clarence 3: 598
Clifford Ball 3: 589
Cline, Patsy 3: 635; 6: 364, 365, 365 (ill.), 439
Clink, Mike 3: 474, 476
Clinton, Bill 1: 193; 2: 315; 5: 276
Clinton, George 1: 149; 2: 276, 285; 3: 503, 541; 4: 85; 6: 403, 403 (ill.)
Clockers (film) 2: 396
The Clones of Dr. Funkenstein 6: 403
Clooney, George 5: 266
Clouser, Charlie 3: 499
Clueless 5: 292
Cobain, Kurt 1: 49, 50, 65-67, 94, 96 (ill.), 97, 98, 175, 206, 208; 2: 238; 3: 573; 4: 150-151; 5: 183, 184; 6: 395
Cobra Verde 3: 570
Cochran, Eddie 6: 374
Cochran, Johnny 6: 343, 404
Code Red 6: 400
Codling, Neil 2: 272
Coed rock 1: 196
Coffey, King 1: 36
Cohen, Lyor 5: 204
Cohn, Marc 5: 293
Coleman, Kevin 6: 389 (ill.), 390-392
Coles, Dennis. *See* Ghostface Killa
Collective Soul 3: 543, 552 (ill.), 553-555; 4: 36, 64 (ill.), 64-68; 6: 429
Colley, Dana 1: 81, 82
Colling, Bootsy 3: 507
Collins, Bootsy 6: 403
Collins, Judy 3: 440
Color Me Badd 5: 188
"Colored People" 4: 100
Colorfringe 4: 142
The Colour and the Shape 4: 151
Colour of My Love 4: 108
Colt, Johnny 3: 546

Columbia Records 3: 444
Columbine High School 5: 271, 283
Colvin, Douglas 1: 138
"Coma White" 5: 271
Combat Rock 6: 449
Combs, Sean "Puffy" 2: 310, 388-390, 424, 426, 428; 4: 34; 5: 266; 6: 340 (ill.), 340-343. *See also* Puff Daddy.
"Come Back to Me" 5: 207
Come on Now Social 5: 202
"Come on Over" (Aguilera) 4: 3
Come on Over (Twain) 6: 437, 440
"Come Out and Play" 1: 108; 6: 319
"Come with Me" 6: 342
Comedy, musical 1: 20
Comess, Aaron 3: 595
The Coming 4: 56
"Coming Out of the Dark" 4: 138
Commerford, Tim 6: 351 (ill.), 351-354
The Commitments 4: 70, 71
The Commodores 2: 404
Compton, California 2: 322, 330, 338, 339, 361
Con Air 6: 366
Concept albums 6: 434
Concert injuries 6: 331, 333-334, 357-358, 395
Confederate flag 5: 231
"Conga" 4: 138
Congregation 1: 8
Conscious rap 2: 392
Conspiracy 5: 254
Conspiracy of One 6: 319
The Contender 6: 377
The Continental Drifters 3: 604
Contra la Corriente 4: 7, 8
Control 5: 207
Cook, Kyle 5: 279
Cooke, Sam 3: 502
"Cookie Puss" 4: 24
Cooking Vinyl label 3: 462
Cool, Tre 1: 60, 61
Coolio 2: 307, 321 (ill.), 322 (ill.), 323-325
Coomer, Ken 3: 608
Cooper, Alice 2: 232; 3: 466; 5: 270
"Cop Killer" 2: 366, 369
Copeland, Andrew 6: 385, 386 (ill.), 387

Copeland, Miles 6: 412
Copeland, Stewart 6: 411–413
Copyright law 6: 332–333
Corgan, Billy 1: 163 (ill.), 164 (ill.), 165; 2: 234; 5: 184–185; 6: 393 (ill.), 393–398
Cornell, Chris 1: 172 (ill.), 172-175; 3: 469; 6: 354
Corr, Andrea 4: 69 (ill.), 71, 71 (ill.), 72
Corr, Caroline 4: 69 (ill.), 70–71, 71 (ill.)
Corr, Jim 4: 69, 69 (ill.), 71 (ill.)
Corr, Sharon 4: 69 (ill.), 70, 71 (ill.), 73
Corrigan, Brianna 2: 223, 225
The Corrs **4: 69 (ill.), 69–74**, 71 (ill.); 6: 322
Cosas Del Amor 5: 197
Cosloy, Gerard 3: 651
Cosmetics 4: 128
Costello, Elvis 1: 1, 2; 2: 220, 240 (ill.), 241-247; 3: 581, 614, 615; 6: 448
Costner, Kevin 5: 191
"Could I Have This Kiss Forever" 5: 197
Counting Crows 3: 541, 542, 556-558; **4: 75–78**, 75 (ill.); 5: 241; 6: 447
Country Grammar (album) 6: 301
"Country Grammar" (song) 6: 302
Country rock 2: 241; 3: 607, 608, 634-637
Court and Spark 5: 221
Cousin Kevin 6: 422
"Cowboy Take Me Away" 4: 114, 115
Cox, Billy 5: 246
Coxon, Gordon 2: 228
Cracked Rear View 5: 187, 188
Cracker 4: 76
The Cranberries 1: 37 (ill.), 38-41; 4: 69, 72, 114
Crash 4: 95
"Crash into Me" 4: 95
Crash Test Dummies 1: 42 (ill.), 43 (ill.), 44
"Crazy" (Cline) 6: 365
"Crazy" (Spears) 6: 407
Crazy Horse 1: 204, 207
Crazy Nights 5: 237
"Crazy Train" 6: 323
CrazySexyCool 6: 428, 429
"C.R.E.A.M." (song) 6: 452

Cream 3: 466
Creed **4: 79 (ill.), 79–83**; 6: 429
Creem 2: 288
Creep (Band) 5: 240
"Creep" (Song) 5: 293; 6: 348, 428
Creepin' On Ah Come Up 4: 45
"Criminal" 4: 12
Criss, Anthony (see Treach)
Criss, Peter 5: 235 (ill.), 235–239
Crisscoula, Peter. See Criss, Peter
Croce, Jim 5: 230
Crooked Rain, Crooked Rain 1: 112
Crosby, Bing 2: 233
Crosby, Stills & Nash 6: 408
Crosby, Stills, Nash and Young 1: 204, 205
Cross, Christopher 6: 408
Cross-dressing 1: 6
The Crow (film) 1: 90; 2: 301
The Crow: City of Angels (film) 2: 348
Crow, Sheryl 3: 550, 615, 626 (ill.), 627 (ill.), 628-629; 4: 114; 5: 284, 284 (ill.); 6: 408
Crowd injuries. See Concert injuries.
"Cruisin" 4: 90
"Crush on You" 5: 254
Cruz, David 5: 266–267
Crystal Method 2: 278
Cuba 4: 137; 5: 202; 6: 322
Cult Heroes 2: 250
Culture Club 1: 2
Cummings, John 1: 138
Cundieff, Rusty 4: 70
"The Cup of Life" 5: 276
Cure 1: 2; 2: 220 (ill.), 248 (ill.), 249 (ill.), 250-252
Cure for Pain 1: 82
Curley, John 1: 7, 9
Curtis, Ian 2: 221
Curtis, Jamie Lee 5: 262
Cuthbert, Scott 4: 142
Cuts Both Ways 4: 138
Cypress Hill 1: 188; 2: 310; 4: 56; 6: 417

D

Da Brat **4: 84 (ill.), 84–87**, 128; 5: 230, 254, 255
Da Game Is to Be Sold, Not to Be Told 6: 404

Da Real World 4: 128
Dahlheimer, Patrick 3: 576
Dali, Douglas 4: 133
Dalsimer, Josh 5: 292
Daltry, Roger 3: 596
Dame, Damian 3: 536
"Dammit" 4: 40
"The Dance" 4: 49
Dance Fools Dance record label 2: 250
Dance Music 2: 275-279
Dancehall 2: 358
Dancing, mosh pit 6: 395, 396
D'Angelo **4: 88–92**, 89 (ill.), 127
Daniels, Charlie 4: 113
Danny Boy. See O'Connor, Daniel
Danzig 3: 467, 470-472
Danzig, Glenn 3: 467, 470-472
Darby, Geoffrey 3: 641
D'Arcy (Wretzky) 1: 164 (ill.), 165
Dark Side of the Moon 6: 434
"Daughter" 6: 332
Dave Matthews Band 3: 543, 584 (ill.), 585 (ill.), 586-587; **4: 93 (ill.), 93–97**, 127; 6: 333
Davey DMX (Dave Reeves) 2: 309
David, Susan Lachter 1: 60
David Copperfield 6: 329
Davis, Clive 5: 193; 6: 370
Davis, Jody 5: 216
Davis, Jonathan (KoRN) 5: 240 (ill.), 240-244, 243 (ill.), 259; 6: 329
Davis, Jonathan (A Tribe Called Quest). See Q-Tip
Davis, Miles 6: 433
Davis, Tamra 4: 26
Day, Morris 1: 29
Daydream 4: 61
"Daylight Fading" 4: 76
dc Talk **4: 98 (ill.), 98–101**, 127
De Artsen 1: 30
De la Rocha, Zack 1: 134 (ill.), 135-137
De La Soul 2: 307, 347
De Lisle, Paul 6: 389 (ill.), 390–392
De Niro, Robert 1: 98
"Dead Bodies Everywhere" 5: 241
Dead Kennedys 1: 33-34

Dead Man Walkin' (album) 6: 404
Dead Man Walking (film) 3: 601
Dean, Dee 4: 119
Dean, Waah 4: 119
"Dear Lie" 6: 429
Death metal 1: 67
Death Row Records 2: 331, 333-336,353,389, 420-422, 427, 428; 4: 123
DeBarge, James 5: 207
December 4: 64
Decoding Society 3: 480
Deee-Lite 2: 278, 283 (ill.), 284 (ill.), 285-286
Deele 3: 507
"Deep Inside You" 6: 422
"Deeper Underground" 5: 212
Def American 1: 46, 71; 2: 416
Def Jam 2: 309, 331, 376, 377; 5: 261
Def Leppard 1: 66; 5: 257
Definitely Maybe 2: 265
Deftones 5: 258
Del-Fi 1: 81
DeLeo, Dean 1: 179
DeLeo, Robert 1: 178 (ill.)
Delicious Vinyl label 1: 26
Dellecave, Lea 6: 307
DeLonge, Tom 4: 38 (ill.), 38–42
Dempsey, Michael 2: 250
Densmore, John 4: 80
Denton, Sandy 2: 410
"Description of a Fool" 6: 433
"Desert Rose" 6: 414
Destiny 4: 138
Destiny's Child 4: **102 (ill.), 102–106,** 104 (ill.), 154
Destroyer 5: 237
Detroit, Michigan 1: 69
Detroit Rock City (film) 5: 238
"Detroit Rock City" (song) 5: 237
Dette, Jon 3: 495
"The Devil Went Down to Georgia" 4: 113
Devil Without a Cause 5: 231, 233
Devils Night Out 5: 292
Devo 2: 277
DeVoe, Ronnie 3: 517
Dewese, Mohandas (see Kool Moe Dee)
DGC Records 1: 27, 67
Diamond, Michael. *See* Mike D
Diamonds and Rust 5: 201
Diary of a Madman 6: 323

Dick, Coby 6: 327 (ill.), 327–330, 328 (ill.)
Dickens, Charles 6: 329
Dido 4: 132, 132 (ill.)
Diff'rent Strokes 5: 207
"The Difference" 6: 447
Digable Planets 2: 307
Diggs, Robert. *See* Prince Rakeem
Digital Underground 2: 425
DiMant, Leor. *See* DJ Lethal
Dinco D. 4: 55
Dinger, Klaus 2: 288
Dinosaur Jr. 1: 45 (ill.), 46 (ill.), 47-48
Dion, Celine 4: 61, 72, 107 (ill.), **107–111,** 109 (ill.), 138; 5: 227; 6: 322
Dirnt, Mike 1: 60, 61; 4: 41; 6: 422
The Dirty Boogie 6: 377
Dirty South rap movement 5: 298
Disciplined Breakdown 4: 64, 65
Disco music 2: 276
"Dissident" 6: 332
Divas 4: 61
"Dixie Chicken" 4: 114
Dixie Chicks 4: **112 (ill.), 112–116,** 113 (ill.), 154
Dixon, Don 3: 573
Dixon, Willie 5: 250
Dizzy Up the Girl 5: 160, 162
DJ Eddie F 2: 356
DJ Hollywood 2: 304
DJ Jazzy Jeff and the Fresh Prince 2: 307, 326 (ill.), 327-329; 6: 399
DJ Kay Gee (Kier Gist) 2: 382
DJ Lethal 4: 147; 5: 258
DJ 618 6: 302
DJ Spinderella 2: 410
DJ Swamp 5: 172
DJing 2: 280, 292, 295, 304, 331
D'Jon, Paris 6: 306
DMX 4: 55, 117 (ill.), **117–121,** 118 (ill.); 5: 203, 204, 226; 6: 303
Do the Right Thing (film) 2: 307, 310, 394
"Do Something" 5: 166
"Do You Remember Rock and Roll Radio?" 1: 140
Document 6: 361
Doggystyle 6: 402, 404
"Doin' It" 5: 262
Doll Congress 3: 459

"Doll Parts" 1: 67
"Domino, Antoine "Fats" 2: 230; 3: 539, 540
The Dominoes 3: 502
Don, Rasa 2: 313
Don Juan De Marco 5: 265
Don't Censor Me 4: 100
Don't Know How to Party 5: 292
Don't Look Back 4: 70
"Don't Speak" 6: 311
"Don't Stand So Close to Me" 6: 412
"Don't Want to Lose You" 4: 138
"Don't Waste Your Time" 4: 36
"Doo Wop" 5: 181
Doo-wop 3: 502
Doobie Brothers 4: 98
Dookie 1: 61, 62; 4: 41
The Doors 1: 119; 6: 395; 4: 77, 80, 81
The Doors (film) 1: 169
"Dope Show" 5: 271
Dorough, Howie D. (Howard Dwaine) 4: 14 (ill.), 14–18, 16 (ill.); 6: 314
Dosage 4: 64, 65
Double Live 4: 50
Double Platinum 5: 237
Doucette, Paul 5: 279
Doug E. Fresh 2: 309, 411
Douglas, Chris 5: 222
"Down" 6: 425
"Down Down Baby" 6: 303
"Down Low" 5: 225
Downloading music 4: 82; 5: 185, 259, 288–289; 6: 319, 332, 353
The Downward Spiral 1: 90, 91
"Dr. Beat" 4: 138
Dr. Doolittle 5: 226
Dr. Dre 2: 307, 310, 330 (ill.), 331-337, 339, 341, 361, 364, 419, 420, 422, 428; 4: 44, 119, 122 (ill.), **122–125,** 131; 6: 241; 6: 404
Dr. Dre Brown 2: 309
Dr. Dre Presents...The Aftermath 4: 123
Dr. Dre 2001 4: 123, 124
Dr. Zoom and the Sonic Boom 3: 598
The Dream of the Blue Turtles 6: 413
Dream Street 5: 207
Dream Syndicate 1: 7
Dreaming of You 5: 265

"Dreamlover" 4: 60
DreamWorks 1: 26, 81, 82
Dressed to Kill 5: 237
Drill 6: 348
Dru Hill 4: 61; 6: 380, 381–382
Dru World Order 6: 382
Drucker, Leon 6: 375
Drugs 6: 395, 426
Drum machines 2: 277, 308, 356
Dub 1: 183; 2: 297, 300
Dublin, Ireland 1: 190
Dude Ranch 4: 40
Dulli, Greg 1: 7 (ill.), 8, 9, 50
Dumont, Tom 6: 309 (ill.), 309–312
Dupri, Jermaine 4: 85, 86
Duritz, Adam 1: 201; 3: 542, 556, 558; 4: 75–78, 75 (ill.)
Durst, Fred 5: 243, 257 (ill.), 257–260
Dust Brothers 1: 26; 2: 280, 281; 3: 499
Dwight, Reginald. *See* John, Elton
Dylan, Bob 1: 3, 199; 2: 275; 3: 440, 599, 612; 4: 30 (ill.), 30–31, 50, 70, 77; 5: 201, 246; 6: 446
Dylan, Jakob 1: 199 (ill.), 200-202; 4: 31; 6: 446 (ill.), 446–450
Dynasty 5: 237
Dyslexia 6: 322, 325

E

E Street Band 3: 598
Earle, Steve 1: 7, 9
Early Mornin' Stoned Pimp 5: 231
The Early Years: Unchained Melody 6: 366
Earth 3: 598
Earth, Wind & Fire 2: 276
The East Bay Sessions 6: 391
East Coast/West Coast rappers feud 2: 388-390, 427-428
Easter, Mitch 1: 113
Easy Mo Bee 2: 388
Eat at Whitey's 4: 148
Eazy-E 2: 307, 310, 332, 334, 338 (ill.), 339, 340 (ill.), 341-342, 361; 4: 44–45, 122, 123, 124
Echo and the Bunnymen 2: 221

The Eclectic 5: 180
Economics 5: 188
Edge 1: 190
The Edge 6: 442 (ill.), 442–445
Edmonds, Kenneth (see Babyface)
Edmunds, Dave 3: 636; 6: 375
Edwards, Eileen Regina. *See* Twain, Shania
"E.I." 6: 303
Eisen, Stanley. *See* Stanley, Paul
Eklund, Greg 4: 141 (ill.), 142, 143
Elastica 1: 113; 2: 221, 253 (ill.), 254 (ill.), 255–256, 270
Eldon, Thor 3: 622
E.L.E.-Extinction Level Event 4: 56
"Elected" 5: 270
The Electric Kool-Aid Acid Test 4: 94
Electric Ladyland 5: 246
Electro/dance 2: 299
Electronica 1: 3, 183; 2: 232, 278, 279, 300 2:
Elektra 1: 8; 3: 448, 487, 589, 622
"Elevators" 5: 298
Elizondo, Rene, Jr. 5: 208
Ellington, Duke 2: 304
Elliot, Missy "Misdemeanor" 4: 61, 85, 86, **126–129;** 5: 253, 254; 6: 421
Ellis, Robert O. 2: 257
Ellis, Terry 3: 524-526
Elton John. *See* John, Elton
Elton John and Tim Rice's Aida 6: 367
Ely, Vince 2: 250
Emergency on Planet Earth 5: 212
Emery, Jill 5: 184
Eminem 4: 2–3, 124, 130 (ill.), **130–135,** 134 (ill.), 144; 5: 230, 259
Emotions 4: 60
En Vogue 2: 410, 413; 3: 504, 505, 524 (ill.), 525 (ill.), 526-527; 6: 435
"End of the World As We Know It" 6: 361
"Endless Love" 4: 61
Enema of the State 4: 40
Enemy of the State 6: 400
English Beat 1: 184; 2: 277
Eno, Brian 1: 191; 2: 219, 233, 297; 6: 397, 443

Enrique Iglesias 5: 197
Enter the Wu-Tang 6: 452
Environmentalism 2: 292
Enya 4: 72
EP (Extended-Play) recordings 6: 353
Epic Records 1: 135, 136; 3: 460, 595
Epitaph Records 1: 3, 107, 146, 147
EPMD 2: 408
Erdelyi, Tommy 1: 138
Eric B & Rakim 2: 419
Erickson, Buke 6: 310
Erikson, Duke 1: 53
Erlandson, Eric 1: 66; 5: 184
Erving, Julius "Dr. J." 4: 122
"Escapade" 5: 207
Eshe, Montsho 2: 313
Esperance, Tobin 6: 327 (ill.), 327–330
Estefan, Emilio 4: 137
Estefan, Gloria 4: 61, 136 (ill.), **136–140,** 139 (ill.); 5: 267; 6: 316, 322, 429
Etheridge, Melissa 3: 541, 542 (ill.), 550, 559 (ill.), 560-561, 615; 4: 51, 134
Eulinberg, Stefanie 5: 232
Eurythmics 5: 270
Evans, Dave 1: 190
Evans, David. *See* The Edge
Evans, Faith 2: 389; 5: 254; 6: 342
Evans, Paula Kaye 5: 176
Evans, Shane 3: 553; 4: 65
Eve 5: 203
Eve of Destruction 4: 119
Eve: Ruff Ryders' First Lady 4: 119
"Evenflow" 6: 332
Everclear **4: 141 (ill.), 141–144,** 143 (ill.); 5: 241; 6: 422, 449
Everlast 4: 55, 72, 146 (ill.), **146–149;** 5: 241
Everly, Erin 3: 475
"Every Breath You Take" 6: 342, 412, 414
"Every Day Is a Winding Road" 5: 284
Every Good Boy Deserves Fudge 1: 85
"Every Little Thing She Does Is Magic" 6: 412
"Every Morning" 6: 417
"Everybody" 4: 16

Index

Everybody Else Is Doing It, So Why Can't We? 1: 38, 39
"Everybody's Everything" 6: 370
Everyday 4: 96
"Everything in Between" 5: 217
"Everything Is Everything" 5: 181
"Everything Zen" 2: 239
Evil Empire 1: 136; 6: 352, 353
"Evil Ways" 6: 370
Evita 4: 72, 139
"Ex-Girlfriend" 6: 311
Exiles 4: 136
Exit Wounds 4: 118, 120
Exodus 3: 622
Extended play albums 6: 353
Extreme 3: 468
Eyes of Innocence 4: 138
Eyes Wide Shut 5: 298

F

Fab Five Freddy 2: 400
Fairley, Colin 2: 244
Fairweather Johnson 5: 188
Faith (Hill) 5: 176
"Faith" (Limp Bizkit) 5: 258
Faith Hill Literacy Project 5: 175
Faith No More 1: 66
Faithless 4: 132
Fajardo, Gloria Maria. *See* Estefan, Gloria
Falkner, Jason 3: 613
Fall 2: 256
"Falling Away from Me" 5: 243
"Falling in Love" 4: 138
Falling Into You 4: 109
"Falls Apart" 6: 417
Fame 4: 70; 5: 207
Fame, fifteen minutes of 6: 417
Fame, views of 1: 115, 173, 205; 2: 269
Family Values Tour 5: 242, 259
Fan injuries 6: 331, 333-334, 357–358, 395
Fanmail 6: 428, 429
Fanning, Shawn 5: 288 (ill.), 288–289
"Fantasy" 4: 61
Fanzines 5: 171
Fareed, Kamal 6: 435
Farm Aid 1: 207; 3: 563; 4: 29, 96
Farrar, Jay 3: 591 (ill.), 592, 606-608

Farrell, Perry 1: 2, 75 (ill.), 76-78, 123 (ill.), 124-126
Farris, Dionne 2: 313, 316
Fat Boys 2: 309, 400
The Fat of the Land 5: 213
"Father Figure" 5: 262
"Father of Mine" 4: 143
Fatone, Joey 6: 313 (ill.), 314
Fear and Loathing in Las Vegas 6: 357
Fear of a Black Hat 4: 70
Fear of a Black Planet 4: 70
Fear of Music 6: 397
Feeling Minnesota (film) 1: 67
Felber, Dean 3: 572; 5: 187 (ill.), 187–190
Female performers. *See* Women
Fenderson, Wardel 6: 342
Fennell, Kevin 3: 568-570
Ferderici, Danny 3: 598
Fife, Nick 5: 212
Fifteen minutes, of fame 6: 417
"Fight for Your Right" 4: 25
"Fight the Power" 2: 307
Filter 3: 469
"Finest Worksong" 6: 361
Fink, Matt 3: 530
Firbank, Louis (see Lou Reed)
"Fire" 5: 246
Fire It Up 5: 231
"Firestarter" 5: 213
First Amendment of the Bill of Rights 1: 76
First releases 6: 408
Fish, Ginger 1: 79; 5: 270
Fishman, Jon 3: 588, 589
F.I.S.T. 6: 357
Fitzgerald, Ella 2: 304
"Five Candles" 5: 217
Five Royales 3: 502
5 Tracks Deep 6: 329
Flack, Roberta 5: 179
Flags 5: 231
"Flashlight" 6: 403
Flavor Flav 2: 393, 395, 396
Flavor Unit Records 2: 384, 401; 6: 345
Flea 1: 77, 148; 3: 641; 6: 310, 355 (ill.), 356, 357
Fleadh Festival 4: 72
Flesh of My Flesh, Blood of My Blood 4: 120
Flesh-N-Bone 4: 43–47
Flip City 2: 242
Flipmode Entertainment 4: 57
Flipmode Squad 4: 57
Flipper 2: 292
Flock of Seagulls, A 1: 2

"Flood" 5: 217, 218
Floored 6: 417
Florida musicians 6: 429
Floyd, Eddie 5: 251
Flur, Wolfgang 2: 288
Fly (Dixie Chicks) 4: 112, 114
"Fly" (Sugar Ray) 6: 416, 417
"Fly Away" 5: 247
"Fly Girl" 6: 345
Flynt 5: 184
Flysher, Roman 5: 293
"Foe Tha Love of $" 4: 45
"A Foggy Day" 5: 164
Foley 2: 315
Folk music and folk rock 3: 439-442; 5: 201
Follow the Leader 5: 243
Fontanelle 1: 17
Foo Fighters 1: 49 (ill.), 50 (ill.), 51-52, 99; 2: 234; 4: 127, 150 (ill.), **150–152**; 5: 241
"For What It's Worth" 5: 293
Ford, Marc 3: 546
Forest for the Trees 1: 3
Forever (Puff Daddy) 6: 342
"Forever" (KISS) 5: 237
"Forget About Dre" 4: 132
Forgiven Not Forgotten 4: 72
Fortress 6: 384, 387
"Fortress Around Your Heart" 6: 413
F.O.S. 6: 390
Foster, Denzil 3: 525
Foster, Eric 6: 407
Four Freshmen 3: 439
"4 My Click/Get the Fortune" 5: 204
Four Tops 2: 276
14 Shots to the Dome 5: 262
Fox, Kim 3: 613
Frankenstein, Jeff 5: 216
Franklin, Aretha 4: 36, 61, 138; 5: 170, 181
Franklin, Farrah 4: 105
Franklin, Gertrude 6: 154
Franklin, Kirk 4: 36, 153 (ill.), **153–157**; 5: 224, 227
Frantz, Chris 6: 397
Frazier, Stan 6: 416 (ill.), 417–419
"Freak on a Leash" 5: 243
Frederickson, Lars 1: 146
Free at Last 4: 99
"Free Bird" 6: 385
"Free Man in Paris" 5: 221
The Freedom Sessions 5: 283
Freedom of speech issues 1: 62, 76, 79; 2: 310, 361, 368,

369, 394-395, 399; *3:* 655-656
Freeman, Matt *1:* 145
Frehley, Ace *5:* 235 (ill.), 235–239
Fresh Air Fund *4:* 62
Fresh Prince of Bel-Air 2: 328, 357; *6:* 400
Friedman, Marty *3:* 483
Friends 5: 188
"Friends in Low Places" *4:* 50
Frischmann, Justine *2:* 253 (ill.), 254-256, 270
"From the Bottom of My Broken Heart" *6:* 407
From the Heart of a Queen 2: 402
From the Muddy Banks of the Wishkah 1: 99
Fruitkwan *2:* 348
Frusciante, John *1:* 149; *6:* 355, 355 (ill.), 356
Fryer, John *3:* 499
Fuel *6:* 422
Fugees *2:* 307, 343 (ill.), 344 (ill.), 345-346; *4:* 56; *5:* 179, 181
Fulfillingness' First Finale 5: 211
Fumbling Towards Ecstasy 5: 282–283
Funhouse 1: 71
Funk music *2:* 276, 277; *3:* 503; *5:* 297
Funk-metal *3:* 480
Funkafied 4: 85
Funky Four Plus One *2:* 306, 308
Funky Four Plus One's Sha-Roc *2:* 400
Furay, Richie *1:* 204
The Furious Five *2:* 308; *6:* 341
Furler, Peter *5:* 216
Furnier, Vincent. *See* Cooper, Alice
Furtado, Nelly *6:* 302
Fush Yu Mang 6: 389, 391
A Future Without a Past 4: 55

G

G Wiz *2:* 356
Gabrels, Reeves *2:* 234, 235
Gacy, Madonna Wayne *1:* 79; *5:* 270
Gaines, Chris *4:* 48, 51, 51 (ill.)

Gallagher, Liam *2:* 221, 265 (ill.), 266, 267 (ill.), 268-269
Gallagher, Noel *2:* 221, 265 (ill.), 266 (ill.), 267-269, 281
Gallup, Simon *2:* 249, 250
"The Gambler" *5:* 180
Gang of Four *2:* 221
Gangsta rap *2:* 299, 305, 310, 321, 330, 339, 390, 419, 424, 429; *5:* 296–297; *6:* 341
"Gangsta's Paradise" *2:* 324
Garage, Inc. 5: 288
Garbage (Band) *1:* 3, 53 (ill.), 54-56; *6:* 310
Garbage (Album) *6:* 310
Garcia, Jerry *2:* 244; *4:* 94
Garcia, Mayte Jannell *3:* 532
Garter, Barry *4:* 73
Gaugh, Bud *1:* 182
Gay Human Rights Commission *3:* 452
Gay/Lesbian Alliance Against Defamation *4:* 133
Gaye, Marvin *4:* 88–89, 90
Gaynor, Adam *5:* 279
Gays. *See* Homosexuality
Geffen, David *1:* 81
Geffen Records *1:* 95, 206; *3:* 474, 475
Gehman, Don *1:* 155
Gein, Gidget *5:* 270
Geldof, Bob *4:* 72
Gender issues *1:* 6, 16; *2:* 258, 271
General Hospital 5: 274
"Genie In a Bottle" *4:* 2
"Genio Atrapado" *4:* 2
Genius *6:* 452, 453
"Genius of Love" *6:* 397
Geographic locations of musicians *4:* 55, 127, 154; *5:* 230, 241; *6:* 322, 429
George and the Dragons *2:* 231
Georgia musicians *6:* 429
Geronimo, Mic *5:* 204
Gersh, Gary *4:* 142
"Get At Me Dog" *4:* 120
"Get It Up" *6:* 429
"Get Money" *5:* 254
"Get On Your Feet" *4:* 138
"Get Over It" *6:* 382
Geto Boys *2:* 310
Gettin' Jiggy Wit It 6: 400
"Getting to Know You" *6:* 364
Ghetto Fabulous 5: 297
"Ghetto Love" *4:* 85
Ghost in the Machine 6: 412

Ghostface Killa *6:* 452
The Ghosts That Haunt Me 1: 43
Gibson, Mel *6:* 443
The Gift (film) *1:* 77
Gilbert, Simon *2:* 270, 272
Gill, Andy *1:* 149
Gill, Johnny *3:* 517
Gillies, Ben *1:* 161
Gillingham, Charles *3:* 557; *4:* 75
Gilman, Billy *4:* 49, 49 (ill.)
"Gimme What Ya Got" *6:* 302
Gin Blossoms *3:* 543, 562-564
Girl bands *1:* 5
Girl groups *4:* 105. *See also* specific groups
Gish 6: 394
Gist, Kier *2:* 382, 383
Gittleman, Joe *5:* 292
Give 'Em Enough Rope 6: 449
"Give It Away" *6:* 356
"Give Me Just One Night (Una Noche)" *6:* 306–307
"Given to Fly" *6:* 332
GLAAD *4:* 133
Glam rock *2:* 222, 232, 271; *3:* 491
Glam-metal *1:* 11; *3:* 466
Glass, Dan *6:* 387
Glaze, Terry *3:* 491
Glenn, John *5:* 252
Glitter, Gary *5:* 293
Glitter rock *2:* 232, 271
The Globe Sessions 5: 284
"Gloomy Sunday" *5:* 164
Gloria! (Estefan) *4:* 138
"Gloria" (U2) *6:* 443
Glove *2:* 250
Glover, Corey *3:* 480
"Go" *6:* 332
The G.O.A.T. 5: 262
"God Bless the Child" *6:* 439
"God of Thunder" *5:* 236
Godflesh *3:* 468
Gods & Monsters *3:* 444
God's Property 4: 155
Godwin, Jeff *4:* 100
Godzilla 5: 212
"Going Back to Cali" *5:* 261
Going Public 5: 216
Gold Mind label *4:* 128
Golden Musicals of Broadway 5: 266
Goldsmith, William *4:* 151
Gong *2:* 296

Goo Goo Dolls *1:* 57 (ill.), 58-59; *4:* 127; *5:* 159 (ill.), **159–162;** *6:* 348
Good God's Urge 1: 125, 126
Good Time for a Bad Attitude 4: 144
Good Times 5: 207
"Good Vibrations" *4:* 20
"Goodbye Earl" *4:* 114
"Goodbye Yellow Brick Road" *4:* 66
Goodridge, Robin *2:* 238
Gordon 4: 20
Gordon, Mike *3:* 589
Gordon, Nina *1:* 197
Gordon, Robert *3:* 599
Gorman, Steve *3:* 546
Gospel *2:* 276, 291, 303; *3:* 462-463, 501-503, 520, 539, 603, 607
Gospel Starlighters *3:* 502
Gossard, Stone *1:* 116, 118; *6:* 331, 333
"Got a Brand New Bag" *5:* 297
"Got 'Til It's Gone" *5:* 208
Goth rock *2:* 221
Gotti, Irv *5:* 204
Goulding, Steve *2:* 250
Gracey, Chad *3:* 576
Graham, Billy *4:* 99
Grand Ole Opry *2:* 243
Grand Wizard Theodore *2:* 304
Grandmaster Flash *2:* 304, 306, 404; *6:* 341, 342
Grandmaster Flash and The Furious Five *2:* 404
Grandmaster Flowers *2:* 304
Grant Lee Buffalo *3:* 565 (ill.), 566-567
Grassroots 6: 425
Grateful Dead *2:* 244; *3:* 542, 548, 584, 588; *4:* 94, 95
Grave Dancers Union 1: 169
Gravediggaz *2:* 300, 347-349
Gray, Macy *5:* **163 (ill.), 163–167,** 165 (ill.), 230
"The Greatest Love of All" *5:* 192
Green 6: 361
Green, James "Woody" *6:* 381
Green, Tony *2:* 336
Green Day *1:* 2, 60 (ill.), 61 (ill.), 62-64; *4:* 39–40, 41; *6:* 422, 449
Green Mind 1: 47
Green River *1:* 85, 118; *6:* 331
Greenbaum, Norman *5:* 293

Greenberg, Steve *5:* 171
Greenwood, Colin *6:* 347 (ill.), 347–350
Greenwood, Jonny *6:* 347 (ill.), 347–350
Grice, Gary. *See* Genius
Grieder, Peter *4:* 94
Griffin, Clive *4:* 108
Griffin, Richard *2:* 393
Griffin, Robert *3:* 569
Griffin, Warren, III. *See* Warren G.
The Grinch 6: 391
Grip *3:* 495
Grits Sandwiches for Breakfast *5:* 231
Grohl, Dave *1:* 49, 50 (ill.), 51-52, 95; *2:* 234, 238; *4:* 150 (ill.), 150–152
"Groove Is in the Heart" *6:* 433
Grunge *1:* 2, 4, 5, 8, 11, 13, 84-86, 95, 115, 174, 178, 179, 207; *2:* 229, 238, 279; *3:* 468, 469
Grym Reaper (Anthony Berkley) *2:* 348
Gudmundsdottir, Bjork (see Bjork)
The Guess Who *5:* 247
Guided by Voices *2:* 227; *3:* 543, 568-571
Guinness Bear *4:* 72
Guitar Slinger 6: 377
Guns N' Roses *3:* 465 (ill.), 467, 473 (ill.), 474–478
Gurewitz, Brett *1:* 107; *6:* 319
Guthrie, Woodie *4:* 30–31
Guy Lombardo Orchestra *6:* 386
GZA. *See* Genius

H

Hagar, Sammy *3:* 468
"Hair bands" *3:* 467
Hairway to Steven 1: 35
Haiti *2:* 346
Haley, Bill *3:* 540
Hall, Richard Melville (see Moby)
Hall, Terry *2:* 300
Halliwell, Geri *5:* 171
Halloween: H20 5: 262
Hammer *2:* 307, 350 (ill.), 351-354; *3:* 512
Hammett, Kirk *3:* 486; *5:* 287 (ill.), 290
Hammond, John *5:* 164

"Hanginaround" *4:* 76, 77
Hank Ballard and the Midnighters *3:* 502
Hanneman, Jeff *3:* 494, 495
Hansen, Beck. *See* Beck
Hanson *4:* 15, 154; *5:* 168 (ill.), **168–173,** 169 (ill.), 251; *6:* 421
Hanson, Isaac *5:* 168 (ill.), 168–173, 169 (ill.)
Hanson, Taylor *5:* 168 (ill.), 168–173, 169 (ill.)
Hanson, Zac *5:* 168 (ill.), 168–173, 169 (ill.)
Happy Mondays *2:* 227, 266, 281
Hard Core 5: 254
A Hard Day's Night 4: 70
Hard Knock Life Tour *5:* 204
"Hard Luck Woman" *4:* 50; *5:* 237
Hard Rain 5: 217
Hardcore rap *2:* 309
"The Hardest Part" *6:* 306
Hargraves, Brad *6:* 420 (ill.), 421–423
Harrell, Andre *2:* 356; *3:* 506; *6:* 340–341
Harris, Eleanora. *See* Holliday, Billie
Harris, Eric *5:* 271
Harrison, George *6:* 434
Harrison, Hank *5:* 183
Harrison, Jerry *1:* 43; *3:* 577; *6:* 396, 397
Harrison, Love Michelle. *See* Love, Courtney
Harrison, Shawtae. *See* Da Brat
Hart, Mickey *4:* 94
Hartley, Mathieu *2:* 250
Harvey, PJ *1:* 6; *2:* 222, 257 (ill.), 258-259
Harvey, Polly Jean (see PJ Harvey)
Harwell, Steve *6:* 389 (ill.), 389–392
Haseline, Dan *5:* 215 (ill.), 215–218
Havens, Richie *3:* 440
Hawkins, Lamont. *See* U-God
Hawkins, Taylor *4:* 150 (ill.), 151
Hayden, Shirley *5:* 232
Haynes, Cornell, Jr.. *See* Nelly
He's the DJ, I'm the Rapper 6: 399–400
Headliner *2:* 313

Parents Aren't Supposed to Like It

Headon, Nicky "Topper" *6:* 448 (ill.), 449
"Heart Shaped Box" *1:* 98
"Heartbreaker" *4:* 85
Heaton, Paul *2:* 223, 225
"Heaven If You Hear Me" *5:* 226
Heavy D & The Boyz *2:* 355 (ill.), 356-359
Heavy metal *1:* 13, 73, 94, 174; *3:* 465-469
"Hell" *6:* 377
Heller, Jerry *2:* 339, 362, 363
"Hello, I Love You" *4:* 80
Hello Nasty 4: 26
"Help" *4:* 98
"Help Me" *5:* 221
"Help Me, Rhonda" *4:* 20
Hemingway, Dave *2:* 223
Hendrix, Jimi *3:* 466, 467, 542; *5:* 245, 246, 246 (ill.); *6:* 370, 395
Hensley, Virginia. *See* Cline, Patsy
Herdman, Bob *4:* 100
"Here We Are" *4:* 138
"Here With Me" *4:* 132
"Hero" *4:* 60
"Heroes" *2:* 233
Heroin *6:* 395
Herring, Dennis *5:* 217
Herron, Cindy *3:* 524-526
Hestla, Brian *4:* 82
Hetfield, James *3:* 482, 483, 485 (ill.), 486; *5:* 287 (ill.), 290
Hewson, Paul. *See* Bono
"Hey Joe" *5:* 246
"Hey Jude" *4:* 77
"Hey Ladies" *4:* 25
Hidalgo, David *3:* 579, 581, 582
Hiedorn, Mike *3:* 592
"Higher" *4:* 82
"Higher Ground" *6:* 356
Higher Ground for Humanity *5:* 222
Higher Learning 4: 57
Highway 61 Revisited 4: 31; *5:* 201
Hill, Brendan *3:* 549
Hill, Dan *5:* 176
Hill, Faith *5:* **174 (ill.),** **174–178,** 177 (ill.), 194; *6:* 429
Hill, Lauryn *2:* 344; *4:* 55, 61; *5:* 179 (ill.), **179–182;** *6:* 370
Hillage, Steve *2:* 296

Hinojosa, Jorge *2:* 367
Hints, Allegations, and Things Left Unsaid 4: 65
Hip-hop and rap *2:* 302-311
The History of Rock 5: 231
Hit singles *5:* 188
Hogan, Mike *1:* 37
Hogan, Noel *1:* 37
Hohman, Thomas *2:* 288
Hold Me Up 5: 160
"Hold My Hand" *5:* 187
"Hold On" *5:* 255, 283; *6:* 370
Holdsworth, Jeff *3:* 588
Hole *1:* 6, 16, 65 (ill.), 66-68; *5:* 183 (ill.), **183–186,** 241
"Holla, Holla" *5:* 204
Holland, Annie *2:* 255
Holland, Dexter *1:* 105, 106 (ill.); *6:* 318-320
Holliday, Billie *5:* 164, 164 (ill.), 250; *6:* 395
Holly, Buddy *3:* 581; *4:* 70
Holtermann, Suzanne *3:* 513
"Home" *5:* 284
Home for Christmas 6: 316
Home states of musicians *4:* 55, 127, 154; *5:* 230, 241; *6:* 322, 429
Homelessness *5:* 279, 283
Homosexuality *1:* 6; *4:* 133; *5:* 207–208
"Honey" *4:* 61
Honor the Earth Campaign *3:* 452
Hooker, John Lee *5:* 250
Hootie and the Blowfish *3:* 541, 543, 544, 572 (ill.), 573, 574 (ill.), 575; *5:* 187 (ill.), **187–190**
Hope Floats 4: 50
Hopkins, Doug *3:* 562, 564
Hopkins, Lightnin' Sam *5:* 250
Hoppus, Mark *4:* 38 (ill.), 38–42
H.O.R.D.E festival *4:* 29; *5:* 283
H.O.R.D.E. tour *1:* 82, 133; *3:* 586, 608
Horner, James *4:* 109
Horovitz, Israel *4:* 24
Horovitz, Adam *4:* 23 (ill.), 23–27, 24 (ill.)
Horror imagery *2:* 347, 497
Horrorcore *2:* 347
Horton, Jerry *6:* 327 (ill.), 327–330
Hot 6: 377
Hot In the Shade 5: 237

Hothouse Flowers *4:* 72
Hotter Than Hell 5: 237
House of Pain *4:* 146, 147, 148; *5:* 258
House Party 3 (film) *3:* 537
Housemartins *2:* 223, 224
Houston, Cissy *5:* 191
Houston, Whitney *2:* 277; *3:* 518, 519; *4:* 55, 61; *5:* 191 (ill.), **191–195,** 197
"How Do I Live" *6:* 366, 367
"How Will I Know" *5:* 192
"How's It Going to Be" *6:* 421
Howlett, Liam *5:* 213
Howlin' Wolf *5:* 250
Howse, Stanley V.. *See* Flesh-N-Bone
Howse, Steven. *See* Layzie Bone
Hudson, Saul (see Slash)
Hughes, Andrew (FMGQ) *2:* 297
Hughes, John *4:* 71
Hugo, Victor *5:* 274, 276
"Human beatbox" *2:* 304, 309
Human Clay 4: 81, 82
Human League *1:* 88; *2:* 289
Human Rights Now! *3:* 448
Humor *1:* 22, 142
Humphrey, Bobbie *3:* 520
The Hunger 2: 233
Hunter, Jason. *See* Inspektah Deck
Hunter, Robert *4:* 94
Husker Du *1:* 8
Hutter, Ralf *2:* 287
Hybrid music styles *1:* 3
Hyenas in the Desert *2:* 396
Hyman, Jeffrey *1:* 138
Hyman, Phyllis *4:* 34
Hynde, Chrissie *2:* 220

I

"I Believe I Can Fly" *5:* 224, 227
"I Can Love You" *4:* 35
"I Do" *6:* 306
"I Don't Like Mondays" *4:* 72
"I Don't Wanna Cry" *4:* 60
"I Drive Myself Crazy" *6:* 316
"I Fall to Pieces" *6:* 365
"I Feel Good" *5:* 297
"I Get Around" *4:* 20
"I Go Blind" *5:* 188
"I Have Nothing" *5:* 192
"I Heard It Through the Grapevine" *4:* 90
I Make My Own Rules 5: 262

"I Need a Beat" 5: 261
"I Need to Know" 4: 5, 8
"I Need Love" 5: 261
I Need More (autobiography) 1: 70, 73
I Need You 6: 367
"I Need You Tonight" 5: 254
"I Still Haven't Found What I'm Looking For" 6: 443
"I Through a Brick Through a Window" 6: 443
"I Turn to You" 4: 2
"I Wanna Be Sedated" 1: 141
"I Wanna Dance with Somebody" 5: 192
"I Want it That Way" 4: 17
"I Want You Back" 6: 315
"I Will Always Love You" 5: 192
"I Will Follow" 6: 443
"I Will Remember You" 5: 283
"I Will Wait" 5: 189
"I Wish" 5: 227
"I Won't Stand in Your Way" 6: 376
"I'll Be Missing You" 6: 342, 414
"I'll Be There for You/You're All I Need" 4: 34
"I'll Fly Away" 6: 342
"I'll Never Break Your Heart" 4: 16
"I'm Eighteen" 5: 270
"I'm Every Woman" 5: 192
"I'm So Happy I Can't Stop Crying" 6: 414
"I'm Your Angel" 5: 227
I'm Your Baby Tonight 5: 192
Iacocca, Lee 3: 600
Ibold, Mark 1: 111
Ice Cube 2: 310, 332, 336, 339, 360 (ill.), 361, 362 (ill.), 363-365, 400, 422; 4: 44, 122; 5: 243
The Ice Opinion (essays) 2: 370
Ice-T 1: 3; 2: 307, 310, 366 (ill.), 367, 368 (ill.), 369-371, 422; 4: 147
"If Anybody Gets Funk Up" 6: 403
"If I Could Turn Back the Hands of Time" 5: 227
"If I Had $1,000,000" 1: 21; 4: 20
If I Left the Zoo 5: 217
"If It Makes You Happy" 5: 284

"If Tomorrow Never Comes" 4: 49
"If You Had My Love" 5: 264, 266
"If You Love Somebody Set Them Free" 6: 413
Iggy Pop 1: 69 (ill.), 70 (ill.), 71-74; 2: 232; 3: 616
Iglesias, Enrique 4: 5; 5: 196 (ill.), **196–199**; 6: 322, 429
Iglesias, Julio 5: 197
Igloo Record Company 3: 619
Ignition 6: 319
Iha, James 1: 164 (ill.), 165; 6: 393–398
Ill Communication 4: 25
Illinois musicians 5: 230
Illtown Records 2: 384
Iman 4: 128
The Imperial 4: 57
"The Impression That I Get" 5: 293
In Blue 4: 69, 72
"In God's Country" 6: 443
In the House 5: 262
In the Life of Chris Gaines 4: 51
In Living Color 5: 266
"In My Bed" 6: 382
In Pieces 4: 50
In Utero 1: 98
Incesticide 1: 98
Independence Day (film) 2: 328; 6: 400
"Independent Woman Pt. 1" 4: 105
Indiana musicians 5: 230
Indies (independent record companies) 1: 3
Indigo Girls 3: 441, 442, 451-453; 4: 137; 5: **200–202**, 200 (ill.); 6: 387, 429
Indigo Girls (Album) 5: 201
Industrial music 1: 78, 87, 90; 2: 278, 287, 297
INET festival 1: 125
The Inevitable 6: 377
Inez, Mike 1: 11, 14
Infest 6: 329
Infinite 4: 131
Injuries, fan 6: 331, 333–334, 357–358, 395
"Inna-Gadda-DaVida" 4: 77
Insane Clown Posse 4: 133
Insomniac 4: 41
Inspektah Deck 6: 452, 453
Inspiral Carpets 2: 266
International Harvesters 1: 207

Internet 1: 22
Internet downloading 4: 82; 5: 185, 259, 288–289; 6: 319, 332, 353
Internet live performances 5: 242
"Interstate Love Song" 1: 180
Interview with the Vampire (film) 3: 477
Into the Light 4: 138
"Invisible Man" 6: 306
Iommi, Tommy 6: 322, 324 (ill.)
Iovine, Jimmy 2: 330, 334
Ireland 1: 37, 190-193
"Iris" 5: 159, 162
Irish music 4: 72
Irish musicians 6: 322
Iron Butterfly 4: 77
"Iron Man" 6: 322
"Ironic" 5: 161
Ironman 6: 452
Irons, Jack 1: 116, 148; 6: 332, 355, 356
Isbelle, Jeffrey (see Izzy Stradlin)
Islamic faith 6: 435
Issues 5: 243
"It Ain't Over Til It's Over" 5: 247
It Matters to Me 5: 176
"It's All Been Done" 4: 21
It's Dark and Hell Is Hot 4: 119, 120
"It's Gonna Be Me" 6: 316
"It's a Man's, Man's, Man's World" 5: 297
"It's Nothing" 4: 85
"It's Your Love" 5: 176
Italian Remix 5: 197
Ivey, Antis, Jr. (see Coolio)
Ixnay on the Hombre 1: 108; 6: 318, 319

J

J. Lo 5: 267
Ja Rule 4: 55; 5: 203 (ill.), **203–205**
Jackson 5 5: 206
Jackson, Janet 4: 56 (ill.), 127; 5: 206 (ill.), **206–209**, 225, 230, 266; 6: 316
Jackson, Michael 2: 292; 3: 627; 4: 127; 5: 206, 207, 224, 225
Jackson, O'Shea (see Ice-T)

Jaffee, Rami 1: 200; 6: 446–447
Jagged Little Pill 5: 161
Jagger, Mick 2: 233; 3: 480
Jam 1: 1; 2: 225
Jam 80 3: 622
Jam, Jimmy 2: 277; 3: 512
Jamaican music 1: 184
James, Alex 2: 228
James, Cheryl. *See* Salt
James Dean Isn't Dead 2: 260
James, Elmore 2: 306
James, Will 6: 328
Jamiroquai 5: **210 (ill.), 210–214**; 6: 322, 421
Jane's Addiction 1: 75 (ill.), 76-77, 123, 166; 6: 356
Janet Jackson 5: 207
Janowitz, Peter 6: 446–447
Jar of Flies 1: 14
Jardine, Al 4: 20
Jars of Clay 4: 100; 5: **215 (ill.), 215–218**, 230
Jason 6: 314
Jason's Lyric 4: 89
Jay-Z 5: 204
Jazz musicians 6: 395
Jean, Wyclef 2: 344; 4: 35 (ill.), 105; 5: 180, 180 (ill.); 6: 370
Jefferes, Justin 6: 305 (ill.), 305–308, 307 (ill.)
Jeffers, Eve Jihan 4: 119, 119 (ill.)
The Jeffersons 5: 245
Jello Biafra 1: 34; 2: 368
Jenkins, Stephan 6: 420 (ill.), 420–423, 422 (ill.)
Jennings, Peter 2: 413
"Jeremy" 6: 332
Jerky Boys 3: 554
Jerry Maguire (film) 3: 601
Jesus Freak 4: 98, 99, 100
"Jesus Is Just Alright" 4: 98, 99
Jesus Lizard 2: 240
Jethro Tull 6: 329
Jewel 5: **219 (ill.), 219–223**; 6: 322, 421
Jimi Hendrix Experience 5: 246
"Jingo" 6: 370
Joannou, Chris 1: 160
Jodeci 4: 36
Joe C. 5: 232, 232 (ill.)
Joel, Phil 5: 216
John 5 5: 271

John, Elton 3: 613; 4: 36, 66, 67, 133, 134 (ill.); 5: 208; 6: 367
John Wesley Harding 4: 31
Johns, Daniel 1: 161
Johnson, Max 3: 608
Johnson, Pamela 4: 33–34
Johnson, Robert 5: 250
Johnson, Scott 3: 563
Johnston, Bruce 4: 20
Johnston, Freedy 3: 613
"Joining You" 5: 161
Jones, David (see Bowie, David)
Jones, George 2: 243
Jones, Kimberly Denise. *See* Lil' Kim
Jones, Maxine 3: 524-526
Jones, Mick 6: 448 (ill.), 449
Jones, Quincy 2: 307, 374; 3: 521; 5: 225
Jones, Russell. *See* Ol'Dirty Bastard
Jones, Steve 3: 478
Jones, Tom 6: 408
Joplin, Janis 6: 395
Jordan, Michael 5: 227
The Joshua Tree 1: 192; 6: 442, 443
Joy: A Holiday Celebration 5: 222
Joy Division 2: 221
J.R.S. Records 3: 573
"Jubilee" 6: 443–444
Judas Priest 3: 466
Judgment Night 4: 147
Juice 2: 425, 426
"Jump Around" 4: 147
Jump blues 3: 501
Jump rope rhythm 6: 303
"Jumpin', Jumpin'" 4: 103
Jungle 2: 235, 278
Jungle Fever 6: 345
Junior M.A.F.I.A. 5: 254
Just a Gigolo 2: 233
"Just a Girl" 1: 101; 6: 311
Just the Two of Us 6: 400
Justified Ancients of Mu Mu (JAMS) 2: 295
"Justify My Love" 5: 247

K

Kain, Gylan 2: 305
Kanal, Tony 6: 309 (ill.), 309–312
Kannberg, Scott "Spiral Stairs" 1: 110

Karges, Murphy 6: 416 (ill.), 417–419
"Kashmir" 6: 342
Kato, Nash 1: 187, 188
Katruud, Nathan 1: 188
Katz, Lawrence 5: 293
Katzenberg, Jeggrey 1: 81
Kay Gee 2: 382, 383, 408
Kay, Jay 5: 210 (ill.), 210–214
K-Ci 4: 36
Keane, Dolores 4: 69
Keith, Ben 5: 221
Keith, Toby 6: 414
Kelly, R. 2: 277, 324; 4: 36, 110, 155; 5: **224 (ill.), 224–228**, 230
Kelly, Robert S.. *See* Kelly, R.
Kennedy, John F. 2: 275; 5: 271
Kerplunk 1: 61
Kerrville Folk Festival 3: 441, 462
Kershenbaum, David 3: 448
Kettle Whistle 1: 77
Khan, Chaka 4: 34; 5: 192
Kid A 6: 349
Kid Creole (Nathaniel Glover) 2: 308
Kid Jonny Lang and the Big Bang 5: 251
Kid Rock 4: 131; 5: **229 (ill.), 229–234**, 232 (ill.)
Kids Cafe 6: 439
Kiedis, Anthony 1: 148 (ill.); 6: 355, 355 (ill.), 356–357
Kilcher, Jewel. *See* Jewel
"Killing Me Softly" 5: 179, 181
"Killing Time" 4: 103
Kilmer, Val 4: 80
Kimble, Paul 3: 565, 566
Kinchla, Chan 3: 549
King, B.B. 5: 250, 251
King Bees 2: 231
King, Dee Dee 1: 142
King, John 1: 26
King, Kerry 3: 493-495
"King of Pain" 6: 412
King's Blank 2: 238
The Kings of Gangster Bop 6: 377
Kinks 1: 60; 2: 221, 227; 3: 465
Kinney, Sean 1: 11 (ill.), 12
Kirby, Kier (see The Lady Miss Kier)
Kirk Franklin and the Family 4: 155

Index

Kirk Franklin's Nu Nation 4: 155
Kirkpatrick, Chris 6: 313 (ill.), 313–317
KISS 2: 232; 3: 466; 4: 50, 55; 5: 235 (ill.), **235–239**, 236 (ill.)
Kittie 5: 185
Klebold, Dylan 5: 271
Klein, Chris 5: 262
KLF 2: 296
Kling Klang 2: 288
Knight, Gladys 2: 306
Knight, Marion "Suge" 2: 333, 334, 335, 353, 389, 421, 422, 427, 428; 4: 123, 124; 6: 404
"Knock on Wood" 5: 251
Knowles, Beyonce 4: 102 (ill.), 102–106, 104 (ill.)
Kool Moe Dee 2: 307, 372 (ill.), 373-375
Koppelman, Brian 3: 447
Koppelman, Charles 3: 447, 448
KoRN 3: 469; 5: 188, 240 (ill.), **240–244**, 243 (ill.), 258; 6: 329, 417
KoRN (Album) 5: 242
Kowalczyk, Ed 3: 576 (ill.), 577-578; 4: 77
Kraftwerk 2: 277-279, 287 (ill.), 288-289
Krasnow, Robert 3: 448
Krause, Jason 5: 232
Kravitz, Lenny 3: 541, 542, 613 (ill.), 614, 630 (ill.) 631-633; 5: 245, 245 (ill.), **247–248**
Krayzie Bone 4: 43–47, 45 (ill.)
Kreisel, Greg 1: 105
Krez, Eric 1: 179
Krieger, Robbie 4: 80, 81
Kriesel, Greg 6: 318–320
Kris Kross 1: 188; 4: 85
Krizan, Anthony 3: 596
KRS-One 2: 304, 309, 317 (ill.), 374, 399, 407
Krusen, Dave 6: 331
Kubrick, Stanley 5: 298
Kukl 3: 622
Kulick, Bruce 5: 237
Kurt and Courtney 5: 184

L

La Bamba 3: 581; 4: 70; 6: 376
"La Copa de la Vida" 5: 276
"La Vida Loca" 4: 5; 5: 197–198, 273, 276
Lachey, Drew 6: 305 (ill.), 305–308, 307 (ill.)
Lachey, Nick 6: 305 (ill.), 305–308, 307 (ill.)
Lack, Steve 1: 197
"Ladies First" 6: 345
Ladies Fresh 2: 400
"Ladies Night" 5: 254
"Ladies Night in Cambodia" 5: 258
"Lady" 4: 90
Lady Miss Kier 2: 277, 283 (ill.), 284 (ill.), 285–286
LaFace Records 3: 508, 536, 538
The Lamb 4: 51
Landau, Jon 3: 598, 599
Lander, Mercedes 5: 185
Lander, Morgan 5: 185
Lang, Jonny 4: 154; 5: 172, 249 (ill.), **249–252**
lang, k. d. 3: 615, 634 (ill.), 635, 636 (ill.), 637, 638; 4: 51
Lang, Kathryn Dawn (see k. d. lang)
Lange, Jessica 6: 365
Lange, Robert John "Mutt" 6: 437, 439
Langer, Clive 2: 239
Langseth, Jon. *See* Lang, Jonny
"Larger Than Life" 4: 17
LaRock, Scott 2: 304, 317
"Last Kiss" 6: 332
The Last Meal 6: 402, 404
Last Poets 2: 305; 6: 434
"Last Resort" 6: 330
The Last Tour on Earth 5: 272
Latin Rascals 4: 7
Latino 5: 196–197
"L.A. Woman" 4: 80
Layzie Bone 4: 43–47, 45 (ill.)
Leaders of the New School 4: 55
"Lean on Me" 4: 155
LeAnn Rimes 6: 367
Learning How to Smile 4: 143, 144
Leary, Paul 1: 33
Led Zeppelin 3: 465, 542; 5: 250, 257; 6: 322, 329, 342, 395
Lee, Brenda 4: 49
Lee, McKinley Malik 2: 420
Lee, Murphy 6: 302
Lee, Spike 2: 385
Lee, Stan 4: 36
Lee, Tommy 5: 254
Leeds, Alan 3: 531
Leeds, Eric 3: 531
Leen, Bill 3: 562
Left Eye. *See* Lopes, Lisa.
The Legend of Bagger Vance 6: 401
Lemonade and Brownies 6: 417
Lenear, Kevin 5: 292, 293
Lennon, John 2: 232; 6: 434
Lennox, Annie 6: 338
Leonard, Sugar Ray 6: 417
Les Miserables 5: 274
Lesbians. *See* Homosexuality
Lesh, Phil 4: 94
Less Than Zero 5: 261; 6: 357
Lessard, Stefan 4: 93, 94, 95 (ill.)
Let 'Em Know 6: 329
"Let Her Cry" 5: 187
Let It Come Down 6: 397
Let It Loose 4: 138
Let Love Rule 5: 247
Let's Face It 5: 293
Let's Get Ready 5: 296, 297
"Let's Make Love" 5: 177
Let's Talk About Love 4: 109
"Let's Wait Awhile" 5: 207
Lewis, Terry 2: 277; 3: 529
LFO 6: 407
Liar Liar 5: 217
Liar's Poker 6: 357
Licensed to Ill 4: 23, 25, 26
Lie to me 5: 249, 251
Liebling, Beth 1: 117
"Life During Wartime" 6: 397
Life Is Peachy 5: 242
Life Of Agony 3: 468
Lifebeat 5: 283
"Light My Fire" 4: 77, 80
"Like a Rolling Stone" 4: 77
Lil' Kim 4: 84, 85, 128; 5: 253 (ill.), **253–256**; 6: 342
Lilith Fair tours 4: 2, 112, 128; 5: 201, 282, 283
Lillywhite, Steve 4: 96
Limon, Leigh 4: 29
Limp Bizkit 5: 231, 243, 257 (ill.), **257–260**, 258 (ill.); 6: 429
The Linguini Incident 2: 233
Linton, Mike. *See* Zum, Zim
Lipson, Steve 5: 217
"Liquid" 5: 217
Liquid Swords 6: 452
"Listen" 4: 65

Parents Aren't Supposed to Like It

Listen Up: The Lives of Quincy Jones 3: 521
Listener Supported 4: 96
Literacy 5: 175
Little Anthony and the Imperials 6: 302
Little Creatures 6: 397
Little Feat 4: 114; 6: 385
"Little Girl's Eyes" 5: 247
"Little More Time on You" 6: 316
Little Richard 2: 230, 232, 244; 3: 540
Little Stevie Wonder 5: 211
Littrell, Brian 4: 14 (ill.), 14–18, 16 (ill.)
Live 3: 543, 576 (ill.), 577-578
Live Aid 1: 191, 206; 2: 233; 6: 324
Live albums 4: 96; 6: 333
"Live For Loving You" 4: 138
Live at Luther College 4: 96
Live From the Middle East 5: 293
Live Internet performances 5: 242
Live at Red Rocks 4: 96
Live Through This 1: 67; 5: 183, 184
Living Colour 1: 2; 2: 394; 3: 467, 479 (ill.), 480–481
Living Out Loud 6: 345
Living Single (TV show) 2: 401, 402; 6: 345
LL Cool J 2: 307, 309, 372-374, 376 (ill.), 377-381, 422; 4: 25, 55; 5: 261 (ill.), **261–263**
Load 5: 288
Lofgrin, Nils 3: 600
Lollapalooza 1: 2, 3, 16, 18, 67, 77, 87, 89, 119, 123, 125, 130, 135, 143, 151; 2: 253, 256, 315, 363, 369, 422; 3: 481, 486; 5: 242, 283; 6: 352
Lombardo, Dave 3: 494, 495
Lombardo, Guy 6: 386
London Calling 6: 448–449, 449
London's FreedomFest 3: 448
"A Long December" 4: 76
The Long Road Out of Hell 5: 271
Long songs 4: 77
"Look into My Eyes" 4: 45

Lopes, Lisa "Left Eye" 3: 535-537; 4: 85; 5: 254; 6: 428 (ill.), 428–431
Lopez, Jennifer 4: 2, 5, 7 (ill.), 55; 5: 264 (ill.), **264–268**, 267 (ill.); 6: 342
Los Angeles punk 1: 2
Los Angeles riots, 1992 2: 341, 363
Los Dinos 5: 265
Los Lobos 3: 543, 579 (ill.), 580-583
"Loser" 1: 3, 24, 27, 28; 4: 28
"Losing My Religion" 1: 157; 6: 361
Louisiana musicians 6: 429
Love, Courtney 1: 6, 16, 65 (ill.), 66-68, 97; 5: 183 (ill.), 183–186
Love Gun 5: 237
"Love Is All We Need" 4: 35
"Love Is the Seventh Wave" 6: 413
Love It to Death 5: 270
Love, Mike 4: 20
Love, Misty 5: 232
Love, Monie 2: 400
The Love Movement 6: 435
"Love of My Life" 4: 96; 6: 372
"Love Takes Time" 4: 60
Lovebug Starski 2: 304, 308
"Lover Man" 5: 164
Low 1: 72, 91; 2: 219, 232
The Low End Theory 4: 55; 6: 432, 433, 434
Lowe, Nick 1: 1; 2: 220, 243, 244
Lowell, Charlie 5: 215 (ill.), 215–218
Lower Third 2: 231
Lowery, John. *See* John 5
Lozano, Conrad 3: 579, 580
L7 1: 5
Lucas, Gary 3: 444
Lucas, Sara Lee 5: 270
Luciano, Felipe 2: 305
"Lucky" 6: 409
Lynyrd Skynyrd 6: 329, 385

M

Ma Rainey 5: 250
Macey, Robin Lynn 4: 113
MACHINA/The Machines of God 6: 397, 398
Machine Elves 3: 566
Mack 10 6: 430
Mack, Bill 6: 365

MacLeod, Brian 3: 628
MacLise, Angus 3: 654
Mad Season 1: 14; 5: 278, 281
Madness 1: 184
Madonna 2: 234, 277; 4: 61, 139; 5: 247, 276
Maggart, Brandon 4: 10
Magnie, John 3: 603, 604
Magnificent Bastards 1: 180
Maguire, Barrie 1: 200; 6: 446–447
Mahoney, Tim 6: 424 (ill.), 424–427
Maines, Natalie 4: 112 (ill.), 112–116, 113 (ill.)
Major releases 5: 188
Major Tom 2: 231
Malcolm X (film) 2: 315
Malibu 5: 185
Malinin, Mike 5: 160
Malkmus, Steve (SM) 1: 110 (ill.), 112-113
Malley, Matt 3: 557; 4: 75
Malone, Tommy 3: 603, 604
Maloney, Samantha 5: 185
Mama Said 5: 247
Mama Said Knock You Out 5: 262
Mami, Cheb 6: 414
Man on the Moon 5: 185; 6: 362
The Man Who Fell to Earth (film) 2: 233
Mana 6: 371 (ill.)
Manchester, England 1: 4; 2: 266, 280
Mandela, Nelson 2: 316
Manic Subsidal 6: 318
Mann, Aimee 3: 612
Manson, Marilyn 1: 78 (ill.), 79-80, 90; 3: 469; 5: 185, 223, 269 (ill.), **269–272**
Manson, Shirley 1: 53 (ill.), 55; 6: 310
Manzarek, Ray 4: 80
Marc Anthony 4: 8
Marching Two Step 3: 552; 4: 65
"Maria, Maria" 6: 372
Mariachi music 6: 369
Mariah Carey 4: 60
"Marigold" 1: 50
Marijuana 6: 395, 426
Marilyn Manson (band) 5: **269–272**
Marked 1: 165; 6: 394
Marker, Steve 1: 53; 6: 310

Marketing in the music industry 1: 2, 5; 2: 244
Marley, Bob 1: 183, 184; 5: 181
Marley, Rohan 5: 181
Marley, Ziggy 3: 550
Maroon 4: 21
Marr, Johnny 2: 221, 260, 261
Marrow, Tracey (see Ice-T)
Marsalis, Branford 6: 414
Marshall, Arik 1: 151; 5: 166; 6: 356
Marshall, Brian 4: 79 (ill.), 79–83
The Marshall Mathers LP 4: 132–133
Marshall Tucker Band 6: 385
Martha and the Vandellas 2: 233; 3: 504; 4: 105
Martin, Dewey 1: 204
Martin, George 2: 221
Martin, Max 6: 407
Martin, Ricky 4: 2, 5; 5: 197–198, 273 (ill.), **273–277**, 275 (ill.); 6: 322
Martinez, Angie 4: 85; 5: 254
Martinez, Eddie 2: 406
Martinez, S.A. (Douglas) 6: 424 (ill.), 424–427
Marvelettes 3: 504
Mary 4: 36
Maryland musicians 4: 127
Mascis, J 1: 45 (ill.), 46-48
Mason, Marilyn 4: 155; 6: 429
Mason, Steve 5: 215 (ill.), 215–218
Massachusetts musicians 4: 127
Massive Attack 2: 278, 299, 300
Masta Killa 6: 451 (ill.)
Master of Puppets 5: 288
Master P 2: 311; 5: 296–297
Matador Records 3: 570, 651
Matchbox Twenty 5: 278 (ill.), 278–281, 280 (ill.); 6: 421, 429
Mathers, Marshall Bruce, III. *See* Eminem
Mathus, Jim 6: 377
Matthews, Dave 3: 543, 584 (ill.); 4: 93 (ill.), 93–97, 95 (ill.); 6: 371, 372
Matthews, Donna 2: 255, 256
Matthews, Eric 3: 613
Maverick Records 3: 641
Max, Kevin 4: 98 (ill.), 98–101
Maxwell, Simon 4: 100

Maybe You Should Drive 4: 20
Mayfield, Curtis 3: 542
M'Boya 2: 304
MC Lyte 2: 400
MC Ren 2: 332, 364
MCA 3: 640
MC5 1: 69
MCs 2: 306
McAfee, Diana 4: 10
McBride, Terry 4: 20
McCarroll, Tony 2: 266
McCartney, Paul 1: 139; 2: 220, 245; 6: 434
McCary, Michael 3: 511, 512
McCollum, Rick 1: 7
McConnell, Page 3: 588, 589
McCready, Mike 1: 116; 6: 331, 332, 334
McDaniel, Darryl "DMC" 2: 404
McDonnell, Jim 6: 375
McElroy, Thomas 3: 525
McEntire, Reba 5: 176
McGinnis, Will 4: 100
McGovney, Ron 3: 486; 5: 288
McGrath, Mark 6: 416 (ill.), 416–419
McGraw, Tim 5: 174, 176, 177 (ill.)
McGuigan, Paul "Guigs" 2: 266
McGuinn, Roger 1: 156
McIntyre, Natalie. *See* Gray, Macy
McKagen, Michael "Duff" 3: 474, 478
McKane, Bryon. *See* Bizzy Bone
McKeehan, Toby 4: 98 (ill.), 98–101
McKenzie, Derrick 5: 210
McKernan, Ron "Pigpen" 4: 94
McKnight, Blackbird 5: 166
McKnight, Duane 6: 356
McLachlan, Sarah 3: 442, 454 (ill.), 455-457; 4: 20; 5: 201, 282 (ill.), **282–286**; 6: 408
McLean, A.J. (Alexander James) 4: 14 (ill.), 14–18, 16 (ill.)
McLean, Don 4: 50, 77
McLin, Lena 5: 225
McManus, Declan Patrick (see Elvis Costello)
McManus, Ross 2: 242
McPhatter, Clyde 3: 502
Me Amaras 5: 274
Meat Is Murder 2: 261

Mechanical Animals 5: 271
Medina, Benny 3: 520
A Medio Vivir 5: 276
Megadeth 3: 467, 482 (ill.), 483-484, 486; 5: 288
Melanie C. 6: 430
"Melissa" 6: 385
Melle Mel 2: 305, 307, 308, 374; 6: 341
Melle Mel & the Furious Five 6: 341
Mellon Collie and the Infinite Sadness 1: 165, 167; 6: 394, 395
Mellor, John. *See* Strummer, Joe
Mellow Gold 1: 24, 27; 4: 29
Melvins 1: 94, 95
Melvoin, Jimmy 1: 167
Melvoin, Jonathan 6: 395
Men in Black (film) 2: 328; 4: 103; 6: 400
Mendel, Nate 4: 150 (ill.), 151
Menudo 4: 7; 5: 274
Menza, Nick 3: 483
Mercury Falling 6: 414
Mercury Records 3: 441, 461-463, 648, 649
"The Message" 6: 341
"Message in a Bottle" 6: 412
Metallica 3: 466, 467, 477, 482, 483, 485-489; 5: 188, 241, 259, 287 (ill.), **287–290**
Metallica (Album) 5: 288
Method Man 2: 307; 4: 34; 5: 259; 6: 338, 451 (ill.), 452, 453
Mexican songs 3: 581
Mi Reflejo 4: 1, 2
Mi Tierra 4: 138
Miami 6: 400
Miami Latin Boys 4: 137
Miami Sound Machine 4: 136, 137–138
Michael Archer and Precise 4: 89
Michael, George 4: 51; 5: 258
Michel, Prakazrel "Pras" 2: 344; 5: 180
Michigan musicians 5: 230
Mickey Mouse Club Show 6: 314, 406, 407
Middle of Nowhere 5: 172
Midnight 2: 237
Midnight Marauders 6: 434
Midnite Vultures 4: 30
Midwest musicians 5: 230

Mighty Mighty Bosstones *1:* 5, 185; *4:* 127; *5:* **291–294**
Mike D *4:* 23 (ill.), 23–27, 24 (ill.)
Milarepa Fund *4:* 25
Miles, Buddy *5:* 246; *6:* 370
Millenium 4: 17; *5:* 258
Miller, Percy. *See* Master P
Miller, Tobi *1:* 200; *6:* 446–447
Milli Vanilli *6:* 408, 408 (ill.)
The Million Dollar Hotel 6: 443
Mills, Mike *1:* 154, 156; *6:* 360 (ill.), 360–363
Milo, Custmaster *4:* 55
Mind of Mystikal 5: 296
Mingus, Charles *5:* 221; *6:* 434
Ministry *1:* 87
Mink, Ben *3:* 635
Minty Fresh record label *1:* 196
The Minus Man 5: 284
Minutemen *1:* 2
Mirror Ball 1: 120; *5:* 285
"Misdemeanor Lipstick" *4:* 128
The Miseducation of Lauryn Hill 5: 179, 181
Misfits *3:* 469–471
Misogyny *4:* 133; *6:* 432
"Miss You Much" *5:* 207
Mission: Impossible Soundtrack 6: 443
Mississippi musicians *6:* 429
Missouri musicians *5:* 230
Mitchell, Joni *3:* 441, 612; *5:* 208, 221
Mitchell, Mitch *3:* 568, 569; *5:* 246
Mitchell, Scott. *See* Berkowitz, Daisy
Mize, Ben *4:* 76
Mizell, Jason "Jam Master Jay" *2:* 404, 405, 408
"MMMBop" *5:* 168, 172
Mo Thugs Family Scriptures 4: 45
Mob Town *4:* 85
Moby *2:* 279, 291 (ill.), 292–294
Molina, Ralph *1:* 204
Molly Hatchet *6:* 385
Money Train 5: 266
Monie Love *2:* 310
"Monkey Wrench" *1:* 51
Monster *1:* 157; *6:* 361
Monsters of Rock Festival *3:* 475, 487, 491
Montana, Tony *6:* 390

Montoya, Craig *4:* 141 (ill.), 142, 143
Moody Blues *6:* 434
Moon, Chris *3:* 529
Moon Records *1:* 185
Moore, Alecia. *See* Pink
Moore, LeRoi *3:* 585; *4:* 93, 94
Morales, Enrique Martin. *See* Martin, Ricky
More Noise and Other Disturbances 5: 292
More Songs About Buildings and Food 6: 397
Morello, Tom *1:* 134 (ill.); *6:* 351, 352 (ill.), 353, 354
Morganfield, McKinley *5:* 250
Morissette, Alanis *1:* 151; *3:* 611 (ill.), 613, 639 (ill.), 640-642; *4:* 61, 96; *5:* 161, 161 (ill.); *6:* 348
Morphine *1:* 81 (ill.), 82-83; *3:* 550
Morris, Nathan *3:* 511, 512
Morris, Steveland. *See* Wonder, Stevie
Morris, Wanya *3:* 511, 512
Morrison, Jim *4:* 72, 80, 80 (ill.); *6:* 395
Morrison, Sterling *3:* 654
Morrison, Van *3:* 541, 542
Morrissey *2:* 221, 260-264
Mosely, Tim "Timbaland" *4:* 127
Mosh pits *6:* 395, 396
Moshing *2:* 277, 279
"Most Girls" *6:* 338
Mother Love Band *6:* 331
Mother Love Bone *1:* 85, 118;
Mother's Milk 1: 149; *6:* 356
Motley Crue *3:* 467
Motown *2:* 243; *3:* 504
Motown Records *2:* 2763: 506, 512, 513
Mottola, Tommy *4:* 60, 61
Mouth of Rasputin *3:* 566
Movies about music *4:* 70
Moyet, Alison *2:* 300
Mp3 format *6:* 332
Mr. Crowes Garden *3:* 546
"Mr. Jones" *4:* 75, 76
Mr. Smith 5: 262
"Mr. Tambourine Man" *4:* 31
"Mrs. Potter's Lullaby" *4:* 76, 77
"Mrs. Robinson" *5:* 201
MTV *1:* 2, 13; *2:* 221, 222, 376, 379, 407; *3:* 441, 459, 467, 498

MTV Unplugged 1: 14, 98, 118; *2:* 376, 379; *3:* 441
Much Afraid 5: 217
Muddy Waters *5:* 250
Mudhoney *1:* 84 (ill.), 85-86, 95
Mueller, Karl *1:* 170
Mugzy's Move 6: 377
Muhammad, Ali Shaheed *4:* 89; *6:* 433–436
Mulan 4: 2; *6:* 306
Mullen, Larry, Jr. *1:* 190; *6:* 442 (ill.), 442–445
Multimedia images *1:* 193
Murmur 1: 154; *6:* 361
Murphy, Daniel *1:* 170
Murphy, Eddie *5:* 208
Murphy, Kyjuan *6:* 302
Music (album) *6:* 425
Music
    alternative metal *6:* 327
    bagpipe *5:* 242
    Blues *5:* 250
    Christian *4:* 79, 100
    downloading *4:* 82; *5:* 185, 259, 288–289; *6:* 319, 332, 353
    folk *5:* 201
    folk rock *5:* 201
    funk *5:* 297
    Irish *4:* 72; *6:* 322
    jazz *6:* 395
    mariachi *6:* 369
    movies on *4:* 70
    neo-soul *4:* 91
    reggae *6:* 390
    rock *4:* 100; *6:* 385, 395
    salsa *4:* 5
    ska *5:* 291–292; *6:* 378
    swing *6:* 377, 378
    teen pop *5:* 170–171
    tejano *5:* 265
Music Box 4: 60
Music 4-Life *2:* 357
Music for the Jilted Generation 5: 213
Music of My Heart 4: 139; *6:* 316
Music of My Mind 5: 211
Musical Chairs 5: 189
Muslim faith *6:* 435
Mustaine, Dave *3:* 482 (ill.), 483–484, 486; *5:* 288
"Mustang Sally" *5:* 251
Mutations 4: 29, 30
My Aim Is True 2: 220, 241
"My All" *4:* 61
"My Baby You" *4:* 8

"My Boy Lollipop" *1:* 184
My Brother the Cow *1:* 85
"My Everything" *6:* 307
My Family *5:* 266
"My Favorite Mistake" *5:* 284
"My Getaway" *6:* 430
"My Gift to You" *5:* 241
"My Heart Will Go On" *4:* 107, 109
My Life *4:* 34
My Life in the Bush of Ghosts *6:* 397
My Love Is Your Love *5:* 193
"My Name Is" *4:* 131
My Own Prison *4:* 80–81
My Own Private Idaho *6:* 357
Mydland, Brent *4:* 94
Myers, Dwight A. *2:* 356
The Mynah Birds *1:* 204
"Mysterious Ways" *6:* 443
Mystikal *5:* **295–299**, 296 (ill.); *6:* 429

N

"N 2 Gether Now" *5:* 259
Nada Como El Sol *6:* 413
Nadirah *2:* 315
Naked Lunch *6:* 329
Naked Toddler *4:* 80
"Name" *1:* 57; *5:* 159, 160
Napalm Death *3:* 468
Napster *5:* 185, 259, 288–289; *6:* 319, 353
Nashville Skyline *4:* 31
Nastanovich, Bob *1:* 111
"Nasty" *5:* 207
Nasty Ness *2:* 416
National anthem *5:* 192
National Ethnic Coalition *3:* 645
National Institute on Drug Abuse *3:* 560
National Organization for Women *4:* 133; *5:* 213
Native Tongues Posse *6:* 433
Natural Born Killers (film) *1:* 90
Nature of a Sista *6:* 345
Naughty by Nature *2:* 307, 323, 382 (ill.), 383 (ill.), 384-386, 408
Naughty Gear *2:* 384
Navarro, Dave *1:* 76, 77, 126, 151; *3:* 641; *6:* 355, 356
Nazz *2:* 231
Nebraska musicians *4:* 154
Nedell, Tiff *5:* 213

Nelly *5:* 230; *6:* 301 (ill.), **301–304**, 303 (ill.)
Nelson, David Jordan, Jr. *2:* 305
Nelson, Prince Rogers (see Prince)
Nelson, Willie *6:* 365
Nemesis *5:* 204
Nemesister *1:* 18
Neo-soul music *4:* 91
"Nervous in the Alley" *6:* 390
Nettwerk Records *3:* 456
Neurotic Outsiders *3:* 478
"Never Be the Same Again" *6:* 430
"Never Let You Go" *6:* 422
Nevermind *1:* 4, 54, 95, 97; *4:* 150
New Adventures in Hi-Fi *6:* 361
New Edition *2:* 277, 369; *3:* 516, 517, 519
New Jack City (film) *2:* 369; *4:* 70
New Jack Swing *2:* 277, 358
New Jersey musicians *4:* 55
New Jill Swing *3:* 505, 524, 535
New Order *1:* 2; *2:* 221
New Orleans, Louisiana *3:* 603
"New Pollution" *4:* 29
New Power Generation *3:* 528, 531, 532
New School Punk *1:* 105
The New Style *2:* 384
New wave *1:* 1, 72, 142; *2:* 277
New York City dance scenes *2:* 284
New York City musicians *4:* 55, 127
New York State musicians *4:* 127
Newell, Ryan *6:* 386, 386 (ill.)
Newport Folk Festival *4:* 31
The Newsboys *5:* 216
Newsted, Jason *3:* 487; *5:* 288, 289–290
Next Plateau Records, Inc. *2:* 411
Nichols, Joseph McGinty *6:* 417
Nico *3:* 654
Nieve, Steve *2:* 243
"Niggaz Done Started Something" *4:* 119
A Night Without Armour *5:* 222

Nine Inch Nails *1:* 3, 79, 87 (ill.), 88, 89 (ill.), 90-92; *2:* 234; *5:* 269
1960s rock music *2:* 275
1979 *6:* 395
"97 Bonnie and Clyde" *4:* 3
98 Degrees *5:* 230, 241; *6:* 305 (ill.), **305–308**, 307 (ill.), 337
"98 Degrees and Rising" *6:* 306
Nirvana *1:* 2, 4, 5, 49-51, 54, 66, 84, 93 (ill.), 94-95, 96 (ill), 97-100, 115, 175; *2:* 222, 238, 240; *4:* 150, 151; *5:* 184; *6:* 332, 394
No Angel *4:* 132
No Code *1:* 121; *6:* 332
No Depression *3:* 607
No Doubt *1:* 101 (ill.), 102-104, 185; *2:* 279; *5:* 241, 291; *6:* 309 (ill.), **309–312**
No Doubt (Album) *6:* 311
No Fences *4:* 49–50
No Limit label *2:* 311
No Limit Records *4:* 34; *5:* 296
"No Me Ames" *4:* 7; *5:* 266
"No More Mr. Nice Guy" *5:* 270
No More Tears *6:* 325
No Need to Argue *1:* 39
"No One to Depend On" *6:* 370
No Rest for the Wicked *6:* 325
"No Scrubs" *6:* 429
"No Sleep Till Brooklyn" *4:* 25
No Strings Attached *6:* 316
"No Time" *5:* 254
No Use for a Name *4:* 151
No Way Out *6:* 342
"Nobody Like You" *5:* 259
North Dakota musicians *4:* 154
Nosebleeds *2:* 260
Not Ashamed *5:* 216
"Not Gon' Cry" *4:* 34
"Not Tonight" *4:* 85; *5:* 254
"Nothing As It Seems" *6:* 332
Nothing Like the Sun *6:* 413
Nothing Records *1:* 78, 90
Nothing's Shocking *1:* 76
Notorious B.I.G. *2:* 310, 387 (ill.), 388-391, 424, 426, 428; *5:* 253, 254; *6:* 341, 342
The Notorious K.I.M. *5:* 255
Novoselic, Krist *1:* 5, 94, 99; *4:* 150
NOW *4:* 133; *5:* 213
Nowell, Brad *1:* 182; *6:* 395

Parents Aren't Supposed to Like It

NPG (New Power Generation) 3: 528, 531, 532
NSync 4: 2, 17, 139; 6: 303 (ill.), 313 (ill.), **313–317**, 315 (ill.), 429
NSync (Album) 6: 316
Nu Nation Project 4: 153, 155
Nu Thang 4: 99
Numbers 6: 426
"Nuthin' But a 'G' Thang" 6: 404
Nutty Professor II: The Klumps 4: 119; 5: 208
NWA 2: 305, 310, 332, 333, 339, 360, 361, 362, 419; 4: 44, 122

O

Oakes, Richard 2: 270, 272
Oasis 2: 221, 227, 228, 238, 265 (ill.), 266 (ill.), 267 (ill.), 268-269, 281; 6: 421
O'Brien, Brendan 1: 150
O'Brien, Ed 6: 347 (ill.), 347–350
Ochs, Phil 3: 439
O'Connor, Daniel 4: 146–147
O'Connor, Sinead 2: 253, 256; 3: 614, 643 (ill.), 644-646; 4: 72
October 6: 443
ODB. *See* Ol'Dirty Bastard
Odelay 1: 3, 24, 26, 28; 4: 29
Odmark, Matt 5: 215 (ill.), 215–218
O'Donnell, Roger 2: 249, 250
The Offspring 1: 105 (ill.), 106 (ill.), 107-110; 5: 241; 6: 318 (ill.), **318–320**
Ohio musicians 5: 230
Ohio Players 2: 276
Oje, Baba 2: 313
O.K. Computer 5: 293; 6: 347, 348-349
Oklahoma musicians 4: 154
"Oklahoma" 4: 49
Ol'Dirty Bastard 6: 452, 453-454
Old Friends From Young Years 6: 328
"Old Man & Me" 5: 188
Old school punk 1: 146, 183
Old school rap 2: 372, 375
Olliver, Ian 2: 258
Olson, Kenny 5: 232
On How Life Is 5: 166
On the 6 5: 264, 266, 267

Onassis, Blackie 1: 187
"Once in a Lifetime" 6: 397
"One" 4: 81; 6: 443
One Foot in the Grave 4: 29
"One Headlight" 6: 447
One hit groups 5: 293
One Hot Minute 1: 151; 6: 356
"The One I Love" 6: 361
One in a Million 5: 226
One Little Indian 3: 624
"One Moment in Time" 5: 192
"One Sweet Day" 4: 61
"One Voice" 4: 49
"One Week" 4: 19
Only Built for Cuban Linx 6: 452
"Only Wanna Be With You" 5: 187
"Only When It Rains" 6: 310
Onyx 2: 408
Ooooooh . . . On the TLC Tip 6: 428–429
Oops . . . I Did It Again 6: 409
Operation Ivy 1: 145, 146, 185
"Orange Crush" 6: 361
The Orb 2: 279, 295 (ill.), 296-298
Orbison, Roy 3: 599, 636
Order in the Court 6: 344, 345
Oregon musicians 5: 241
The Organisation 2: 288
"Original Prankster" 6: 319
Original Soundtrack, Vol. 1 6: 443
Orioles 3: 502
O'Riordan, Caitlin 2: 243
O'Riordan, Dolores 1: 37 (ill.), 38-41
Osborne, Joan 3: 615, 647 (ill.), 648-649
Osbourne, John Michael. *See* Osbourne, Ozzy
Osbourne, Ozzy 3: 465, 466; 6: 321 (ill.), **321–326**, 324 (ill.)
Osbourne, Sharon 6: 321, 323–324, 397
Oseary, Guy 3: 641
Osman, Mat 2: 270
Osterberg, James Jewell (see Iggy Pop)
Otra Nota 4: 7
Otto, John 5: 257
Out Da Gutta 2: 426
Out of Sight 5: 266
Out of Time 1: 157; 6: 361
OutKast 5: 298, 298 (ill.)

Outlandos d'Amour 6: 412
Outlaws 6: 385
Owen, Mark 2: 240
Owens, Dana Elaine. *See* Queen Latifah
Oyawole, Abiodun 2: 305
"Oye Como Va" 4: 6; 6: 370
"Oye Mi Canto" 4: 138
Ozzfest tour 6: 325
Ozzmosis 6: 325

P

Pablo Honey 6: 348
Pacino, Al 4: 39
Padham, Hugh 3: 628
Page, Jimmy 3: 466; 5: 250; 6: 342
Page, Stephan 1: 20; 4: 19 (ill.), 19–22, 21 (ill.)
Pain Killers 1: 18
Paisley Park 3: 531
Palmer, Bruce 1: 204
Pantera 3: 468, 490 (ill.), 491-492
Papa Roach 5: 241; 6: 327 (ill.), **327–330**
"Papa Was a Rollin' Stone" 4: 77
"Papa's Got a Brand New Bag" 4: 77
"Paranoid" 6: 322
Parental Advisory Labelling 1: 62
Parents Just Don't Understand 6: 400
Parents Music Resource Center (PMRC) 3: 530
Parker, Alan 4: 71
Parker, Charlie 6: 395
Parker, Graham 2: 220
Parker, Laurence Krisna (see KRS-One)
Parker, Maceo 1: 149
Parliament/Funkadelic 2: 276, 285; 4: 85
Parsons, Dave 2: 237
Parton, Dolly 5: 192
"The Party Continues" 4: 85
"Party Up" 4: 117, 120
"The Passengers" 6: 443
Patterson, Alex 2: 295-297
Patti Smith Group 1: 139
Patton, Antwan, "Big Boi" 5: 298, 298 (ill.)
Paul's Boutique 4: 25, 26
Pavement 1: 110 (ill.), 111 (ill.), 112-114, 166; 2: 227

Pavitt, Bruce 1: 173
Pay Attention 5: 293–294
Peacock, Charlie 4: 100
Pearl Jam 1: 2, 14, 85, 115 (ill.), 116, 117 (ill.), 118-122, 149, 207, 208; 2: 269; 5: 241; 6: **331–334**
Pearl, Lucy 6: 435
Pearlman, Lou 4: 14–15, 16–17; 6: 316
Pebbitone 3: 538
Pebbles 3: 536
Peltier, Leonard 1: 136; 6: 352
Pendergrass, Teddy 5: 192
Penn, Michael 3: 442, 458 (ill.), 459-460
Penn, Sean 5: 222
Penniman, Richard (see Little Richard)
Pennsylvania musicians 4: 127
People of the Sun 6: 353
The People vs. Larry Flynt (film) 1: 67
People's Instinctive Travels and the Paths of Rhythm 6: 433, 434
Pérez, Louie 3: 579–582
Perez, Rosie 5: 266
Perez, Rudy 4: 3
Perez, Selena Quintalla. *See* Selena
"Perfect Day" 4: 67
Perkins, Stephen 1: 76
Perry, Audrey Faith. *See* Hill, Faith
Perry, Joe 2: 406
Perry, Pat 5: 175
Pet Shop Boys 2: 292; 4: 51
Peters, Joey 3: 566, 567
Peterson, Roberta 3: 449
Pfaff, Kristen 5: 184
P-funk style 6: 403
Phair, Liz 3: 614, 650 (ill.), 651-652
Phenomenon 5: 262
Phife 6: 433–436
Philadelphia (film) 3: 601
Phillips, Duncan 5: 216
Phillips, Grant Lee 3: 565 (ill.), 566, 613
Phillips, Julianne 3: 600, 601
Phillips, Scott 4: 79 (ill.), 79–83
Phish 3: 542, 543, 588 (ill.), 589-590
Phoenix, River 1: 151
Picadilly Boys 4: 6
Pickett, Wilson 2: 276; 5: 251

Pickwick Records 3: 654
Piece of Cake 1: 85
Pieces of You 5: 219, 221, 222
Pierce, Allison 4: 114
Pierce, Catherine 4: 114
PIL 2: 296
"Pinhead" 1: 139
Pink 4: 127; 6: 336 (ill.), **336–339**, 337 (ill.)
Pink Floyd 2: 232, 296; 3: 543; 4: 77; 5: 180; 6: 329, 434
Pinkett, Jada 6: 400
Pioughd 1: 35
Pirner, David 1: 169 (ill.), 170, 171
Pittsburgh Steelers 4: 2
Plant, Robert 3: 465, 466
Platoon (film) 3: 480
"Players Anthem" 5: 254
Please Listen to My Demo 4: 124
"Please, Please, Please" 5: 297
"The Pleasure Principle" 5: 207
Plummer 2: 304
P-Nut 6: 424 (ill.), 424–427
Pod 2: 240
Poetic Justice 2: 426; 3: 537; 5: 207; 6: 429
Poetry 5: 222
Pogo dancing 2: 277
The Pogues 2: 243; 4: 72
Poison 3: 467
The Police 6: 342, 411, 412–413
Political action 6: 353
Political music 1: 191; 2: 285, 305, 392
Political rap 2: 305, 392
Pollard, Bob 3: 568–570
Poltz, Steve 5: 220
The Polyfuze Method 5: 231
Pop 6: 443
Pop Art Records 2: 411
Pop, Iggy (see Iggy Pop)
Pop Mart Tour 1: 192; 6: 443
Pop metal 3: 466
Pop rap 2: 327
Pop Will Eat Itself 1: 90
Popper, John 3: 542, 548 (ill.), 549-550; 5: 172, 251
"Por Siempre Tu" 4: 2
Pork Guys 2: 292
Pork Soda 1: 130
Porno for Pyros 1: 77, 123 (ill.), 124 (ill.), 125-126
Portishead 1: 3; 2: 300

Portrait of an American Family 5: 270
Post, Louise 1: 197
"The Power of Love" 4: 108
"The Power of the Dream" 4: 109
Power pop 2: 221
Prakazrel Michel 2: 344
Prawn Song (label) 1: 131
The Preacher's Wife 5: 192, 193
"Precious Declaration" 4: 65
The Presidents of the United States of America 1: 127 (ill.), 128-129
Presley, Elvis 2: 244; 3: 540; 4: 59; 5: 175; 6: 374
The Pretenders 2: 220
"Pretty Fly" 6: 318, 319
Pretty Hate Machine 1: 89
Pretty on the Inside 5: 184
Preysler, Isabel 5: 197
"Pride" 6: 443
Pride, Charlie 2: 243
Primitive Love 4: 138
The Primitives 3: 654
Primus 1: 130 (ill.), 131-133; 3: 550
Prince 2: 277; 3: 503, 504 (ill.), 521, 528 (ill.), 529-534; 4: 89
Prince and The Revolution 3: 530
Prince of Egypt 4: 61; 5: 217
Prince Paul (Paul Huston) 2: 347
Prince Rakeem 6: 452
Prince Rogers Trio 3: 529
Prison Song 4: 36
Private Music Records 3: 461, 463
Prodigy 2: 278; 3: 469; 4: 26; 5: 213
Psychedelic Furs 2: 221
Psychedelic rock 1: 71
Psychedelic Stooges 1: 71
Psycho 6: 357
Psycho Circus 5: 238
Public Affection 3: 576, 577
Public Enemy 2: 307, 309, 328, 331, 392 (ill.), 393-397, 407; 4: 55
Puente, Tito 4: 6, 6 (ill.); 5: 274
Puerto Rican musicians 6: 322
Puff Daddy 4: 34, 55, 61; 5: 227, 254, 266; 6: 340 (ill.), **340–343**, 414, 421, 454. *See also* Combs, Sean

Pulp Fiction 1: 187
Pulsford, Nigel 2: 237
Punk 1: 1, 2, 25, 60, 61, 63, 69, 72, 94, 105, 139, 141, 147, 183; 2: 277
Punk/ska/reggae 1: 182; 2: 241
Purple 1: 180
"Purple Haze" 5: 246
"Push" 5: 278, 279
"Put Your Hands Where My Eyes Could See" 4: 56
"Put Your Lights On" 4: 148; 6: 372
Puterbaugh, Parke 2: 224

Q

Qawwali 3: 648
Q-Tip 2: 408; 6: 433 (ill.), 433–436
Queen 2: 233
Queen Latifah 2: 306, 307, 310, 384, 399 (ill.), 400-402; 4: 51, 55; 6: 344 (ill.), **344–346**
Queensryche 3: 469
The Quest for Camelot 4: 72
A Question of Balance 6: 434
Question the Answers 5: 292
Quiet Riot 3: 466
"Quit Playing Games" 4: 15
Qwest 3: 521

R

R. 5: 227
R. Kelly 5: 224
Radical chic 6: 353
Radio 5: 261
Radio airtime 4: 77
"Radio Free Europe" 6: 361
"Radio Song" 6: 361
Radioactive Records 3: 577
Radiohead 2: 221; 4: 25; 6: 322, 347 (ill.), **347–350**, 421
Raekwon 6: 452, 453
Rage Against the Machine 1: 134 (ill.), 135-137; 4: 25, 137; 5: 241; 6: 351 (ill.), **351–354**, 425, 449, 453
Rahiem 2: 304
Rain 2: 266
"The Rain" 4: 128
"Rain King" 4: 76
Rainbow 4: 62
"Ramblin' Man" 6: 385
Ramirez, Twiggy 1: 79; 5: 270
Ramone, C.J. 1: 142

Ramone, Dee Dee 1: 138
Ramone, Joey 1: 138
Ramone, Johnny 1: 138
Ramone, Richie 1: 142
Ramone, Tommy 1: 138
The Ramones 1: 1, 138 (ill.), 139-144
Rancid 1: 145 (ill.), 146-147, 185; 2: 279
Rant'n Rave with the Stray Cats 6: 375
Rap 2: 299, 302-429
    Dirty South 5: 298
    gangsta 5: 296–297; 6: 341
    metal 6: 352
Rap and the Grammys 2: 307
Rap Olympics 4: 131
Rape, Abuse and Incest National Network (RAINN) 3: 617, 619
"Rapper's Delight" 2: 306; 6: 341
Rattle and Hum 6: 443
Rave parties 2: 278, 280
Ravens 3: 502
Raw Power 1: 71
Rawls, Lou 5: 192
Ray, Amy 3: 442, 451, 452; 5: 200–202, 200 (ill.)
Ray, Anthony (see Sir Mix-A-Lot)
Raynor, Scott 4: 39, 40
RCA Records 3: 459, 460
"Ready to Run" 4: 114
"Real Love" 4: 34
"The Real Slim Shady" 4: 2, 130, 132
"Rebel" 4: 7
"Rebel Heart" 4: 69
Recently 4: 95
Reckoning 1: 155
The Reclines 3: 635
Record Industry Association of America 1: 62
Recovering the Satellites 4: 75, 76
Red Hot Chili Peppers 1: 77, 117, 148 (ill.), 149, 150 (ill.), 151-152; 5: 241; 6: 352, 355 (ill.), **355–359**, 403
"Red Light Special" 6: 428
Redding, Noel 5: 246
Redding, Otis 2: 276; 3: 541
Redline 6: 385
Reed, Brett 1: 145
Reed, Dizzy 3: 475

Reed, Lou 3: 614, 653 (ill.), 654, 655 (ill.), 656-657; 6: 434
"Reflection" 4: 2
Refugee Camp Youth Project 5: 181
Regatta de Blanc 6: 412
Reggae 1: 183, 184; 2: 241, 299; 6: 390
Reggae-flavored rap 2: 343
Reid, Antonio "L.A." 2: 277; 3: 507, 508, 517, 536, 537
Reid, Perri M. (see Pebbles) 3: 536
Reid, Vernon 2: 394; 3: 479 (ill.), 480-481
Relapse tour 1: 77
Religion 4: 153
Religious imagery 1: 191
"Religious Love" 5: 226
R.E.M. 1: 2, 153 (ill.), 154, 155 (ill.), 156-159; 3: 441, 543; 6: 348, 360 (ill.), **360–363**, 376, 429
Remain in Light 6: 397
Remember Two Things 4: 94
"Reminisce" 4: 34
Remixes 2: 281, 292
Renegades 6: 351, 354
The Replacements 1: 2
Return of Dragon 6: 383
The Return of Satan 6: 309, 311–312
Return of the Space Cowboy 5: 212
Reveal 6: 362
Revelation 6: 307
Revenge 5: 238
"Revolution" 4: 153
Revolver 6: 349
Reynolds, Tim 4: 94, 96
Reznor, Trent 1: 78, 87 (ill.), 89 (ill.); 2: 234; 5: 269
Rhoads, Randy 6: 323, 325
Rhodes, Philip 3: 563
Rhone, Sylvia 4: 128
Rhyme Syndicate label 2: 366, 369
Rhythm and blues 2: 241, 300; 3: 501-505
"Rhythm Divine" 5: 197
"Rhythm Is Gonna Get You" 4: 138
Rhythm Nation 1814 (Album) 5: 207, 208
"Rhythm Nation" (Song) 5: 207
"Ribbon in the Sky" 5: 225

Richards, Keith 5: 250
Richardson, Bill 4: 65
Richardson, Jiles Perry (see the Big Bopper)
Richardson, Kevin Scott 4: 14 (ill.), 14–18, 16 (ill.)
Richling, Greg 1: 200; 6: 447
Ricky Martin 5: 274, 276
"Ride on the Rhythm" 4: 7
Ride with the Devil 5: 222
Ridenhour, Carl (see Chuck D)
"Riders on the Storm" 4: 77, 81
Right On (film) 2: 305
Riley, Ted 2: 358, 373, 374
Rimes, LeAnn 4: 154; 6: 364 (ill.), **364–368**, 408, 429
Rimes, Wilbur 6: 364, 366, 367
Riot Grrrls movement 1: 16
The Rise and Fall of Ziggy Stardust and the Spiders from Mars 2: 219, 232
Ritchie, Lionel 4: 61; 5: 207
Ritchie, Robert James. See Kid Rock
Rites of Passage 5: 201
Ritual De Lo Habitual 1: 76
Rivers, Sam 5: 257
"Roadhouse Blues" 4: 81
ROAR Tour 1: 74
Robbin' the Hood 1: 183
Roberson, La Travia 4: 103, 104
Roberts, Brad 1: 42, 43 (ill.)
Roberts, Elliot 3: 448
Robertson, Ed 1: 20; 4: 19 (ill.), 19–22
Robinson, Bobby 2: 306
Robinson, Chris 3: 541, 545 (ill.), 546
Robinson, Dawn 3: 524-526; 6: 435
Robinson, Rich 3: 545 (ill.), 546
Robinson, Ross 5: 258
Robinson, Sylvia 2: 306
Robison, Charlie 4: 115
Robison, Emily 4: 112 (ill.), 112–116, 113 (ill.)
Roc-a-Fella 5: 204
Rocha, Zach de la 6: 351 (ill.), 351–354, 354
Rock and Roll 3: 539–544
"Rock and Roll All Nite" 5: 237
Rock and Roll Hall of Fame 1: 119; 2: 234
Rock 'n' Roll High School 1: 141; 4: 70
"Rock and Roll Is Dead" 5: 247

Rock and Roll Over 5: 237
"Rock and Roll, Part 2" 5: 293
Rock Bottom 3: 573
Rock for Choice benefit concerts 1: 136
Rock, Chris 5: 188
Rock establishment 1: 1
Rock music
 Christian 4: 100
 drugs and 6: 395
 Southern 6: 385
Rock, Pete 2: 408
Rock in Rio II Festival 3: 475
Rock Spectacle 1: 22; 4: 20
"Rock the Casbah" 6: 449
Rock the House 6: 399
"Rock This Town" 6: 375
Rockabilly 2: 243
Rockabilly Rebel 6: 375
Rockathon 3: 569
Rocker, Lee. See Drucker, Leon
"Rocket Man" 4: 66
"Rockin' in the Free World" 1: 207
Rocksteady 1: 184
Roeder, Klaus 2: 288
Roeser, Ed 1: 188
Rogers, Kenny 5: 180
Roker, Roxie 5: 245
Roland, Dean 4: 64, 65
Roland, Ed 3: 552 (ill.), 553-554; 4: 64 (ill.), 64–68
Rolison, D'Mon. See Mack 10
Rollerball 5: 262
Rolling Stones 2: 233, 257, 267, 276; 3: 480, 541, 596; 5: 251, 284; 6: 395, 409, 421
Rollins Band 1: 3
Romeo and Juliet 5: 271
Romeo Blue (see Lenny Kravitz)
Romeo Must Die 4: 120; 5: 226
The Ronettes 4: 105
Ronson, Mick 2: 232
"Rooster" 1: 13
Roper, Deidra (see DJ Spinderella)
Ropin' the Wind 4: 50
"Rosa Parks" 5: 298
Rosas, Cesar 3: 579, 580
Rose, Axl 3: 465 (ill.), 467, 473, 474-478, 480
"A Rose Is Still a Rose" 5: 181
Rose, William (see Axl Rose)
Roskilde, Denmark concert 6: 331, 333–334
Ross, Diana 2: 276; 3: 525; 4: 61, 105; 6: 337, 342

Rossdale, Gavin 1: 103; 2: 222, 237 (ill.), 238-240
Rosse, Eric 3: 619
Roswell 4: 132
Roswell Records 4: 151
Roth, David Lee 3: 468
Rotheray, Dave 2: 223
Rotten, Johnny 1: 1 (ill.), 2, 206; 2: 296
"Round Here" 4: 76
Rowan, John 1: 187
Rowland, Kelly 4: 102 (ill.), 103, 104 (ill.)
Rowlands, Tom 2: 280
Rowntree, Dave 2: 228
"Roxanne" 6: 412, 414
Roxy Music 2: 222
Royal Crown Revue 6: 377
Royal Sons 3: 502
Rubber Soul 5: 201
Rubin, Rick 1: 150; 2: 309, 331, 377, 393, 416; 3: 467, 471, 494, 546; 4: 24, 25
Rucker, Darius 3: 572 (ill.), 575; 5: 187 (ill.), 187–190
Ruckett, Le Toya 4: 103, 104
Rue, Caroline 5: 184
Ruff Ryders 4: 119; 5: 204
RuffHouse label 2: 344, 345
Ruffin, David 1: 9
Ruffin, Tamir "Nokio" 6: 381–382
Rugrats in Paris 6: 430
The Rugrats Movie 4: 57
Rule 3:36 5: 205
"Run" 4: 65
"Runaway" 5: 207
The Runaway Bride 4: 115
"Runaway Train" 1: 169
Rundgren, Todd 3: 613
Run-DMC 2: 308, 309, 403 (ill.), 404, 405 (ill.), 406-408
Runt 5: 259
Russell, Keri 6: 314
"Russians" 6: 413
Ruthless 6: 407
Ruthless Records 2: 331, 332, 338, 339, 361
The RZA. See Prince Rakeem
Rzarector (RZA) 2: 348
Rzeznik, Johnny 1: 57 (ill.); 5: 159 (ill.), 159–162

S

S & M 5: 288
Saadiq, Raphael 6: 435
Sabec, Christopher 5: 171

Sadler, Eric 4: 55
Sailing the Seas of Cheese 1: 130
St. John, Mark 5: 237
St. Lunatics 6: 302, 304
Sainte-Marie, Buffy 3: 439
Salazar, Arion 4: 41; 6: 420 (ill.), 421–423
Sales, Hunt 2: 234
Sales, Tony 2: 234
Saliers and Ray 5: 200
Saliers, Emily 3: 442, 451 (ill.), 452; 5: 200–202, 200 (ill.); 6: 387
Salsa music 4: 5
Salt (Cheryl James) 2: 410; 4: 155
Salt-N-Pepa 2: 307, 310, 400, 410 (ill.), 411, 412 (ill.), 413-414; 4: 155
Samhain 3: 470, 471
Samples, digital 1: 3, 26; 2: 279, 281, 297, 309, 372, 374; 3: 498
Sandinista! 6: 449
Sandman, Mark 1: 81-82
"Santa Monica" 4: 143
Santana 4: 6, 96, 148; 5: 241, 246, 278, 280; 6: 369 (ill.), **369–373**, 371 (ill.)
Santana Blues Band 6: 370
Santana, Carlos. *See* Santana
Santana III 6: 370, 371
"Santeria" 1: 182
Sap 1: 13
Satanism 1: 78, 79; 3: 494; 5: 271
"Satisfaction" 6: 409
"Satisfy You" 5: 227
Saturday Night Fever 2: 276
Saturday Night Live 1: 135; 2: 244; 3: 459, 557, 644, 645
Save the Music Foundation 4: 96
"Saving All My Love for You" 5: 192
"Say It Loud, I'm Black and I'm Proud" 5: 297
"Say My Name" 4: 103, 105
SBK 3: 447
"Scar Tissue" 6: 358
Scarface 4: 39; 6: 390
Scary Movie 5: 255
Scat Records 3: 569
Scattered, Smothered & Covered 5: 189
Scatting 2: 304; 3: 444
"Scenario" 4: 55

Schemel, Patty 5: 183 (ill.), 184
Schenkman, Eric 3: 595, 596
Schneider, Florian 2: 287
Schon, Neil 6: 370
School shootings 5: 271, 283
"School's Out" 5: 270
Schools of Thought 6: 337
Schrody, Erik. *See* Everlast
Schubert, Franz 4: 29
Scialfa, Patty 3: 600, 601
Scorcher 6: 385
The Score 5: 180–181
Scratching 2: 304
"Scream" 5: 207
Screaming Trees 1: 14
Scruggs, Charles. *See* Wish Bone
Seagal, Steven 4: 118 (ill.)
"Seal Our Fate" 4: 138
Seattle, Washington 1: 4, 5, 13, 49, 66, 84, 85, 95, 118, 172, 173, 175; 2: 15; 3: 468
Second Harvest Food Bank 6: 439
Second Nature 3: 536
"Seether" 1: 196
Seidel, Martie 4: 112 (ill.), 112–116, 113 (ill.)
The Selecter 1: 184
Selena 5: 265
Selena (Movie) 5: 265, 266
Self-destructive behavior 5: 271
"Self Esteem" 1: 108
Selway, Phil 6: 347 (ill.), 347–350
"Semi-Charmed Life" 6: 420, 421
Sepultura 3: 468
Serletic, Matt 5: 279
Set It Off 2: 402
Setzer, Brian 4: 55; 6: 374 (ill.), **374–379**, 376 (ill.)
Sevens 4: 50
Severin, Steve 2: 250
Severson, Edward Louis, III (see Eddie Vedder)
Sex Maggots 5: 160
"Sex Me" 5: 225
Sex Pistols 1: 1 (ill.), 60, 139, 206; 2: 219, 225; 6: 449
Sexsmith, Ron 3: 613
Sexton, Chad 6: 424 (ill.), 424–427
"Sexual Healing" 4: 90
"Sexy and Seventeen" 6: 375–376

Seymour, Stephanie 3: 475
SFW (film) 1: 18
Sgt. Peppers Lonely Hearts Club Band 4: 31; 6: 347, 349, 434
Shades 3: 654
"Shadowboxer" 4: 11
Shaffer, James "Munky" 5: 240, 240 (ill.), 242
Shaft 4: 57
"Shake It Fast" 5: 295, 297–298
"Shake Your Bon-Bon" 5: 276
Shakespeare, William 5: 271
ShaKim Compere 6: 345
Shakur, Tupac 2: 311, 335, 389, 422, 424 (ill.), 425-430; 4: 123, 124; 5: 207, 254, 296; 6: 341, 452
"Shame on You" 5: 201
"Shameless" 4: 50
Shaming of the Sun 5: 201
"Shamrocks and Shenanigans" 4: 147
Shango 6: 370
"Shape of My Heart" 4: 17
Shapiro, Jim 1: 197
Share My World 4: 35
"She's All I Ever Had" 5: 276
She's All That 5: 255
"She's On It" 4: 25
Sheehan, Bobby 3: 549
"Sheena Is a Punk Rocker" 1: 140
Sheik, Duncan 5: 217
Shepherd, Ben 1: 174
Sheppard, Rodney 6: 416 (ill.), 417–419
Sherman, Jack 6: 355
Sherrill, Billy 2: 243
Sheryl Crow 5: 284
Shiflett, Chris 4: 150 (ill.), 151
"Shimmy, Shimmy, Ko-Ko-Bop" 6: 302
Shindig label 4: 142
"Shine" 4: 64, 65
Shining Path 6: 353
"Shiny Happy People" 6: 361
The Shirelles 4: 105
Shiva Burlesque 3: 566
Shock G 2: 425
Shock-rock 1: 78
Shocked, Michelle 3: 441, 442, 461 (ill.), 462-463
Shocking Pinks 1: 206
Shocklee, Hank 4: 55
"Should I Stay or Should I Go?" 6: 449
"Show Me the Way" 4: 17

"The Showman" 5: 293
Shur, Itaal 5: 280
Siamese Dragon 6: 394
Siamese Dream 1: 163
Sickle-cell anemia 6: 430
Significant Other 5: 258, 259
Silverchair 1: 160 (ill.), 161-162
Silveria, David 5: 240, 240 (ill.)
Simmons, Daryl 3: 507, 536
Simmons, Earl. *See* DMX
Simmons, Gene 5: 235 (ill.), 235–239
Simmons, Joseph "Run" 2: 404
Simmons, Russell 2: 309, 377
Simon and Garfunkel 3: 440; 5: 201
Simon, Carly 3: 441
Simon, Paul 3: 440, 581, 612
Simone, Nina 4: 11
Simonon, Paul 6: 448 (ill.), 449
Simons, Ed 2: 280
"Simple Kind of Life" 6: 311
Simple Machines label 1: 50
Simpson, Jessica 6: 306
Simpson, Michael 1: 26
"Sin Wagon" 4: 114
Singer, Eric 5: 238
Singers/Songwriters 3: 611–616
Singles, hit 5: 188
Singles (film) 1: 13, 175
Siouxsie and the Banshees 1: 1, 3; 2: 250
Sir Mix-A-Lot 2: 407, 415 (ill.), 416-417; 5: 188
Sire Records 3: 635
Sirois, Joe 5: 292
Sisqo 4: 61, 120, 127; 6: 380 (ill.), **380–383**, 381 (ill.)
Sisqo's Shakedown 6: 382
Sista 4: 127
Sister Hazel 4: 114; 6: **384–388**, 386 (ill.), 429
Sisters of Mercy 2: 395
Sittin' On Top of the World 6: 367
Six Degrees of Separation 2: 328; 6: 400
Sixteen Stone 2: 239
"6th Avenue Heartache" 6: 446, 447
Ska music 1: 102, 184, 185; 2: 277, 279; 5: 291–292; 6: 378
Skacore 1: 146, 185
Skanking 2: 279

Ski Hard 6: 357
Skillings, Muzz 3: 480, 481
Skinner, Leonard 6: 329
Skinny Puppy 1: 87
Skunk Records 1: 183
Skye, Ione 4: 26
Slacker culture 1: 27, 45, 111
Slam dancing 2: 277
Slam Jamz 2: 396
Slanted and Enchanted 1: 112
Slash 3: 474, 475, 477, 478
Slash Record Company 1: 3, 54; 3: 566, 580
Slash's Snakepit 1: 14; 3: 477
Slater, Andrew 4: 11; 5: 166; 6: 447
Slayer 3: 467, 493 (ill.), 494–495
Sleep Now in the Fire 6: 353
"Sleep to Dream" 4: 12
Sleepless in Seattle 4: 108
"Sleepwalker" 6: 446, 448
Slick Rick 2: 411, 419
"Slide" 5: 162
Slim Jim Phantom. *See* McDonnell, Jim
Slim Shady EP 4: 131
Slovak, Hillel 1: 148, 149; 6: 355, 356
Slow Train Coming 4: 31
Sly and the Family Stone 2: 276
"Smack My Bitch Up" 5: 213
Small, Millie 1: 184
Smalls, Biggie (see The Notorious B.I.G.)
Smart Studios 1: 53
Smash 1: 105, 107; 6: 318, 319
Smash Mouth 5: 241; 6: 389 (ill.), **389–392**, 449
Smashes, Thrashes, and Hits 5: 237
Smashing Pumpkins 1: 163 (ill.), 164 (ill.), 165-168; 2: 234; 5: 184, 230; 6: **393–398**, 394 (ill.)
Smear, Pat 4: 151
Smells Like Children 5: 270
"Smells Like Teen Spirit" 1: 97, 175
Smith, Bessie 5: 250
Smith, Chad 1: 149; 6: 356, 357
Smith, Clifford. *See* Method Man
Smith, Elliott 3: 613

Smith, James Todd. *See* LL Cool J
Smith, Jean Kennedy 4: 71–71
Smith, Patti 1: 158; 2: 222
Smith, Robert 2: 221, 248 (ill.), 249-251
Smith, Toby 5: 210
Smith, Trevor. *See* Busta Rhymes
Smith, Will 2: 326; 4: 127; 6: 399 (ill.), **399–401**
The Smiths 2: 221, 260, 261
Smokey Robinson and the Miracles 2: 276
Smokin' 5: 251
"Smooth" 5: 278; 6: 371
Sneaker Pimps 1: 3
Snipes 6: 304
Snoop Dogg 2: 310, 334, 336, 418 (ill.), 419, 420 (ill.), 421-422; 4: 84; 5: 241; 6: 402 (ill.), **402–405**
Snoop Dogg Presents Tha Eastsidaz 6: 404
Snowed In 5: 172
"So Emotional" 5: 192
So Much for the Afterglow 4: 143
"So Much to Say" 4: 95
"So Pure" 5: 161
"So Sad to Say" 5: 294
Social activism 3: 462
Socialist revolutionaries 6: 351
"Sock It 2 Me" 4: 85, 128
Soft Cell 1: 2; 2: 277
Soft Wolf Tread 3: 566
Solace 5: 282
Solar Records 2: 419
Some Kind of Zombie 4: 100
"Someday" 4: 60; 6: 417
"Sometimes" 6: 407
Somewhere More Familiar 6: 387
Son in Law 6: 357
Son Volt 3: 543, 591 (ill.), 592-593, 606
Sonefeld, Jim "Soni" 3: 573; 5: 187 (ill.), 187–190
S1W (Security Of The First World) 2: 393
"Song for the Man" 4: 26
The Song Remains the Same 4: 70
Songs 4: 77; 5: 188
Songs from an American Movie, Vol. One: Learning How to Smile 4: 143, 144

Parents Aren't Supposed to Like It

Songs from an American Movie, Vol. Two: Good Time for a Bad Attitude 4: 144
Songs in the Key of Life 5: 211
Sonic Youth 1: 18, 95; 2: 234
Sood, Ashwin 5: 283
Sordid Humor 4: 75
Sorum, Matt 3: 475, 478
Soul Asylum 1: 2, 169 (ill.), 170-171
Soul Caddy 6: 377
The Soul Cages 6: 413
Soul music 1: 8, 9; 2: 276, 277; 3: 502, 503, 505
Sound Loaded 5: 276
Soundgarden 1: 2, 95, 172 (ill.), 173, 174 (ill.), 175-177; 2: 269; 3: 469
The Sounds of Silence (Album) 4: 26
"The Sounds of Silence" (Song) 5: 201
Soundsystem 6: 426–427
South Bronx, New York 2: 304
South Carolina musicians 6: 429
South Central Los Angeles 2: 322, 360
Southeast musicians 6: 429
Southern rock 3: 544; 6: 385
Southernplayalisticadillacmuzik 5: 298
Space Jam 2: 414; 5: 227
"Space Oddity" 2: 231
Space rock 2: 296
Spade, David 5: 233
Spanish musicians 6: 322
Sparkle and Fade 4: 143
Speak of the Devil 6: 324
Speaking in Tongues 6: 397
Spears, Britney 4: 1, 40, 132; 6: 303 (ill.), 314, 406 (ill.), **406–410**, 407 (ill.)
"Special" 6: 310
The Specials 1: 184; 2: 277, 300
Spector, Phil 1: 140; 3: 599; 4: 105
Speech 2: 312
Speed metal 3: 466, 483, 490, 495
Spence, John 6: 309
Sphere 6: 345
Spice 5: 171
Spice Girls 4: 15; 5: 170 (ill.), 170-171
"Spiderweb" 6: 311
Spielberg, Steven 1: 81

Spin 6: 434
Spin Doctors 3: 543, 550, 594 (ill.), 595-596
"Spin the Black Circle" 6: 332
Spinderella 2: 410
"Spirit in the Sky" 5: 293
Spiritual music 4: 153
Spit 5: 185
Spoonie Gee 2: 308, 373
Springsteen, Bruce 3: 541 (ill.), 597 (ill.), 598-602, 615; 4: 50
Sprout, Tobin 3: 570
Squeeze 2: 220
The Squires 1: 204
Squirrel Nut Zippers 6: 377
Stage behavior 1: 60, 63, 71, 150; 2: 262, 301
Stahl, Franz 4: 151
Staley, Layne 1: 11 (ill.), 12 (ill.), 13
Stamp, Terence 2: 272
"Stan" 4: 132
"Stand" 6: 361
Stankonia 5: 298
Stanley, Paul 5: 235 (ill.), 235–239
Stansfield, Lisa 6: 342
Stapp, Scott 4: 79 (ill.), 79–83
Starland Vocal Band 6: 408
Starr, Brenda K. 4: 60
Starr, Ringo 6: 434
Stasauskas, Jim 3: 651
Stead, David 2: 223
Steel Mill 3: 598
Steely Dan 6: 329
Stefani, Eric 1: 102; 6: 309, 311
Stefani, Gwen 1: 101 (ill.), 102-104, 183; 6: 309 (ill.), 309–312
Stein, Seymour 3: 635
Stephenson, Karl 1: 27
Stereolab 1: 3
Stereopathetic Soulmanure 4: 29
Stern, Howard 1: 44
Stetsasonic 2: 347
Stetsasonic's Daddy-O 2: 399
Stevens, Cat 3: 612
Stewart, Mark 2: 300
Stewart, Martha 4: 56
Stewart, Rod 3: 541; 5: 208; 6: 414
Stewart, Tyler 4: 19 (ill.), 19–22
Stills, Stephen 1: 204
Sting 3: 543; 6: 322, 353, 411 (ill.), **411–415**, 413 (ill.)

Stipe, Michael 1: 153 (ill.), 154, 156; 6: 360 (ill.), 360–363
"Stir My Soul" 6: 443
Stirling, Scott Monroe (see Scott LaRock)
Stirratt, John 3: 608
Stockman, Shawn 3: 511-514
"Stomp" 4: 153, 155
Stone, Angie 4: 91
Stone, Rose 5: 172
Stone Roses 2: 227, 266, 281
Stone Temple Pilots 1: 178 (ill.), 179, 180 (ill.), 181
Stop the Violence: Overcoming Self-Destruction (book) 2: 374
Stradlin, Izzy 3: 474, 477
Strange Fire 5: 200–201
"Strange Fruit" 5: 164
The Stranglers 1: 1; 2: 253
Strauss, Neil 5: 271
"Stray Cat Strut" 6: 375
Stray Cats 6: 374, 375, 376
The Stray Gators 5: 221
Streithorst, Fred. *See* Lucas, Sara Lee
"Stronger" 6: 409
Strummer, Joe 6: 448 (ill.), 449
Stuart, Mark 4: 100
Stunt 4: 19, 21
"Stupid Girl" 6: 310
Styler, Trudie 6: 412
Sub Pop Records 1: 3, 8, 54, 85, 95, 172
subdudes 3: 543, 603 (ill.), 604-605
Sublime 1: 182 (ill.), 183-186; 2: 279; 6: 395
The Substitute 4: 7
"Subterranean Homesick Blues" 4: 30
SubUrbia (film) 1: 113; 6: 357
Suede 2: 222, 238, 254, 255, 270 (ill.), 271-272
Sugar Hill Records 2: 306, 308, 309, 373
Sugar Ray 5: 241; 6: 416 (ill.), **416–419**, 421, 422 (ill.), 449
Sugar Ray 6: 418
Sugarcubes 3: 622, 623
Sugarhill Gang 6: 341
"Suicide Solution" 6: 325
"Sullen Girl" 4: 11
Summer, Donna 2: 276
Summers, Andy 6: 411–413

Index   lxxi

Sumner, Gordon Matthew. *See* Sting
"Sunday Bloody Sunday" 6: 443
"Sunday Morning" 6: 311
Sundquist, Scott 1: 173
Supa Dupa Fly 4: 128
Super Bowl 4: 139; 5: 192; 6: 303 (ill.)
Supernatural 4: 100; 5: 280; 6: 369, 370, 371
Supernature 2: 411
Superstar Car Wash 5: 160
Superunknown 1: 175
Supposed Former Infatuation Junkie 5: 161
The Supremes 2: 276; 3: 504, 505, 525; 4: 105
Surfacing 5: 283
"Surfin' U.S.A." 4: 20
Survivor 4: 106
Swamp Ophelia 5: 201
Swarm I 6: 454
Sweet Dreams (Movie) 6: 365
"Sweet Dreams" (Song) 5: 270
"Sweet Home Alabama" 6: 385
Sweet, Matthew 3: 612
"Sweet Surrender" 5: 283
"Sweet Thing" 4: 34
Swing, Devante 4: 127
Swing music 6: 377, 378
Swing revival bands 6: 377, 378
Swingers 4: 70; 6: 377, 378
Swingle Sisters 6: 408
Synchronicity 6: 412
Synkronized 5: 212
Synth-pop 1: 88
Synthesizers 1: 88; 2: 277, 296, 310
Synthetic sound 2: 288
Synthetic vocals 2: 288
System 7 2: 296

T

T. Rex 2: 222, 271, 272
Tabitha's Secret 5: 279
Tairrie B. 4: 147
Tait, Michael 4: 98 (ill.), 98–101
Takac, Robby 1: 57 (ill.), 58; 5: 159 (ill.), 159–162
Take Me As I Am 5: 176
"Take Me to the River" 6: 397
Take Me to Your Leader 5: 216
Take Off Your Jacket & Pants 4: 42

Take That 2: 240
Talbot, Billy 1: 204
Talena 5: 185
Tales from the Punchbowl 1: 133
Talk on Corners 4: 72
Talking Book 5: 211
Talking Heads 1: 1, 139; 2: 277; 6: 396 (ill.), 396–397
Tallent, Gary 3: 598
Tank Girl (film) 1: 180; 2: 370
Tappi Tikarrass 3: 622
Tarabay, Michael 4: 115
A Taste of Honey 6: 408
Tate, Robert 3: 447
Taupin, Bernie 4: 66
Taylor, Chad 3: 576, 577
Taylor, Chuck 4: 49
Taylor, James 3: 441, 612; 6: 414
Taylor, John 3: 478
Taylor, Malik. *See* Phife
Taylor, Shante 6: 404–405
T-Boz. *See* Watkins, Tionne.
"Tearing Up My Heart" 6: 316
Tears for Fears 5: 270
Techno 2: 278, 287
Techno dance 2: 293
Techno-rap 2: 308
Teen pop 5: 170–171
Tei, Towa 2: 283–285
Tejano music 5: 265
Television 1: 1, 139
"Tell Me" 6: 382
The Temptations 1: 9; 2: 276; 4: 77
Ten 1: 118, 119; 6: 332
Ten Summoner's Tales 6: 414
"Tennessee" 2: 312, 314
Terrorism 6: 353
Texas musicians 4: 154
Tex-Mex music 2: 243; 3: 579, 580; 5: 265
"Tha Crossroads" 4: 43, 45
Tha Dogg Pound 2: 334, 421, 422
Tha Doggfather (Album) 6: 404
Tha Doggfather: The Times, Trials, and Hardcore Truths of Snoop Dogg (Book) 6: 405
"Thank God I Found You" 6: 306
"Thank U" 5: 161
"Thank You" 4: 132
"That Don't Impress Me Much" 6: 440
"That I Would Be Good" 5: 161

"That's the Way Love Goes" 5: 207, 266
"That's What I'm Looking For" 4: 85–86
Thayil, Kim 1: 173, 177; 3: 469
There Is Nothing Left to Lose 4: 151
"There U Go" 6: 338
"There's Only One Year Left" 4: 56
"There's Your Trouble" 4: 114
Theron, Charlize 6: 421
These Are Special Times 4: 110
Thin Lizzie 4: 72
Thin White Duke 2: 219, 232
"The Things You Do" 4: 128
Third Eye Blind 4: 41, 76; 5: 241; 6: 420 (ill.), **420–423**
Third World countries 6: 444
30 on the Rail 5: 189
This Beautiful Life 6: 377
This Christmas 6: 306
This Desert Life 4: 75, 76–77
"This Gift" 6: 306
"This I Promise You" 6: 316
This Is Spinal Tap 4: 70
"This Kiss" 5: 174, 176
This Time Around 5: 172
Thomas, Bruce 2: 243
Thomas, Damon 4: 123
Thomas, Pete 2: 243
Thomas, Rob 5: 278 (ill.), 278–281, 280 (ill.); 6: 371
Thomas, Rozanda "Chilli" 3: 536; 6: 428 (ill.), 428–431
Thomas, Rufus 2: 276
Thompson, Derek 2: 250
Thompson, Gina 4: 128
Thompson, Porl 2: 249, 250
"Thong Song" 6: 380, 382
Thornley, Phil 2: 250
Thoughts 6: 430
Thrash (Kris Weston) 2: 296, 297
Thrash-metal 3: 467, 468, 482, 494
3 AM 5: 280
Three Car Garage 5: 172
Three Dollar Bill, Y'all 5: 258, 259
311 4: 154; 6: 424 (ill.), **424–427**
311 6: 425
"Three Marlenas" 6: 447
Thriller 5: 207
Throwin' Tantrums 4: 85
Thug Life 2: 426

"Thuggish Ruggish Bone" 4: 45
"The Thunder Rolls" 4: 48, 50
Tibetan Freedom Concerts 4: 25, 26; 6: 362
Ticketmaster 1: 121, 122; 6: 333
Ticketron 6: 333
Tidal 4: 11, 12
Tim C.. *See* Commerford, Tim
Timberlake, Justin 4: 2; 6: 313 (ill.), 314
Time 3: 530
T.I.M.E. 4: 55
"Time" 5: 187
"Time of Your Life" 4: 41
Time Out of Mind 4: 31
"Time to Build" 5: 204
Timmons, Jeff 6: 305 (ill.), 305–308, 307 (ill.)
Tin Machine 2: 233-235
Tinsley, Boyd 3: 585; 4: 93, 94
Tiny Music: Songs from the Vatican Gift Shop 1: 180
Titanic 4: 107, 109
TLC 3: 505, 535 (ill.), 537, 538; 6: 428 (ill.), **428–431**
TNT 6: 348
"To Make You Feel My Love" 4: 50
To Mother 1: 17
To Reach a Star 5: 274
To the Faithful Departed 1: 39
"To Zion" 5: 181
The Toasters 1: 185
Tobias, Jesse 1: 151; 6: 356
Todo a Su Tiempo 4: 7
"Together Again" 5: 208
Tolhurst, Lol 2: 250
Tom and Jerry 3: 440
Tom Cats 6: 375
Tom Tom Club 6: 397
Tommy 6: 434
Tommy Boy record label 2: 323, 425
"Tomorrow" 1: 161
Tomorrow Never Dies 5: 284
Tone Loc 2: 307, 328
"Tonight, Tonight" 6: 395
"Tonight's the Night" 5: 208
Tony! Toni! Toné! 6: 435
Too Poetic 2: 348
Top Dogg 6: 404
"Top O' the Morning to Ya" 4: 147
Topley Bird, Martina 2: 300, 301
"Torn" 4: 81

Torres, Dayanara 4: 8
Tosh, Peter 1: 183, 184
Touch 5: 282, 283
"Touch Me, I'm Sick" 1: 84, 85
"Touch of Grey" 4: 94
Touched by an Angel 4: 110
The Tour 4: 35
Townes, Jeff 2: 326; 6: 399–400
Townsend, Pete 2: 265; 6: 329
Toys (film) 2: 379
Tragic Kingdom 1: 101-103; 6: 309, 311
"Train in Vain" 6: 449
Transistor 6: 426
Transvision Vamp 2: 237
Tranzlator Crew 5: 180
Travelling Without Moving 5: 210, 212
Tre Cool 4: 41
Treach 2: 323, 382 (ill.)
Treacherous Three 2: 308, 373
Tremonti, Mark 4: 79 (ill.), 79–83
Tresant, Ralph 3: 517
A Tribe Called Quest 2: 404, 408; 4: 56; 6: 432 (ill.), **432–436**, 452
A Tribe Called Quest 4: 55
Tribute 6: 324–325
Tricky 2: 278, 299-301, 348
Trip-hop 1: 3; 2: 278
Triple X (indie label) 1: 76
Trojanowski, Mark 6: 386, 386 (ill.)
Trouble T-Roy 2: 356
"True to Your Heart" 6: 306
The Truthful Night 4: 11
"Try Again" 5: 226
Tucker, C. Delores 1: 79; 2: 324
Tucker, Maureen 3: 654
Tuesday Night Music Club 5: 284
Tull, Jethro 6: 329
Tupac Shakur 2: 310, 334-335, 424 (ill.), 425-429
Turn It Up 5: 205
"Turn the Beat Around" 4: 138
Turner, Big Joe 3: 501
Turner, Elgin. *See* Masta Killa
Turner, Jeff 5: 331
Turner, Steve 1: 85
Turpin, Will 3: 553; 4: 65
Tutuska, George 5: 159 (ill.), 159–162

Twain, Shania 4: 61,138; 5: 174–175, 176; 6: 322, 409, 437 (ill.), **437–441**
Tweedy, Jeff 3: 543, 591, 592, 606 (ill.), 607-608
12 Play 5: 225
Twin Peaks 2: 292
Twin/Tone Records 1: 3, 17, 54, 170
Twisted Brown Trucker Band 5: 232
Twisted Kites 6: 360
Two Live Crew 2: 399
"Two of a Kind" 4: 50
2001: A Space Odyssey 2: 231
Two-Tone 1: 184
Tyler, Mike. *See* Mystikal
Tyler, Steven 2: 404, 406

U

"U Will Know" 4: 89
U-God 6: 452
Ulrich, Lars 3: 482, 486, 487; 5: 287 (ill.), 287–290, 289 (ill.)
Ultimate Sin 6: 324
Ultrasuede label 1: 8
Ultravox 2: 289
"Unanswered Prayers" 4: 50
Uncle Kracker 5: 232
Uncle Tupelo 3: 543, 591, 592, 606, 607
"Under the Bridge" 1: 151; 6: 356
Under the Cherry Moon 3: 530
Under the Table and Dreaming 4: 95
Underdog 4: 100
The Unforgettable Fire 6: 443
"Uninvited" 5: 161
Unison 4: 108
"U.N.I.T.Y." 6: 345
Unleash the Dragon 6: 380, 382
Unmasked 5: 237
Unplugged 5: 262
Unpredictable 5: 297
"Unpretty" 6: 429
Unrestricted 4: 86
"Unsent" 5: 161
Untitled 4: 91
Up 6: 361
Up in It 1: 8
"Up in Smoke" 4: 124
Uptown Avondale 1: 8
Uptown Records 2: 356, 388
Urban Soul 3: 501-503, 505

Urge Overkill *1:* 187 (ill.), 188-189
Uriah Heep *6:* 329
UTFO *2:* 309
U2 *1:* 190 (ill.), 191, 192 (ill.), 193-195; *3:* 543; *4:* 36, 72; *6:* 322, 353, 376, 390, 442 (ill.), **442–445**
U2: The Best of 1980-1990 *6:* 443
Uzi/Suicide label *3:* 474

V

Valens, Richie *3:* 581; *4:* 70
Valentine, Eric *6:* 390
Valenzuela, Jesse *3:* 562
Van Dijk, Carol *1:* 30
Van Halen *3:* 466, 468
Van Halen, Eddie *3:* 466
Van Morrison *4:* 72
Van Outen, Denise *5:* 212
Van Winkle, Robert. *See* Vanilla Ice
Van Zandt, Steve *3:* 598, 600
Vandross, Luther *4:* 61
Vanilla Ice *4:* 147; *5:* 231
Vanity 6 *3:* 530
Varsity Blues *4:* 65
Vatican Commandos *2:* 292
Vaughan, Steven *2:* 258
Vaughn, Sarah *2:* 304
Vaughn, Stevie Ray *2:* 219
Vavoom! *6:* 378
Vedder, Eddie *1:* 6 (ill.), 115 (ill.), 116-122, 175; *4:* 25, 81; *6:* 331 (ill.), 332, 334
Vega, Louis *4:* 7
Vega, Suzanne *3:* 449
Vegetarianism *2:* 291; *3:* 637
The Velvet Rope *5:* 207–208; *6:* 316
Velvet Underground *2:* 231; *3:* 614, 653-655
Venni, Vetti, Vecci *5:* 204
Version 2.0 *6:* 310
Veruca Salt *1:* 196 (ill.), 197-198
VH-1 *2:* 244; *3:* 459
The Vibrators *1:* 1
Vickery, Dan *3:* 557; *4:* 76
Vietnam War *1:* 12
Vig, Butch *1:* 53, 54; *6:* 310
"Vincent, Eddie "Cleanhead" *3:* 501
Vincent, Vinnie *5:* 237
Violence *4:* 133; *5:* 213, 271, 279; *6:* 341, 353

V.I.P. (TV show) *4:* 86; *5:* 255
VIP Records *2:* 419
Virgin Records *3:* 631
Virginia musicians *4:* 127
"Virtual Insanity" *5:* 210, 212
"Vision of Love" *4:* 60
Visser, Peter *1:* 30
Vitalogy *1:* 119; *6:* 332
Vivir *5:* 197
"Vivrant Thing" *6:* 435
"Vomit Heart" *1:* 17
Voodoo *4:* 88, 91
Vs. *1:* 119; *6:* 332
Vuelve *5:* 276

W

Waiting to Exhale (film) *3:* 508
Waiting to Exhale (album) *4:* 34; *5:* 192
"Walk On" *6:* 444
"Walk on the Wild Side" *6:* 434
"Walk This Way" *2:* 309
Walker, Lyle *6:* 366, 367
Walker, Matt *6:* 395
Walker, T-Bone *3:* 501, 540
"Walkin' After Midnight" *6:* 365
"Walkin' in Memphis" *5:* 293
"Walkin' on the Sun" *6:* 389, 390
Walking with the Panther *5:* 261
"Wall of Sound" *1:* 140, 163
Wallace, Christopher (see The Notorious B.I.G.)
The Wallflowers *1:* 199 (ill.), 200-202; *4:* 11, 31, 76, 148; *5:* 241; *6:* 421, 446 (ill.), **446–450**
The Wallflowers (Album) *6:* 447
Walmart *3:* 629
Wander This World *5:* 251
Wangdu, Dechen *4:* 26
Wannabe *5:* 171
War *6:* 389
"War Pigs" *6:* 322
Ward, Bill *6:* 322, 324 (ill.)
Ward, Billy *3:* 502
Ward, Christopher Joseph *1:* 142
Ward, Michael *1:* 200; *6:* 447
Warhol, Andy *2:* 231, 233; *3:* 654, 656; *4:* 28; *5:* 276; *6:* 417
Warner, Brian. *See* Marilyn Manson

Warner Bros. Records *3:* 449, 520, 528, 531, 532, 656
Warped Tour *4:* 40
Warren G. *2:* 310, 336, 419; *6:* 402, 404
Warren, Patrick *3:* 459
Warwick, Dionne *5:* 191
Was, Don *1:* 73; *5:* 160
Washington state musicians *5:* 241
Wasserman, Kevin "Noodles" *1:* 107, *6:* 318
The Watcher *2:* 416
"Watching the Detectives" *2:* 241
"Waterfalls" *6:* 428
Waters, Muddy *3:* 540
Watkins, Tionne "T-Boz" *3:* 536; *4:* 85; *6:* 428 (ill.), 428–431
Watt, Mike *1:* 2
Watts, Charlie *2:* 257
Wax Trax *1:* 4
"The Way I Am" *4:* 133
"The Way You Love Me" *5:* 176
Wayne's World *5:* 270
"We Are the World" *5:* 207
"We Shall Be Free" *4:* 48
"We'll Be Together" *6:* 413
"We've Got It Goin' On" *4:* 15
Weavers *3:* 439
The Wedding Planner *5:* 267
Weiland, Scott *1:* 178 (ill.), 179-180; *5:* 259
Weinberg, Max *3:* 598
Weir, Bob *4:* 94
Welch, Brian "Head" *5:* 240, 240 (ill.), 258
Welch, Justin *2:* 254, 255
Welch, Sean *2:* 223
Welcome to the Freak Show *4:* 99
Welty, Ron *6:* 318
West Coast rap *2:* 310, 323
West, Steve *1:* 112
Westerberg, Paul *1:* 2
Wet Willie *6:* 385
Weymouth, Tina *6:* 397
Whalen, Katharine *6:* 377
"What About Your Friends" *6:* 429
"What 'Chu Like" *4:* 86
"What Have You Done for Me Lately" *5:* 207
"What It's Like" *4:* 148
What You Want *4:* 120
What's Going On *4:* 90

"What's It Gonna Be?" 5: 208
"What's My Age Again?" 4: 40
What's the 411 4: 34
What's This Life For (album) 4: 79
"What's This Life For" (song) 4: 81
Whatcha Lookin 4 4: 155
When Disaster Strikes 4: 56
"When I Fall in Love" 4: 108
"When I Grow Up" 6: 310
"When I Think of You" 5: 207
When the Pawn . . . 4: 12
"When You Believe" 4: 61
"When You Gonna Learn?" 5: 211
"Where Do Broken Hearts Go" 5: 192
"Where Does My Heart Beat Now" 4: 108
"Where It's At" 4: 29
Where the Red Ferns Grow 4: 96
"Where the Streets Have No Name" 6: 443
"Where You Are" 6: 306
Whilhelmina Modeling 4: 86
Whispers 3: 507
White, Alan 2: 268
White, Jeordie. *See* Ramirez, Twiggy
White, Mark 3: 595
White Zombie 3: 469, 497 (ill.), 498-499
Whitesnake 2: 284
Whitey Ford Sings the Blues 4: 147–148
Whitney (1987) 5: 192
Whitney Houston (1985) 5: 192
Whitten, Danny 1: 204
The Who 2: 221; 3: 543; 6: 333–334, 395, 434
"Who Will Save Your Soul" 5: 221
Whoa Nelly! 6: 302
Whodini 2: 309
"Why Can't We Be Friends" 6: 389, 390
"Why Didn't You Call Me" 5: 166
"Why Didn't You Get a Job" 6: 319
Wide Open Spaces 4: 112, 114
Widespread Panic 3: 542
Wiggins, Keith "Cowboy" 2: 306
Wilco 3: 543, 550, 591, 606 (ill.), 607-609
Wild Bunch 2: 299

"Wild One" 5: 176
Wild Wild West 5: 197; 6: 400–401
Wilk, Brad 6: 351, 354
Willennium 6: 401
Williams, Boris 2: 249, 250
Williams, Hank 6: 439
Williams, Hank, Jr. 5: 231
Williams, Michelle 4: 102 (ill.), 104 (ill.), 105
Williams, Victoria 3: 613
Williams, Willie 3: 604
Willie, Pepe 3: 529
Wills, Aaron. *See* P-Nut
Wilson, Brian 4: 20
Wilson, Carl 4: 20
Wilson, Dennis 4: 20
Wilson, Eric 1: 182
Wilson, Kenny. *See* Fish, Ginger
Wilson, Robin 3: 563
Wimbash, Doug 3: 481
Wind-Up Records 4: 81, 82
Wingate, Dick 3: 456
Winley, Paul 2: 306
"Winning" 6: 370
Winslow, Vernon 3: 502
Winstanley, Alan 2: 239
Wire 2: 253
Wish Bone 4: 43–47, 45 (ill.)
"With Arms Wide Open" 4: 81, 82
With Arms Wide Open Foundation 4: 82
"With or Without You" 6: 443
Without A Sound 1: 47
"Without You" 4: 60
The Wizard of Oz 6: 346
Wobble, Jah 2: 296
Woldemariam, Phillip 2: 420, 421; 6: 404
Wolf Brothers 5: 187
Wolfe, Tom 4: 94; 6: 353
The Woman in Me 6: 439
Womanly Hips Records 3: 648
Women, performers 4: 101; 5: 283
Women, violence against 4: 133; 5: 213
Wonder, Stevie 2: 276; 5: 211, 211 (ill.), 225; 6: 306, 337, 356, 414
"Wonderful" 4: 144
"Woo Hah!! Get You All in Check" 4: 56
Wood, Andrew 1: 118; 6: 331
Wood, Brad 1: 197
Woods, Cory. *See* Raekwon

"Woodstock" (Mitchell) 5: 221
Woodstock '94 1: 63, 87, 91; 3: 554, 629
Woodstock '99 6: 357–358
"Wordy Rappinghood" 6: 397
The World I Know 4: 64
World of Noise 4: 142
World Vision 5: 283
A Worm's Life 1: 44
"Would?" 1: 13
"Wrapped Around Your Finger" 6: 412
Wretzky, D'Arcy 6: 393–398
Wright, Donna 4: 15; 6: 313
Wright, Eric. *See* Eazy-E
Wright, Frank Edwin, III. *See* Tre Cool
Wright, Johnny 4: 15; 6: 313
The Writing's on the Wall 4: 103
"Written in the Stars" 6: 367
The Wu 6: 454
Wu Wear 6: 454
Wu-Chronicles 6: 454
Wu-Tang Clan 2: 310, 347; 4: 34, 55; 6: 421, **451–455**, 453 (ill.)
Wu-Tang Forever 6: 452–453
Wyclef Jean Presents the Carnival 5: 180

X

X 1: 2

Y

Y Kant Tori Read 3: 618
Yale, Brian 5: 279
Yamamoto, Hiro 1: 173
Yankee Stadium 1: 193; 2: 304
Yanowitz, Peter 1: 200
Yauch, Adam 4: 23 (ill.), 23–27, 24 (ill.)
Yearwood, Trisha 6: 366
yes 1: 82
Yield 6: 332
Yo! MTV Raps 2: 309, 331, 382, 400
"Yo-Da-Lin in the Valley" 5: 231
Yoakam, Dwight 5: 284
Yorke, Thom 6: 347 (ill.), 347–350
"You and Me" 5: 270
"You and Me and the Bottle Makes Three Tonight" 6: 377
"You Are Not Alone" 5: 225

"You Can't Kill Rock and Roll" 6: 323
"You Learn" 5: 161
You Light Up My Life-Inspirational Songs 6: 366
"You Make Me Sick" 6: 338
"You Oughta Know" 5: 161
"You Remind Me of Something" 5: 226
"You Sang to Me" 4: 8
"You Were Meant for Me" 5: 220, 221, 222
You Were Meant for Me 5: 222
"You Were Mine" 4: 114
You're Living All Over Me 1: 47
"You're Still the One" 6: 440
Young, Adrian 6: 309 (ill.), 309–312
Young Americans 2: 219
Young and the Useless 4: 24
Young, Andre Ramelle. *See* Dr. Dre
Young, Grant 1: 170
Young, Jeff 3: 483
Young MC 2: 307
Young, Neil 1: 119, 120, 122, 203 (ill.), 204–209; 3: 550, 614, 616; 5: 221, 293; 6: 332
Young, Nicole 4: 123
Youngblood, Jennifer 4: 151
"Your Body's Callin'" 5: 225
"Your Song" 4: 66
Yourself or Someone Like You 5: 278, 279
Youth 2: 296
Yseult, Sean 3: 498

Z

Z Music Television 3: 513
Zebop 6: 370
Zender, Stuart 5: 210, 212
Zenyatta Mondata 6: 412
Zeppelin, Led 4: 70
Zimmermann, Robert. *See* Dylan, Bob
"Zombie" 1: 39
Zombie, Rob 3: 497-499
The Zombies 2: 221
Zoo TV Tour 1: 193
Zooropa 6: 443
Zoot Suit Riot: The Swinging Hits 6: 377
Zulu Nation 2: 304
Zum, Zim 1: 79; 5: 270